Love on Inishcoo, 1787

Edmund Cobb Hurry (1762-1808)

Love on Inishcoo, 1787

A Donegal Romance

Edited by

Martin Sheppard

Matador
9 Priory Business Park,
Wistow Road, Kibworth Beauchamp,
Leicestershire. LE8 0RX
Tel: 0116 279 2299
Email: books@troubador.co.uk
Web: www.troubador.co.uk/matador
Twitter: @matadorbooks

ISBN 978 1789010 237

British Library Cataloguing in Publication Data.
A catalogue record for this book is available from the British Library.

Printed and bound by CPI Group (UK) Ltd, Croydon, CR0 4YY
Typeset in 11pt Minion Pro by Troubador Publishing Ltd, Leicester, UK

Matador is an imprint of Troubador Publishing Ltd

Contents

Illustrations

To

Patrick Boner and Debonnaire Perceval

Edmund, if you ever see these papers, I intreat you to burn them when perused. Think how mortified I should be that you should have it in your power to bestow a second reading on them. Consider that I write, at any time and in any humour, surrounded by *five* noisy children.

Eliza Liddell to Edmund Cobb Hurry, 20 September 1787

Introduction

In the summer of 1787 a young couple, Edmund Cobb Hurry and Eliza Liddell, met and fell in love on the small island of Inishcoo, or Inniscoo, in an area known as the Rosses off the coast of Donegal. He was a Great Yarmouth merchant visiting a promising trading hub on nearby Rutland Island. She was on Inishcoo as a governess, teaching the five daughters of Robert Corbet, an Irish gentleman from Wexford. They declared their love for each other but had only five weeks together, as Edmund had to sail away to the Baltic, leaving Eliza behind him.

Over the next thirteen months, the couple wrote to each other whenever they were apart, as they mostly were, frustrated not only by their separation but by the unpredictability of the arrival of letters in an age when ships could be delayed for weeks by adverse winds. These delays were made worse by the prohibitive cost of postage to and from the Baltic. While Edmund was in Latvia, then part of an area known as the duchy of Courland, Eliza moved east from Rutland Island, to Dublin, to Chester and finally to London.

Both Edmund and Eliza suffered agonies from their separation, but the story ended happily. The couple were married in St Mary's church in Putney on 20 August 1788, a week after Edmund sent off his last letter from Great Yarmouth, discussing details of their future housekeeping and telling Eliza that he was setting out for London on the 18 August.

If the survival of individual love letters from so long ago is unusual, the survival of over fifty reciprocal letters between lovers is remarkable. They are also not the letters of aristocrats or celebrities but of an ordinary, if intelligent and well-educated, couple who happened to have fallen in love.

The circumstances of their meeting on Inishcoo were also exceptional. Both Edmund and Eliza were drawn there, in different ways and for different reasons, by an ambitious though ephemeral plan to create an industrial hub on Rutland Island, next to Inishcoo. The letters shed light on this remarkable episode in the history of Donegal and indeed of Ireland.

Edmund came from a dynasty of 'Russia' merchants, trading with the Baltic but based in Great Yarmouth. His letters describe life as a merchant in the days of sailing ships, at the mercy of winds and other uncertainties. Eliza's letters reflect the loneliness and tribulations felt by an educated woman without fortune who was obliged to make her own way in life by becoming a governess. This was almost the only way open to a woman at the time to do so, if she wished to keep her status of gentility. Eliza expresses, despite the difficulties she had encountered in life and as a governess, a clear sense of her own worth and of the right of women to be treated by men as rational creatures. While paying deference, with a degree of irony, to men as the Lords of Creation, Eliza letters show her determination to stand up for herself as a woman with a mind of her own.

Both Edmund and Eliza's letters contain many attitudes typical of the Romantic period, with its emphasis on the importance of the individual; and on the priority of love over prudential and monetary considerations. The agonies of separation, including longing, sleeplessness and despair, as well as the sublime happiness of assured mutual affection, are quintessential Romantic emotions. Eliza's rescue from her solitary life on Inishcoo by Edmund, sailing in from far away, could be taken for the stuff of Romantic fiction, were it not so memorably documented.

In the end, the appeal of the story is the timeless one of mutual love, tried and tested by separation and doubt, reaching the happy ending of marriage. Edmund and Eliza's letters allow us intimate access to their lives and loves, to Inishcoo and to the world of the late eighteenth-century Ireland. Sadly, no likeness of Eliza survives, though we know she was small. There is, however, a silhouette of Edmund, who was tall.

There is a description of the exact moment when Eliza first heard of Edmund's arrival on Inishcoo. 'I was sitting at this little desk writing to my sisters the day you came into the harbour ... Mrs Corbet sent for me down to welcome Mr Hurry'.[1] We also know that they had five weeks together on

---

1   Eliza to Edmund, Letter 8, p. 64.

the island, in June and July 1787, before Edmund sailed north, leaving Eliza behind.

In the days before Edmund sailed the couple exchanged six letters. The first three of these letters do not survive, though their contents can be deduced from the exchanges which followed immediately afterwards and from later letters. In a first letter, Edmund declared his love for Eliza, at the same time confessing faults in his own character. Eliza's replied by expressing strong feelings of friendship for Edmund, but denying that she loved him. She also admitted her own poverty. Her reserve was due to a determination not to be seen to be acting from monetary motives, given the discrepancy in their financial positions. Edmund then replied with an offer to take Eliza with him on his ship, the *Fly*, as he knew that she wished to return to England.

The first letter to survive is Eliza's response to Edmund's offer of a passage to England via Riga, refusing it on the grounds of the damage that acceptance would have done to her reputation.[2] This is followed by a letter expressing her agony at their parting.[3] Edmund's first surviving letter, while promising to write to Eliza, sets out the places to which he is sailing and his likely schedule.[4] After these letters were written and exchanged, his departure was delayed for several days by unfavourable winds before the *Fly* finally sailed early on Wednesday 18 July.

As soon as they were apart, Edmund and Eliza wrote to each other.[5] Edmund began a long letter to Eliza, written over ten days, while still in sight of Inishcoo.[6] In it he repeatedly expressed his love for her and his agony at their having been parted. This he posted from Stromness in the Orkneys on 26 July, but it did not reach Eliza until 24 August. The delay of over a month in hearing from Edmund caused Eliza to wonder whether their encounter had been merely ephemeral. As she expressed it in a letter sent from Inishcoo on 3 August:

you may depend on this being the last time I shall thus force myself

---

2   Eliza to Edmund, Letter 1, pp. 31-32.

3   Eliza to Edmund, Letter 2, pp. 33-34.

4   Edmund to Eliza, Letter 3, p. 35.

5   Eliza to Edmund, Letter 4, pp. 36-38.

6   Edmund to Eliza, Letter 5, pp. 39-49.

on your remembrance unless I receive assurances from your pen that my writing continues to be your wish and expectation … I will not, maybe it would be improper I should, dwell on what the supposition costs me: that perhaps here closes for ever a correspondence with one that – but on you this depends …[7]

Her doubts were reinforced when Mr Corbet received a business letter from Edmund in early August, sent from Elsinore, before she herself had received a letter from him.[8]

At last, after nearly five weeks, on 19 August Eliza received a letter from Edmund, to which she immediately replied, though her reply is lost.[9] Five days later, she received his letter sent from the Orkneys.[10] 'Your lamented, your valuable pacquet, my Edmund, is not lost. 'Tis this moment pressed to my heart.'[11] She now knew that Edmund felt the same towards her as she felt towards him:

You know not how highly I am gratified that ideas similar to mine should have occupied your mind: the gloom, the dejection to which I have been a prey, the inability of applying to anything you have felt, while Eliza's image has been no less present to your imagination than Edmund's to hers.[12]

In two letters, written over the next three weeks, Eliza wrote freely about her feelings and principles.[13] As well as providing news from Inishcoo, and a perceptive character sketch of its leading inhabitant, Robert Corbet, she admitted her inability to concentrate on her work as a governess:

---

7   Eliza to Edmund, Letter 7, pp. 53-56.

8   Eliza to Edmund, Letter 7, p. 56.

9   Edmund to Eliza, Letter 6, pp 50-52. This letter, although written after Letter 5, reached Eliza five days before it.

10   Edmund to Eliza, Letter 5, pp. 39-49.

11   Eliza to Edmund, Letter 8, p. 57.

12   Eliza to Edmund, Letter 8, p. 59.

13   Eliza to Edmund, Letter 8, pp. 57-65; Letter 9, pp. 66-76.

My mornings are now filled up by attending to the children's improvements, but what ever avocations I think I ought to mind I may be said to perform mechanically. They read to me, etc, etc, I correct their pronunciation, their blunders, their errors, without knowing I am doing it. The five weeks I spent with you has destroyed my relish for any other society. Alas, in vain do I look at the chairs you sat on; you occupy them no longer.[14]

She also explained why she had not immediately admitted her love for Edmund while he was still on Inishcoo:

Only consider how very delicately I was circumstanced. It was repugnant to my pride you should know what my refractory heart betrayed, tho' it was never repugnant to either my pride or principles. Could you know me for what I am, could you see the purity, the disinterestedness of my regard, I had nothing to apprehend from your inspection. But you could not see by intuition and had not known me long enough to form an established opinion in my favour. For you to mistake my character was dreadful to me and to prevent your doing so, in growing my friendship for you, I at the same time studiously sought to inform you I was destitute of fortune.[15]

Eliza also continued to agonise about his safety and about whether they would ever meet again.

Edmund, have I seen you for the last time, the last? Reason, religion strengthens my soul to support an evil I have myself created, and yet not I brought you here. I bid you not appear, to have a feeling, a generous, a good heart to engage my regard, my esteem, my affections, my too anxious interest in your health, your peace, your honour. I have not written a line since Thursday. It is become a too painful task. Need I any memorialist of you, of your absence? Alas! Do I think of anything else?[16]

---

14   Letter 8. p. 63.

15   Letter 9, p. 67.

16   Letter 9, p. 75.

Not knowing, however, where Edmund was, and not having heard again from him, she did not send off the two letters, or two subsequent ones, which contain a great deal of well-observed information about life on Inishcoo, about the characters of its inhabitants, and about two unusual visitors, the geologist William Hamilton and his wife.[17] She only despatched all four letters when Mr Corbet again received a business letter from Edmund, without one coming to her.

> Edmund, may you never experience the sorrow you have this day occasioned me. What if you did not receive my letters? Was it not more reasonable to suppose that was owing to your quick removal from place to place than to my neglect of writing? Recollect. Oh how could you so soon forget how much I regretted your departure? Regret. How incompetent that word to express what passed in my soul! If you had regarded me, would you have written to Mr Corbet to tell him of your arrival in England (he who, though he regards you, comparatively speaking it was of no consequence to) in your letter from Windau?
>
> You say you could have written ten sheets to me, if opportunity had offered of sending them; and the moment you got to Yarmouth from whence you might write twice ten sheets, you neglect *one*. You write a formal letter of business to Mr Corbet (he gave it to me to read) and you coldly desire your respects to the family. Well, and have you not a right to do as you please? And you did not chuse to write.[18]

Until she received Edmund's first two letters to her after he sailed from Inishcoo, in the second half of August, Eliza had been prey to anxiety and depression.[19] Edmund himself in the Baltic was in no better position, as he did not receive Eliza's first two letters to him until he read them at Elsinore in early September.[20] He had found it difficult to write again before then.

> I was also uneasy at being so long detained on the sea between Windau and Elsinore, a whole fortnight, and yet in all that time did

---

17   Eliza to Edmund, Letter 11, pp. 84-97; Letter 12, pp. 98-99.

18   Eliza to Edmund, Letter 11, pp. 94-95.

19   Edmund to Eliza, Letter 5, pp. 39-49; Letter 6, pp. 50-52.

20   Eliza to Edmund, Letter 4, pp. 36-38; Letter 7, pp. 53-56.

I not so much as write one single line to my dearest Eliza. Yet you were scarce from my thoughts ...[21]

Landing at Hull on 10 September, Edmund wrote to Eliza before he sailed back to the Baltic, posting his letter from Great Yarmouth just before he sailed on the twenty-ninth. This had no time to reach Eliza before, in renewed despair at not hearing a letter from him, she sent four of her letters to him at Great Yarmouth, missing him only by days.[22] With a covering note addressed to Edmund's father, her letters were opened by his uncle, Samuel Hurry. This brought Eliza's existence of Eliza to the knowledge of the Hurry family as a whole.

Despite their strong mutual commitment, it is not surprising that both Edmund and Eliza suffered greatly from not knowing what the other was doing or thinking. After an agonisingly slow first exchange after their parting on Inishcoo, their subsequent exchanges continued to take many weeks, especially when Edmund was in the Baltic. While their letters answer one another's, if after a considerable time lag, they also reflect their individual separation, loneliness and depression.

Only when Edmund's letter of 29 September reached Eliza on 8 October did her anxiety about their long-term relationship cease, though not before she had sent off another despairing letter to Edmund.[23] By this time Mr Corbet had taken the decision to move his family, with Eliza, to Dublin.[24] Eliza sailed from Inishcoo on Tuesday 17 October.

Many people have helped in the production of this book. I am first and foremost grateful to my cousin Debonnaire Perceval for allowing me to transcribe and publish the letters. She and Sandy Perceval have made my visits to Ballymote not only productive but highly enjoyable. I am also very greatly indebted to Patrick Boner for his encouragement and help, and for supplying many of the images in this book, including the photographs of the originals of the letters. He and Carrie Boner have also been most hospitable to my wife, Lucy, and me in Burtonport, as have Anna and Philip Dunlop at Lodge in Castlebar, Bob Maxwell at Dunfanaghy and Sarah Willert at Kiltarnaght.

---

21   Edmund to Eliza, Letter 10, p. 77.

22   Eliza to Edmund, Letters 8, 9, 11, 12, pp. 57-76, 84-99.

23   Edmund to Eliza, Letter 10, pp. 77-83; Eliza to Edmund, Letter 13, pp. 100-3.

24   Eliza to Edmund, Letter 14, p. 106. See also Letter 15, pp. 115-16.

It was a great pleasure to spend a day on Inishcoo itself as the guest of Celia Ferguson, one of the current owners of Inishcoo House. I have been encouraged in editing these letters by the other owner, Michael Mitchell. I have also enjoyed discussing the letters and the later history of Inishcoo with Michael Dover.

Anthony Malcomson, John Perry and Gilbert Hughes, and the Public Record Office of Northern Ireland, by their invaluable listing of the Templehouse Papers, introduced me to Edmund Cobb Hurry and Eliza Liddell, and to their letters. Wesley Forsythe's help and advice, based on his groundbreaking reconstruction of William Burton Conyngham's extraordinary project on Edernish, Inishcoo and Rutland Island, has been indispensable. Rosie Lowe has provided expert help in producing this book.

I have been helped, while working on *Love on Inishcoo*, by my wife, Lucy Sheppard, my brother, Peter Sheppard, my daughters Catherine Turbett, Eleanor Morrison and Matilda Sheppard, my cousin Roger Scarlett-Smith, my friends Alison Kemp and Caroline Powell, and my dogs, Anna and Conor, both of whom were born in Ireland.

I am grateful to the National Archives of Ireland for permission to publish four previously unpublished letters from the Cliffe-Vigors Papers as Appendix, A1, A2, A5 and A6, pp. 281-84, 287-90. I also thank the following for permission to reproduce images: Patrick Boner, pp. xvi, xviii, 5, 7, 11, 13, 14, 25, 30, 34, 99, 170, 206 and 272; Andrew Cline 87, 118, 136, 157, 172, 186, 195, 216, 219, 220, 253 and 274; Donegal County Archives, Lifford, Donegal 14, 20 and 21; and the Victoria and Albert Museum 60. The silhouette of Edmund Cobb Hurry on p. ii was given to me by Debonnaire Perceval.

The Letters

As Eliza Liddell wrote to Edmund Cobb Hurry on 9 October 1787, 'It is a sad thing my happiness should be in the keeping of post boys – depend on the uncertain receipt of letters and such like wayward contingencies'. The originals of the fifty letters between Eliza Liddell and Edmund Cobb Hurry are at Temple House, Ballymote, County Sligo. Listed by PRONI, the Public Record Office of Northern Ireland, they are part of the Templehouse Papers, as N13 (Edmund Cobb Hurry) and N14 (Eliza Liddell). Of these letters, thirty are by Edmund and twenty-one by Eliza. In terms of length, Edmund's letters contain 41,537 words against Eliza's 24,252. This discrepancy, however, largely arises from the loss of Eliza's letters between March and August 1788, when Eliza was in London or Putney and Edmund was in the Baltic. For this period sixteen letters of Edmund's survive (totalling 21,126 words), as opposed to only one of Eliza's (of 450 words).

For the critical first period of the correspondence, while Eliza was on Inishcoo, eleven of her letters survive (totalling 15,826 words), as against four of Edmund's (totalling 7849 words). For the second phase of the correspondence, when Eliza was in Dublin, there are four letters by Edmund (6947 words) and four by Eliza (6624 words). For the month after Eliza arrived in Chester, but before she came to London, there are six letters by Edmund (5615 words) as opposed to four by Eliza (2088).

This count of the letters is not definitive. A number of both Eliza's and Edmund's longer letters were written over days or even weeks, sometimes seemingly finished, only to be begun again on the next day or on later ones before finally being posted. A number of other, earlier letters are also lost,

Eliza Liddell to Edmund Cobb Hurry, Letter 1 (below, p. 31), July 1787

including the earliest three letters exchanged, hand-delivered on Inishcoo, before Edmund sailed. The correspondence also contains one letter from Edmund to George Coldham, his stepbrother; and one from Eliza (signing herself for the first time as Eliza Hurry, after her marriage) to George's mother, Dorothy Hurry.

In 1995, in an inspired initiative by the Public Record Office of Northern Ireland (PRONI) to catalogue records still held privately in Irish country houses, Anthony Malcomson, John Perry and Gilbert Hughes made a thorough listing of the remarkable archive then held at Temple House, Ballymote, Sligo. This archive, listed under PRONI, MIC.597, contains a wealth of material on English, Irish and Indian history. The correspondence between Edmund Cobb Hurry and Eliza Liddell, MIC.597, N13 and N14, forms part of a larger holding on the history of the Hardcastle family. Edmund's letters (N13) are available at PRONI in Belfast on microfilm, where I first started to read them. On my first visit to Ballymote, I was delighted to see the originals of Edmund's letters emerge from PRONI envelope N13. I was then thrilled to find in the next envelope, N14, the originals of Eliza's letters. Until that moment I had not known whether any of her letters had survived.

There are also gaps in the correspondence, reflecting letters which were either not delivered or have subsequently been lost. During Edmund's second voyage to the Baltic, in 1788, Eliza wrote to him on 5 and 30 April, 3 and 25 May and 3 June. Just before the couple married, she wrote to him on 8 and 12 August. These and other earlier letters do not survive. Eliza burnt some of her letters before sending them (Letter 8). Twice Eliza also urged Edmund to burn her letters: once (in Letter 11) for fear of their being read by anyone else; and once (in Letter 23) because she regretted sending Edmund evidence of her despair.

Even after the marriage, Edmund and Eliza continued to write to each other when they were apart. Almost 250 of their later letters, containing just under 150,000 words and dating between 1789 and 1796, survive in the Templehouse Papers, N15-19, N22-25, as well as letters from Edmund's sister, Priscilla (N20), and his father, William (N21). There are also many letters, dating from 1802-8, between Edmund and his daughter Anne Cobb Hurry (N26). Anne's own life, and tragic death in childbirth, is itself exceptional well documented in Templehouse Papers, N26-41, as is the birth and early life of Edmund and Eliza's only grandson, Joseph Alfred Hardcastle, N41-84.

Edmund Cobb Hurry to Eliza Liddell, Letter 5 (below, p. 40), July 1787

The letters passed down via Anne Cobb Hardcastle (née Hurry), the daughter of Eliza and Edmund Cobb Hurry, and her husband, Alfred Hardcastle, to Edmund and Eliza's only grandson, Joseph Alfred Hardcastle MP. They were then inherited by Joseph Alfred Hardcastle's son, Henry Hardcastle, and, in turn, by his grandson, Joseph Alfred Hardcastle junior, before passing to the latter's daughter Felicité Hardcastle and, finally, to the latter's niece Debonnaire Perceval (née Hardcastle).

Two of the letters in the Appendix, both from Edmund's grandmother, Ann Cobb, are also in the Templehouse Papers. The other four letters are from the Cliffe-Vigors Papers in the National Archives of Ireland.

The handwriting of both Edmund and Eliza is mainly easily legible, though occasional words, especially names, remain conjectural. The words of the letters are sometimes crammed onto the paper, so as to get more writing onto the page. There is also far more underlining in the original than has been kept in the transcript. The main problem, however, facing the modern reader of the original letters is that of punctuation, which is sparse. Many new thoughts are added after a comma, while sentences sometimes run on for many lines. I have therefore modernised the punctuation throughout, keeping as much of the original as possible but inserting additional paragraphs and breaking up sentences into shorter extents. I have also modernised spelling where this might lead to confusion and have changed 'wrote' to 'written' as the past tense of to write. In addition, I have made verbs agree in number in a modern way (changing, for instance 'was' to 'were' to agree with 'they') and have united obvious couplings, including myself, tonight and everyone (where the original reads 'my self', 'to night' and 'every one' etc.) A very small number of other words have been added to make the sense clearer. These are shown in square brackets. There are a number of tears to the original and some words are obscured by blots and seals. These are noted in italic inside square brackets, as are unclear words. Finally, I have standardised the format of the dates given in the letters.

Rutland

1

Rutland

Donegal is one of the least industrialised counties in Ireland. It is therefore astonishing to discover that in the late eighteenth century there were plans to turn a small island just off its coast into a major fishing port, industrial hub and trading entrepôt. For a few years in the mid-1780s, Rutland Island hummed with building works and commercial activity, backed by substantial investment and attracting large numbers of workmen from across Ireland.

Rutland Island, between the larger island of Arranmore and the coast in the area known as the Rosses, also drew those from further away. Edmund Cobb Hurry and Eliza Liddell met there in June 1787 and fell in love. Edmund, from a wealthy family of merchants in Great Yarmouth, had come on behalf of his father and uncle to see the progress being made, with a view of investment. There was a possibility, once he had reported back, that he would return there as his family's agent. Eliza, originally from Cheshire, was working as a governess on Inishcoo, a smaller island next to Rutland. After a stay of five weeks, Edmund sailed away. He invited Eliza to come with him, as she had expressed a wish to return to England. She, however, refused, not because she did not have faith in his honourable intentions and integrity, but because, in the eyes of the world, sailing away with him unchaperoned would have led to lasting damage to her own reputation.

Separated after their short time together, the lovers promised to write to each other. Both began immediately after Edmund's ship, the *Fly*, sailed north early on Wednesday 18 July 1787. This was the beginning of a prolonged exchange of correspondence over the next year, most of which has survived.

As well as expressing the lovers' agony on parting, their longing for each other, their inability to think of other matters, their sleeplessness, and their anxiety about each other's safety and spirits, the letters reveal much about their lives, including their beliefs, hopes and values. The not unpredictable failure of some of Edmund's letters to arrive, given the problems of postal delivery to Donegal from places as far away as Riga, caused Eliza to despair at times of ever seeing him again.

The existence of love letters following a meeting so long ago in such a Romantic location is remarkable. The survival of both sides of the correspondence is doubly so, adding greatly to the completeness, depth and appeal of the story. We hear not only about Edmund and Eliza's love for one another but about their past lives and their families, as well as their present activities and attitudes to those around them. The letters reveal the social and religious views of both writers. We learn why Eliza became a governess and her view of the five small girls of whom she was in charge on Inishcoo. Her strong sense of her own dignity as an educated and independent woman, despite her poverty and lack of a supportive family, comes over clearly. Her letters, while she was on Inishcoo before she sailed with her charges to Dublin in October 1787, also provide numerous sidelights on life on Rutland and Inishcoo. Beginning with a vivid account of the *Fly*'s voyage through a storm to Stromness in the Orkneys, after he left Eliza on Inishcoo, Edmund's letters describe his life as a ship's captain and merchant. Fortunate in coming from a strong and united family, his letters are full both of his travels and of his high esteem for his relations. An unusual feature of the Hurry family was that they were Unitarians, who considered Christ was human and therefore denied the Trinity. Edmund's outlook, however, was largely the tolerant and optimistic one of the Enlightenment.

Edmund and Eliza's meeting, their courtship, correspondence and eventual marriage were only made possible by the existence a highly ambitious plan to develop a north-western fishery in Donegal. It brought Eliza to Inishcoo as a governess; and Edmund to Rutland Island to deliver a cargo of timber from the Baltic and assess the future prospects of the scheme. This provided the opportunity for the lovers' meeting and is an extraordinary story in its own right.

The eighteenth century was a great age of improvement, with many plans being put forward to promote transport, agriculture and commerce, in Ireland as well as in England. In the early 1770s William Burton Conyngham, of Slane in County Meath, an aristocratic, wealthy and well-connected landowner, came up with a grandiose scheme to build a commercial herring fishery, as the centre of a trading and industrial hub, off the coast of Donegal. He invested £30,000 of his own money in the project, but also persuaded the government of Ireland to provide £20,000 towards it.[1]

Conyngham, who was born William Burton, was the nephew of the first Earl Conyngham. He took the name Conyngham when he inherited half of his childless uncle's estate in 1781. A connoisseur, he rebuilt Slane Castle extensively, employing James Wyatt and James Gandon, though he spent little time there.[2] He made an outstanding collection of antiquarian records, commissioning many drawings in Ireland, notably of Glendalough. With his friend, Colonel Tarant, he also visited Portugal and Spain to record ancient buildings, including the medieval monastery of Batalha in Portugal and the Roman theatre at Saguntum near Valencia. He was one of the thirty-eight founding members of the Royal Irish Academy and was its treasurer from 1785 until his death.

*William Burton Conyngham
(1733-1796), by C.G. Stuart, 1792*

---

1   For an account of the project, see James Kelly, 'William Burton Conyngham and the North-West Fishery of the Eighteenth Century', *Journal of the Royal Society of Antiquaries of* Ireland, 115 (1985), pp. 64-85. For detailed information on the modern remains on Rutland Island, Inishcoo and Edernish, see Wesley Forsythe, 'Improving Landlords and Planned Settlements in Eighteenth-Century Ireland: William Burton Conyngham and the Fishing Station on Inis Mhic an Doirn, Co. Donegal', *Proceedings of the Royal Irish Academy*, C, 112 (2011), pp. 301-32.

2   For Conyngham's life and antiquarian interest, see C.E.F. Trench, 'William Burton Conyngham (1733-1796)', *Journal of the Royal Society of Antiquaries of Ireland*, 115 (1985), pp. 40-63. His activities in Donegal are described, ibid., pp. 55-57. William Burton Conyngham used only William Conyngham as a name after 1781, but he is here referred to as William Burton Conyngham for convenience. He never married.

An MP from 1761, Conyngham held several public offices, including those of Teller to the Exchequer and of Comptroller and Commissioner of the Barrack Board, following an earlier career in the army. He took a particular interest in the development of Dublin, sitting on the Wide Streets Commission for over twenty years. He was an influential early supporter of James Gandon's plans for a number of major buildings, though he fell out with Gandon over his design of the Customs House.

Conyngham was in some ways well placed to promote an ambitious scheme of improvement. At a time when Irish landowners monopolised political, social and economic power, he had the capital and the influence to promote it. He had previous experience of commercial success, having built the largest flour mill in Ireland at Slane in 1763, at a total cost of £20,000, with the aid of a £5000 interest-free loan from Parliament.[3]

Conyngham had inherited 100,000 acres in Donegal in 1781 and, having administered them for his uncle before the latter's death, knew the area well. He also had long had an interest in navigation and fisheries, providing a report on the latter to Parliament which Arthur Young relied on is his account of Ireland, published in 1780.[4] As Conyngham later explained:

> Having had various opportunities of visiting the western coast of Ireland from the situation of my family property and from my service as an officer upon this establishment, I saw much reason to lament that no advantage whatever was taken of its harbours, so peculiarly happily situated for commerce; but that the country lay uncultivated and these harbours rendered useless from want of communication by roads with the interior country.
>
> I had in consequence early determined that, if I should be in possession of any of that property, I would dedicate part of it to the improvement of that coast and raise, if possible, a commercial spirit in its inhabitants. The acquisition of a considerable tract of country in the County of Donegal has furnished me an ample field … I entered eagerly upon a plan by which I flattered myself with the expectation of

---

3   Forsythe, 'Improving Landlords and Planned Settlements in Eighteenth-Century Ireland', p. 3. Conyngham built the mill at Slane with his neighbour, Blayney Townley Balfour of Townley Hall.

4   Trench, 'William Burton Conyngham', p. 48. Arthur Young, *A Tour in Ireland*, 2 vols (Dublin, 1780).

Slane Castle, County Meath, rebuilt by William Burton Conyngham. Detail from a copy by Gabriel Beranger of a lost painting by Thomas Roberts

rendering productive a large tract of dreary country by the introduction of trade grounded upon the immediate object of a fishery ...[5]

In February 1785, having already begun work in the Rosses, Conyngham submitted his plan to the Irish Parliament, with the support of the Duke of Rutland, the Lord Lieutenant. Despite objections from existing fishery interests, the Irish Parliament voted him £20,000 towards it under the Donegal Fisheries Act without any serious opposition. As John Parnell, later Chancellor of the Exchequer, said:

What can be greater economy than in laying out a part of the public money at present, to secure an inexhaustible source of wealth for the future? What can be greater economy than in erecting towns where there are none now, and spreading population in a part of the kingdom now almost a desert? And what can be greater economy

---

5   William Burton Conyngham to the Marquess of Buckingham, 1788, British Library, MS 40180, fol. 38.

than providing a nursery for seamen, the best defence of our country against foreign enemies?[6]

Strategically, Conyngham's plan, which aimed at bringing commercial prosperity to Donegal and at stimulating the Irish economy as a whole, had much to recommend it. The magnet of the ports of Liverpool and Glasgow drew shipping from America, the West Indies, Spain and the Mediterranean. Access to a port on the north-west coast of Ireland, offering supplies, ship repairs, an opportunity to receive and send post, and to load and unload goods for the Irish market, would be a great attraction and convenience to ships sailing round the north of Ireland. This was especially so when the northern route also allowed ships to avoid the dangers of sailing up the English Channel. Britain, including Ireland, was at war with France repeatedly during the eighteenth century, and French warships and privateers posed a serious threat to British trade.[7] This threat had recently been increased by the French government's plan for a major expansion of the port of Cherbourg as a naval and privateering base.

As Conyngham explained to the Lord Lieutenant, the Marquess of Buckingham, in 1788:

> Your Excellency's attention to every branch of commerce will I am convinced induce you to see the advantage of establishing a port in such a happy situation on the north-west coast of Ireland, where the trade of Great Britain (in time of war particularly, when a great part of it is induced to avoid approaching the coasts of France) may without deviating from their course supply themselves with provisions and water, repair their vessels and receive intelligence from their owners. Should the scheme of the French at Cherbourg succeed, the trade of England will be necessitated to take this route; and the completion of the canal between the Friths of Forth and Clyde will render this a central port between the Mediterranean and Baltic Seas.[8]
>
> Led into an expence of near £30,000 of my own property to forward these views, having opened communications through the

---

6   Kelly, 'William Burton Conyngham and the North-West Fishery of the Eighteenth Century', p. 74.

7   France and Britain were indeed to be at war almost without a break between 1793 and 1815.

8   Frith was the contemporary form of firth.

country, built a town, established a building yard for ships and prepared everything to encourage commercial exertion, I trust your excellency will countenance my expectations and afford to them the protection of Government so indispensably necessary to such an undertaking.[9]

The centrepiece of Conyngham's plan was a large-scale fishery, with a saltworks to allow the preservation of the fish, and a shipyard to repair and indeed build ships. This in turn depended on the known abundance of the herring in the waters off Donegal. (Herring, once caught, were described as 'red' when smoked and as 'shotten' when dried.) In 1775 he had offered leases in the Rosses, underlining the opportunity offered to Protestants:

To be let from the first of May next, on leases of twenty-one or thirty-one years, or for three lives, to Protestants, the islands of Arranmore, Innis M'Adurn,[10] Inniscoe, Eddenis and Lackenagh; lying and being in the Rosses, in the barony of Boylagh and Banagh, containing many acres of good arable and pasture, with a quantity of seaweed.
     The lands are well known and remarkable for their commodious situation for the purposes of carrying on a most extensive fishery for herrings, cod and other sea-fish. There are now a number of store-houses for curing such fish on said ground, and there are safe harbours for any number of ships at two of the said islands.[11]

The early 1780s saw a series of remarkable catches, drawing a host of small boats, but on an individual rather than a commercial basis. In the winter of 1782-83, £118,170 worth of herring was caught off the Rosses. It was said, 'as many herrings might have been caught off the Rosses in 1782 as would have loaded all the ships in England'.[12] According to James M'Parlan, writing in 1801:

---

9   William Conyngham to the Marquess of Buckingham, 16 August 1788, British Library, Add. MS 40180, fos 37-38. In the original, Cherbourg is given as Cherburg.

10   Later renamed Rutland Island.

11   *Dublin Post*, 14 February 1775.

12   Forsythe, 'Improving Landlords and Planned Settlements in Eighteenth-Century Ireland', p. 24.

In the years 1784 and 1785, the winter fishery produced to the inhabitants of Rosses a sum of £40,000, having loaded with herrings upwards of three hundred ships each of those years. This induced Colonel Conyngham to expend a sum of £50,000, in building houses and stores on the island of Innismacdurn, in the manner of a town, which he called Rutland; and in making roads, through the mountains, to the champain parts of the county.[13]

The fishery was, however, by no means the limit to Conyngham's ambitions. He wished to attract Protestant immigrants to Donegal, rather than relying on the local Catholic population, to run improving farms, capable of supplying the workforce at Rutland. As he explained in a letter to Arthur Young:

You cannot form an idea of that part of my estate called the Rosses from what you saw at Mount Charles.[14] The former is an almost entire moor, not very deep or wet; so much otherwise that a fine pointed grass which it produces is esteemed very good winter food, for which purpose the farms are let, which in summer are put out to cattle. Cultivation, however (of which there are but few traces) renders them capable of producing barley and oats, but the immense amount of fish to this coast enriches the inhabitants so much in a few weeks in winter that they are careless of improvement inland.

My object is to invite strangers to settle and engage in the fishery, which may be carried on to so much more advantage by residents than by a temporary resort in vessels during the winter season. For this purpose I have begun building a town. But it is necessary that the land in the neighbourhood to be rendered capable of furnishing subsistance to the inhabitants; and, for this purpose, I propose to give large farms at a very trifling rent and to pay half the expence of settling the tenants in their buildings, their houses and farmyards.[15]

---

13 James M'Parlan, *Statistical Survey of the County of Donegal: with Observations on the Means of Improvement; Drawn up in the Year 1801 for the Consideration, and under the Direction of the Dublin Society* (Dublin, 1802), pp. 71-72.

14 Mount Charles, or Mountcharles, between Donegal and Killybegs, was the seat of the Conynghams before Slane. William Burton Conyngham was MP for Killybegs.

15 William Conyngham to Arthur Young, 11 July 1783, British Library, Add. MS 35126, fol. 246.

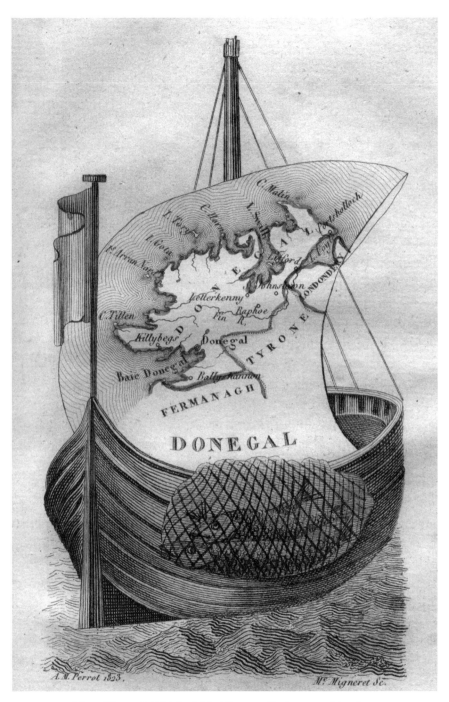

Map of Donegal, 1823, by Michel Perrot, with three netted herrings.
The Rosses are sheltered by the island of 'Arran Nord' on this French map

He even had hopes of recruiting 'loyal American' farmers, who would find farming in Donegal far preferable to colonising the wilds of Nova Scotia or clearing the forests of North America.[16]

To support his plans, Conyngham also started building a road to connect the coast of Donegal to the interior of Ireland. Replacing a road that was almost unpassable, he built one declared to be one of the finest in Ireland from Mount Charles to Glenties, and on to what was at first called Burton's Port, opposite Rutland Island.

Conyngham's chosen site for his fishery was Inis Mhic an Doirn, which he renamed Rutland Island in honour of the Lord Lieutenant of Ireland, the Duke of Rutland. Rutland Island itself, with a safe, deep-water anchorage, was immediately next to two other islands, Edernish and Inishcoo. Although a few fisherman and other inhabitants were living there before the development, it was to all intents and purposes a completely new settlement. Here he set out to build a town and port, with several quays, complemented by a dockyard on Inishcoo.

Conyngham sought to draw 'merchants, boat-builders, sail-makers, rope-makers, coopers employed in fishery … masons, carpenters, sail-makers, slators and other persons employed in building' to Rutland.[17] Begun in 1785, his new town, laid out on a grid, with the streets named after his friends, was to include warehouses, stores, ropeworks, saltworks, cork stores, lime kilns, a brewery and a pub, as well as a dockyard. The next few years saw hectic construction and many visitors.

As a Dublin newspaper reported in 1785, Conyngham was 'building a town with a view to establish a market in the centre of the Rosses', supported by a new road from Mount Charles. At Lackbeg, 'where the ferry is established to pass to Rutland, he has established another inn, where travellers are accommodated as well as in any part of Ireland … It is unnecessary to say anything of the advantageous and secure port of Rutland, where upward of three hundred vessels lay several months during last winter in perfect security, besides which there is very good lying at Cruitt and at Dauras.'[18]

Conyngham himself took an active part in the project. He also, however, had an agent in the Rosses to supervise the works there.

---

16   Trench, 'William Burton Conyngham', p. 56.

17   *Dublin Evening Post*, 15 March 1785.

18   *Evening Post*, 1785.

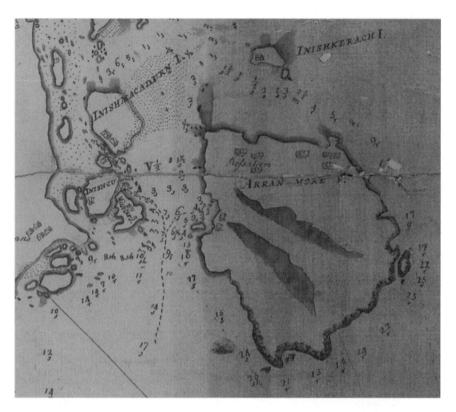

Murdoch Mackenzie, chart of Arranmore, Inishcoo and Inishmacadurn
(later Rutland Island), 1759, with soundings

Mr Corbet, his agent, is actually settled at Rutland; and, from the known abilities of this gentleman, there is no doubt of a rapid progress in the conveniences for trade: a dockyard is already established, and a vessel of sixty tons completed; a most regular and beautiful town is laid out with convenient quay, stores, salt works etc; and nearly twenty houses are covering in; in addition to this, he has brought farmers from different parts of this kingdom to improve the ground and give subsistence to those who will undoubtedly settle themselves in a situation so convenient, not only for the fisheries but for the general trade to the West Indies and America.[19]

---

19 Ibid.

Rutland Island, early 1780s, before the building of Inishcoo House on the neighbouring island

Rutland Island, mid 1780s, showing outline of streets and buildings, and Inishcoo House on the neighbouring island

Unfortunately, Conyngham's ambitions were greater than his business acumen. While a man of energy and taste, Conyngham had little relevant business experience. From an early stage, expenditure outran revenue. Despite the remarkable scale of building activity, and continuing good catches of herring, he was soon experiencing difficulties in paying his bills. From having £37,088 available in March 1786, he was down to £8995 by December 1787 and in debt for £6665 by the end of 1788.[20]

Thomas Mathews of Drogheda, who in March 1786 had agreed to build a saltworks on Edernish and a brewery on Rutland Island, was soon regretting it:

> I never suffered so much as I have done since I came to the Rosses. My men turned out twice, obliged to humer them and very distressing to account them. Up at work every morning at six; often I don't taste a morsel until six in the evening. What I take in hand I will finish. No price fixed on the bullocks or horses at Croi.
>
> Wrote several letters to the Right Hon. William Conyngham and received no answer. Mr Conyngham must see my situation and put matters in some satisfactory form to setle his humble servant Thomas Mathews.[21]

By the middle of 1787, when Edmund Cobb Hurry arrived at Rutland Island in the *Fly*, Conyngham was desperate for further investment, putting his difficulties down to the lack of available capital in Ireland. As he wrote in November that year to the new Lord Lieutenant, the Marquess of Buckingham, who had replaced the Duke of Rutland after the latter succumbed to an overfondness for claret:

> I have had great satisfaction in communicating with some very sensible merchants relative to the Irish fisheries, and I have great expectations of engaging a very considerable House at Yarmouth to settle one of their connexions at Rutland; but if my countrymen

---

20   Kelly, 'William Burton Conyngham and the North-West Fishery of the Eighteenth Century', p. 80.

21   Thomas Mathews to William Burton Conyngham, 29 June 1786, Cliffe-Vigors Papers, National Archives of Ireland. The Cliffe-Vigors Papers, which include material to do with Robert Corbet, William Burton Conyngham's agent on Rutland, contain a number of letters to do with Rutland. The spelling in the letter is the original. Croi was another nearby island used for pasturing cattle. For the full version of two letters from Thomas Mathews to William Burton Conygnham, see below, pp. 281-84.

could be roused to make it a national object, as the Scotch have done, and to enter into a subscription, I have no doubt that it would succeed, as our difficulties arise from want of capital and mercantile knowledge.[22]

The 'very considerable House at Yarmouth' was that of the Hurrys, in which the principals were Edmund Cobb Hurry's father, William, and his uncle, Samuel. William and Samuel Hurry were, however, highly experienced businessmen and unlikely to risk their money in such a hubristic venture. They must have also been alerted, as a danger signal, by the failure of Robert Corbet, Conyngham's agent on Rutland Island, to settle the invoice for the cargo which Edmund had brought.

With credit exhausted, there was no way forward. Corbet, Eliza's employer, sailed away from Rutland with his family, taking Eliza with them, to Dublin in October 1787, though Corbet himself remained involved.[23] While the fishery continued to make good catches in the remaining years of the decade, in 1790 the catch fell to below 10,000 barrels. There was then a disastrous fall in the herring catch in 1793, to a mere 364 barrels, from which the fishery never recovered, leading to its abandonment in 1800. The reason for the collapse remains unclear. It is probable that overfishing, including that of sprats which were not recognised as young herring, led to this catastrophe.[24] More fancifully, it was suggested that Conyngham frightened the fish 'by the noise of hammering onshore by building habitations for fishermen, sheds and warehouses for curing and barrelling the fish'; and even that 'sharks with heads like Dutchmen … drove the fish out to sea'.[25]

In the years that followed, the buildings put up so recently became dilapidated. Then a series of sand storms after 1813, stemming from the loose sand to the west of Rutland Island, buried the new town, leaving only parts of it showing. In April 1820, Nassau Forster, the agent of the Conyngham estate, told his master: 'As the blowing sand continues to infuse

---

22   William Burton Conyngham to the Marquess of Buckingham, 16 August 1788, British Library, Add. MS 40180, fos 37-38.

23   Robert Corbet returned to Rutland and was there at least some of the time during the following years.

24   Forsythe, 'Improving Landlords and Planned Settlements in Eighteenth-Century Ireland', p. 24.

25   Kelly, 'William Burton Conyngham and the North-West Fishery of the Eighteenth Century', p. 82; Trench, 'William Burton Conyngham', p. 57.

the places of Rutland – in the same ratio they have done for the last seven years, your lordship … must be prepared to hear of their becoming totally unproductive and waste altogether'. By March 1822 Forster reported that the sand was 'now twenty feet high close to the door of the sailors' inn and has rendered the whole island a desert. I fear in a little time the whole island must be abandoned'. Another witness described the scene in 1827: 'the sands began to blow and now large ranges of lofty buildings, three or four stories high, are covered on the sea side with sand; you can walk up to the ridge-poles of the roof'.[26]

Painstaking archaeology has now reconstructed the buildings of Rutland Island, Edernish and Inishcoo, rescuing them from the sands of time.[27] This has provided a reconstruction of an extraordinary planned settlement, the result of the ambition by an eighteenth-century connoisseur who was unwise enough to rely on the red herring. Conyngham's abortive scheme also left behind it the correspondence between Eliza Liddell and Edmund Cobb Hurry.

26   Forster to Marquis Conyngham, April 1820 and March 1822, National Library of Ireland, MS 35392/12 and 14; C. Otway, *Sketches in Ireland: Descriptive of Interesting and Hitherto Unnoticed Districts in the North and South* (Dublin, 1827), p. 16. All quoted in Forsythe, 'Improving Landlords and Planned Settlements in Eighteenth-Century Ireland', p. 25.

27   This has been done in admirable detail by Wesley Forsythe in 'Improving Landlords and Planned Settlements in Eighteenth-Century Ireland', which provides a full account of the buildings on Rutland, Edernish and Inishcoo.

Inishcoo

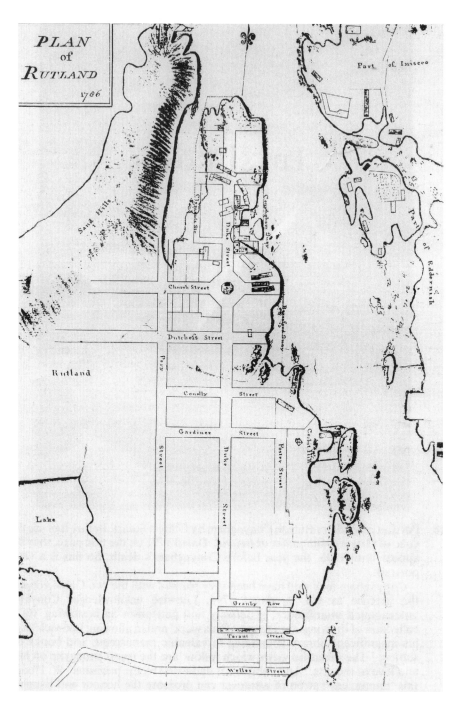

Rutland Island, 1786, from the family papers of Montgomery of Convoy, Donegal

2

Inishcoo

Inishcoo, or Inniscoo as Edmund and Eliza themselves called it, is only separated from Rutland Island itself by the narrow but deep shipping channel between the mainland and Arranmore; and by a much narrower channel from the island of Edernish, the site of William Burton Conyngham's saltworks. Inishcoo, only part of which is shown on a 'Plan of Rutland' dating to 1786, was the site Conyngham's dockyard. This had a wall around it and its own large quay. There was also a house for the shipbuilder, accommodation for labourers and a lime kiln. The bay in front of the quay may have provided space at low water to ground fishing vessels. Otherwise the rocky island was used for grazing.[1]

The most imposing house on Inishcoo, however, and indeed the best house on any of the three islands, was Inishcoo House, a three-story house with pretensions to Georgian elegance. While a number of its features suggest a date of around 1750, its omission from all early maps proves that it was only built at the time of the Rutland Island project, as a suitable house for the agent overseeing it.[2]

Conyngham himself seems to have spent little time at Rutland, leaving

---

1   For the buildings on Inishcoo, see Wesley Forsythe, 'Improving Landlords and Planned Settlements in Eighteenth-Century Ireland: William Burton Conyngham and the Fishing Station on Inis Mhic an Doirn, Co. Donegal', *Proceedings of the Royal Irish Academy*, C, 112 (2011), pp. 20-21.

2   According to Michael Bidnell of the Georgian Group, 'If this rather wonderful-looking staircase were in or around London and the home counties, I would have little hesitation in placing it in the early part of the eighteenth century or even, possibly, the end of the seventeenth century. I am not sure how this would equate to the current location. Architraves look later, but could be mid-eighteenth century; doors look mid-eighteenth century'. I am grateful for this information to Patrick Boner and Wesley Forsythe.

supervision of the works there to his agent Robert Corbet (1741-1804), who lived with his family in Inishcoo House. Corbet, an Irish gentleman from Arneston, County Wexford, came from an ancient Irish ascendancy family, his father having been Dean of St Patrick's Cathedral, Dublin.[3] He and his wife Susannah had eight children, three boys and five girls. While the boys, Francis, Robert and Samuel, were elsewhere, the five Corbet girls, Sarah, Elizabeth, Henrietta, Anne and Ellinor, were on Inishcoo for most of 1786 and 1787.[4] It was as governess to these girls that Eliza herself was living there.

Eliza Anne Liddell had been born in 1762. She was the daughter of James Liddell, a naval surgeon born in Dundee, and of Elizabeth Sharples, whom he had married at Neston, in the Wirral, on 3 January 1756. They may have lived in Liverpool for some time and later at Chester. James Liddell, however, had been lost at sea, leaving his widow only his naval pension.[5] Eliza, who was clearly well educated, had come to Ireland with her mother at the invitation of her sister, Barbara, who was married to an Irishman named Collier. Elizabeth Liddell, however, had died in Dublin and her pension had died with her, while Barbara Collier and her husband had returned to London.

Left destitute and alone in Ireland, Eliza determined to support herself as a governess, taking advantage of her education. Becoming a governess, although it involved many trials, was almost the only career open to women. It allowed educated but impoverished women to earn their own living without losing their residual status of gentility. As Eliza explained in an early letter to Edmund:

---

3   Corbet Hill, Robert Corbet's house, was in Arnestown, County Wexford. In tribute to this house, the highest point on Rutland Island was also named Corbet Hill. The house in Wexford was subsequently known as Corbet Hall and Talbot Hall.

4   Mrs Corbet and some, at least, of her children were away at times. See Eliza Liddell to Edmund Cobb Hurry, Letter 7, p. 55; Letter 8, p. 61. Harriet Corbet was certainly on the island while Edmund was there, Letter 7, p. 55.

5   Many years later, in 1859, Edmund and Eliza's only grandchild, Joseph Alfred Hardcastle, met Eliza's great niece, Eliza Teasdale, in Weymouth. In a letter to him of 25 November that year, she told him: 'With regard to my maternal grandfather and grandmother, strange to say, I know but little. My dear mother doubtless thought it wisest and best not to imbue her children's minds with ideas which never could be realized. My grandfather James Liddell was I think born in Dundee and surgeon in the navy. The ship was lost and my grandmother Elizabeth Sharples, I believe of Liverpool, with her four children received a pension. They lived some time at Chester but my grandmother died I think in Ireland'.

When death tore from me a mother most dear, when my sister returned with her husband to England, I resolved to remain here, deprived of the gifts of fortune. I determined to be as independent as I now could – neither pride nor principle would permit my looking up to my relations for support – by commencing preceptoress to some young people; the situation you now find me in. I considered I would then have the satisfaction of earning my own subsistence, avoid the cruel insolence of proud prosperity, and be gratified by the consideration that I was fulfilling an important duty by my uniform attentions to inspire my young friends with those sentiments of rectitude they could not derive from a mere mercenary.[6]

We learn that for three years Eliza had worked for Robert Corbet's sister-in-law, Mrs Ashworth, followed by two years on Inishcoo. By 1787 Eliza's two sisters, Mary and Barbara, were both living in London, where she also had a cousin, Mr Barnes, who had an elegant house in Westminster. She was a member of the established church.[7] Eliza's sisters, who were more committed religiously than she was, were followers of Methodism, to which they were keen to convert her.[8]

The letters record, in Eliza's words, the moment when Edmund first arrived at Inishcoo House:

I was sitting at this little desk writing to one of my sisters the day you came into the harbour. Mrs Corbet, who knows I dislike being interrupted from her children to attend to the chit chat of morning visitors, contrary to her usually leaving me to follow my own devices, sent for me down to welcome Mr Hurry; but I was fine lady enough to desire being desired. Would I now do so, would I now sit contented upstairs and know you were below? Impossible![9]

---

6   Eliza Liddell to Edmund Cobb Hurry, Letter 1, p. 31.

7   Edmund to Eliza, below Letter 44, p. 252, refers to 'your church' in terms which make it almost certain that this was the Church of England.

8   Methodists, the followers of John Wesley (1703-1791), were still part of the Church of England at the time these letters were written. Methodism was a movement to restore spirituality and personal belief to the largely formal beliefs of the established church of the day. Eliza's sisters were followers of Garnet Terry, a Methodist engraver and preacher who wrote under the name of Onesimus.

9   Eliza to Edmund, Letter 8, p. 64.

Edmund Cobb Hurry, born in 1762, was a member of a prominent family of Great Yarmouth 'Russia merchants', who specialised in trade with the Baltic. The dominant figures in the business were his father, William Hurry, and his uncle, Samuel Hurry, though two other uncles were actively involved. According to a later memoir:

> The four brothers, Thomas, Samuel, William and George, were, in my younger days, all fathers of families, and men of considerable property, and extensive connection in business, and of such weight in the town that they disputed the power of returning the parliamentary representatives with the corporation, and defeated them in the memorable contest of 1784.[10]

The family, including Edmund, were Unitarians, with distinctive nonconformist beliefs, notably a rejection of the doctrine of the Trinity. Edmund himself is described:

> Like most of his family, Edmund Cobb Hurry was a tall and powerful man, and an ardent politician. In 1796 he supported the candidature of Sir John Jervis, afterwards Earl St Vincent, in opposition to Mr Joddrell, who was the government candidate. At the nomination, which took place at the guildhall, Mr Hurry pressed so much upon Mr Joddrell, who was about to speak, as to push him off his legs, 'which led to a great uproar'.[11]

Edmund was the eldest of a family of seven, with two brothers and four sisters. He invariably signed himself using his middle name, Cobb, which was his mother's maiden name. One of his brothers, Ives Hurry, was with him on the trip to Donegal on their ship, the *Fly*. Edmund, already a freeman of Yarmouth by birthright, had spent much of his time over the previous five years living in Courland, in what is modern-day Latvia, working for his father in the family business.

---

10   Dawson Turner, *Spiritual Reminiscences* (1848), p. 44.

11   C.J. Palmer, *Memorials of the Family of Hurry* (1873), p. 67.

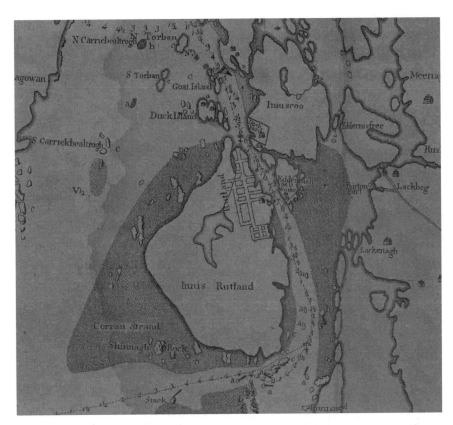

Rutland Island and the Rosses, 1788, by Captain William O'Brien Drury, showing Inishcoo House and Lackbeg, the site of the inn built by William Burton Conyngham

The letters introduce us to the other residents on Rutland and Inishcoo, as well as occasional visitors, seen mainly through the eyes of Eliza. Of these the most prominent were of course the Corbets:

> Mr Corbet, though possessed of some good and praiseworthy dispositions, is the slave of pride, prejudice and passion. Variable, inconstant, he weighs not the chances for or against any scheme he takes in his head. Hence the measures he adopts are all precipitate and too often he has reason to repent having acted in such a rash manner as must hurt himself and those connected with him.[12]

Eliza clearly got on well with Mrs Corbet and describes her at length:

---

12   Eliza to Edmund, Letter 8, p. 61.

Mrs Corbet is the only one I can love here. Her I do sincerely. Though, from her unhappiness of mind, which I cannot help participating, from a peevish and unequal temper, I have little pleasure in her society. She possesses some great and good qualities: the most generous disdain of those who have nothing but rank to recommend them; the most exquisite sensibility for the misfortunes of others; and an integrity of heart that thinks no ill. But her temper is soured by frequent disappointments, too many of them brought on by indiscretions that nothing will I fear ever convert.

Her attachments are all sudden – ardent to enthusiasm. She dresses out those she regards with more than human excellence. She ceases to approve or reject but as they do. She adopts their opinions, their manners, their tone of voice. Hence, when she cannot remain blind to imperfections incident to human nature, to errors the best minds may be surprised into and the worst at times feel compunction for, she is inconsolable, accuses with severity her fate, talks of the dreadful deceit of the world with the utmost acrimony and bitterness, and at times is quite a misanthrope. 'Tis a pity, but where shall we find perfection?[13]

Eliza clearly did her best to educate the girls in her charge but often found it an uphill battle, especially when her mind was fixed on Edmund:

My mornings are now filled up by attending to the children's improvements, but whatever avocations I think I ought to mind I may be said to perform mechanically. They read to me, etc, etc, I correct their pronunciation, their blunders, their errors, without knowing I am doing it. The five weeks I spent with you has destroyed my relish for any other society.[14]

She was not deeply attached to her charges: 'I love Mrs Corbet, but her children I cannot'.[15] She also felt that her own effort at improving the girls were jeopardised by their mother:

---

13 Eliza to Edmund, Letter 11, pp. 85-86.

14 This allows the arrival of Edmund to be calculated. Eliza to Edmund, Letter 8, p. 63.

15 Eliza to Edmund, Letter 16, p. 127.

I think I shall not be long with Mrs Corbet after she leaves this place. I cannot love her children. They are by nature the very reverse of what I would wish them to be. Their understandings are good, but their tempers bad; and they possess a degree of art or cunning, for it is not penetration, which exceeds what I could have had an idea of in creatures of their age; Harriet alas, before I knew her, poor wretched girl. I have done all in my power to check what was wrong in them all and to strengthen what I thought right, but Mrs Corbet, without intending it, counteracts what I do. She holds them at a distance. She is severe for trifles and, though she wishes their confidence, will never gain it, but would not give up her opinions to any other person.[16]

More succinctly, when faced with the prospect of the voyage by ship to Dublin, Eliza wrote, 'I dread the thought of being shut up in it, for perhaps several days, with such a troop of sick and troublesome brats …'[17] Eliza's letters were also written in the midst of hubbub. 'Consider that I write, at any time and in any humour, surrounded by *five* noisy children.'[18]

Two other frequent visitors to Inishcoo House were the local clergyman, John Stewart, the vicar of Templecrone; and Nassau Forster, William Burton Conyngham's agent for his Donegal estates, who lived opposite Inishcoo on the mainland at Lackbeg:

Stewart is generous to profusion. He is not a bad man, but he aims at wit, or rather buffoonery. People laugh with him and at him, but in so doing cease to value or respect him. He makes me angry, more particularly because he is a clergyman. Forster is a man of more refinement but, shall I say it, it appears to me more the refinement of policy than the native inmate of his breast. He likes to be well with everyone. He studies your disposition, he applauds, he flatters. If you can be caught by it, his manners are wary, elegant, insinuating; or coarse, vulgar etc, etc, according to the company he is in. I love these accommodating tempers, or rather principles. Then he is a philosopher and talks to use his own words scientifically on

---

16   Eliza to Edmund, Letter 11, pp. 90-91.

17   Eliza to Edmund, Letter 9, p. 71.

18   Eliza to Edmund, Letter 11, p. 92.

every subject: scientifically on the formation of the heavens and scientifically on the drawing on of his gloves.[19]

Eliza found some of the conversation on offer offensive: 'The people of this kingdom are satirical. They possess lively dispositions which often gives to their satire a humorous turn. To indulge this their women, no less than their men, often forget what is due to themselves and others'.[20] She wished men to treat women with respect:

> Those of you who I will not say condescend (I like not abject expressions when the female part of the world are in question); no, well then, those of you who please to think us of sufficient consequence to ingage your attention, may be of essential service to us; nay enlighten and enlarge our minds, if instead of degrading yourselves and insulting us by the poison of flattery, you treat us as rational creatures, companions, friends.[21]

A particular trial was the boisterous humour of Robert Symes, Mr Corbet's deputy:

> Can I better illustrate this than by telling you (a mortification to conceit) that when Mrs Corbet and I have been in the clouds, and have talked our very best in the midst of our fine speeches, Symes has jumped up, not in ecstacy, not to admire some fine woman passing by, not even to admire himself in the glass, but to examine his *rat traps*. And if his devices, to entrap the unwary rats, have succeeded, with strings fastened to their legs or tail, whatever number he has caught, he marches before him into the room we are sitting in and enjoys the confusion and screaming he occasions, the tumbling over tables and clang, much more than the conversation or company of any woman in the world.[22]

---

19   Eliza to Edmund, Letter 9, pp. 69-70.

20   Eliza to Edmund, Letter 9, pp. 68-69.

21   Eliza to Edmund, Letter 14, p. 106.

22   Eliza to Edmund, Letter 14, pp. 113-14.

In contrast, Eliza found the prospect of a morning spent with Mrs Lawrence, the wife of a merchant, living on Rutland Island, unwelcome for another reason:

The boat is waiting to convey me over to Mrs Lawrence. Church is you know almost out of the question here. What a tiresome morning shall I spend. She will talk me to death and scold me too, or I have great good fortune, for I have not been to see her but twice since your departure. Your departure, alas![23]

There were also occasional visitors. Of these the most interesting were William Hamilton and his wife. Hamilton was an early geologist and the first person to give anything like an accurate description of the Giant's Causeway. He was travelling around Ireland in pursuit of scientific knowledge, notably about the Irish weather:

Mr Hamilton is a Fellow of Dublin College.[24] He seems a man of much information and, if I mistake not, of an eccentric turn. I imagine he is a deep researcher into nature and is travelling more for information than pleasure; or rather that he makes the latter subservient to the former. Accompanied by his wife, he has made the tour of England, Ireland and Scotland. They do not make use of a carriage, but she has rode the entire tour on a single horse.[25]

There is an added piquancy in the description of the Hamiltons in that, thirteen years later, William Hamilton, a staunch supporter of the government, was brutally murdered by a mob at Stratton in County Londonderry.

A more august visitor to the area, if not to Inishcoo itself, was no less a person that the Lord Lieutenant himself, the Duke of Rutland:

But before I go let me, least I forget, communicate a most important piece of intelligence. The Duke of Rutland was three hours on board

---

23 Eliza to Edmund, Letter 9, p. 72.

24 Trinity College Dublin, restricted to Protestants, the only university in Ireland.

25 Eliza to Edmund, Letter 11, p. 90.

the brig.[26] The *Duke of Rutland*, eat beef steaks, on board the brig, this at Killala! Oh how we love to bow down to the great. For, from Mr Corbet down to the little dirty cabin boy, we are all elated at this most extraordinary honour.[27]

The letters which follow are written in the formal, elaborate and sometimes convoluted style of the late eighteenth century. They convey, however, passionate feelings and agonised uncertainty, as well as allowing privileged access both to the hearts of the main protagonists and to an extraordinary moment in the history of Donegal.

The letters written while Eliza was still on Inishcoo begin with the drama of Edmund and Eliza's first exchanges, and the passionate feeling expressed in the first letters written to each other after the *Fly* sailed from the Rosses. Following weeks without hearing from Edmund, Eliza despaired, especially after Mr Corbet received a letter from him without one for her:

Edmund, have I seen you for the last time, the last? Reason, religion strengthens my soul to support an evil I have myself created. And yet not I brought you here. I bid you not appear, to have a feeling, a generous, a good heart to engage my regard, my esteem, my affections, my too anxious interest in your health, your peace, your honour.[28]

Inishcoo House, 1900, also showing the fishing station on Edernish Beag

---

26   Robert Corbet's brig, the *Dutchess*. Charles Manners, fourth Duke of Rutland (1754-1787), Lord Lieutenant of Ireland, 1784-87, toured midland and northern Ireland in the summer of 1787. His death a few months later, on 24 October 1787, from liver disease, was attributed to an excessive love of claret.

27   Eliza to Edmund, Letter 11, pp. 86-87.

28   Eliza to Edmund, Letter 9, p. 75.

Letter 1

Eliza Liddell to Edmund Cobb Hurry
Rutland in the Rosses

Written and delivered by hand before 13 July 1787

You heard me say, sir, I had some intention of going to London – perhaps that I wished to be there – and kindly offered to conduct me yourself.[29] Apprehensive that you may mistake the motive that will compel me to decline this offer, I think it but what is due to you that I should inform you why I must not go. I cannot bear that you should entertain the shadow of doubt that I should be afraid to place myself under your protection. I do not date our acquaintance from the few weeks I have known you, but consider you as an old and approved friend.

Should I then hesitate to go with you, if it was only to procure to myself the happiness of your society, a society too valuable to be given up without regret? But it is not sufficient that we profess the delightful consciousness of upright intentions. We must avoid the appearance as well as the reality of acting wrong. Would not the world condemn me as rash and giddy? Perhaps suspicions more injurious might take place in the minds of many if I were to accompany you – particularly as you are not going immediately to England.

And if you were going immediately to England, I could not go at present, for reasons I will now inform you of. It has long been my intention to go to England. I have no tie to induce me to stay, and in this kingdom I have known nothing but bitter calamity. When death tore from me a mother most dear, when my sister returned with her husband to England, I resolved to remain here, deprived of the gifts of fortune.[30] I determined to be as independent as I now could – neither

---

29   The first written exchanges between Edmund Cobb Hurry and Eliza Liddell have not survived. They both wrote three times to each other before the *Fly* sailed. Only two of Eliza's letters survive (Letters 1 and 2, pp. 31-34) and one of Edmund's (Letter 3, p. 35). Edmund's first missing letter declared his affection for Eliza and listed his own faults. Her reply may have welcomed his friendship but denied that she loved him. His second letter offered to take Eliza with him, to which her reply was this letter. His third told her about his likely movements. Edmund was about to sail from Inishcoo, off the north-west coast of Donegal in an area known as the Rosses, to Derwinda, the modern-day Ventspils in Latvia. He had been in the Rosses for five weeks.

30   Born in England, Eliza Liddell was the orphaned and impoverished daughter of a naval surgeon, James Liddell, and his wife Elizabeth, née Sharples. Together with her sister, Barbara Collier, and her mother, Eliza had come to Ireland, where her mother had died in Dublin.

pride nor principle would permit my looking up to my relations for support – by commencing preceptoress to some young people; the situation you now find me in.[31] I considered I [would] then have the satisfaction of earning my own subsistence, avoid the cruel insolence of proud prosperity, and be gratified by the consideration that I was fulfilling an important duty by my uniform attentions to inspire my young friends with those sentiments of rectitude they could not derive from a mere mercenary. But many things have occurred to render my residence here very, very irksome, some that make me think it a duty to leave it for ever. I have often attempted to do so, but some unexpected obstacle intervened and I have at times been too much lost in apathy and disappointment to forward my own intentions. Pardon me for the length I have undesignedly run on to.

And now I will tell you why I cannot go to London yet. My resolution still remains fixed not to reside with any person but on the terms I now am. I have some relations in London in affluent circumstances, but I know not their dispositions well enough to be certain whether I should like to remain with them until I could procure a situation similar to my present one.[32] One worthy family has long intreated my going to them until convenient to me to leave them.[33] They urge me to leave this place, so hateful because I am chained down to the company of many I cannot love or respect, except one and she by indulging melancholy destroys my spirits.[34] But this family, who I mean to go to for a while, live in Chester. London is the place of your destination. So that you find it is not a distrust injurious to you and foreign to my opinion of you that obliges me to decline an offer that I am truly grateful for.

Cover, none. Postmark, none. Delivered by hand.

---

31 Eliza had been a governess for over five years, for three years to the daughter of Mrs Susannah Corbet's sister, Mrs Ashworth, near Dublin, and then to the five daughters of Robert and Susannah Corbet on the island of Inniscoo for two years.

32 The Barnes family in Westminster.

33 The Eltoft family in Chester. Mr Eltoft's sister was married to Eliza's cousin, John Barnes, with whom he was in partnership in the wine trade.

34 Mrs Corbet had a melancholic disposition. See Eliza to Edmund, Letter 11, p. 85.

Letter 2

Eliza Liddell to Edmund Cobb Hurry
Rutland in the Rosses

Written and delivered by hand before 13 July 1787

Common forms may be necessary to guard from dangerous errors common minds. May I flatter myself mine is not of that stamp; and that it will not be considered a breach of decorum, by him I address, that I should take this method of saying farewell: that I should give him this testimony of regard in what consists the difference between writing and speaking. If agitated, as I am at this moment, the latter will perhaps be denied me.

A few short hours and I may look for you in vain. I shall see you no more. What a thought is that. How shall I stifle the distress it occasions me? The beings that surround me understand not any language but that of interest (one only excepted). They would laugh at, perhaps deride, my lamenting the loss of a companion whose value they know not, whose worth they could never comprehend. My soul shrinks from a communication of even opinion (sentiment they know not); is sunk in reserve; is oppressed beyond endurance with people of the cast I am doomed to drag out my time with.

Is it any wonder, bred in elegant retirement, early taught to relish the intrinsick value of merit, early taught to despise people who had nothing to recommend them but the fortuitous advantages of fortune? Is it any wonder that meeting with one so congenial in mind to the friends I have lost that I should pay him the tribute of esteem?

Ah, how different the hours I have spent with you from those I have so long set down as lost! Hours of pleasure, of instruction, of happiness. Were you indeed my brother, could I treat you with a greater degree of unsuspecting confidence? Could I feel more forcibly the earnest hope that you might think me worthy to be ranked among the number of your friends? Shall I own to you that I am not a little proud that I have been able so far to discriminate, to distinguish, as to enable me to select for my friend one who does honour to my head and heart? And am I to root out these better feelings of my soul to conform to vulgar and low-minded prejudices? Ah me! I will cherish your idea ever. Ever will you be most dear to me. Your health, your happiness – have you a sister who would be more tremblingly alive to ought that might interrupt them? That you may be a stranger to anxiety, that God Almighty may bless and prosper you, is (and can it ever cease to be?), the first wish of Eliza Anne Liddell.[35]

Cover, none. Postmark, none. Delivered by hand.

Inishcoo House, 2017, retaining many of its original features

---

35 This reveals Eliza's middle name. It was the name that she and Edmund gave their first child, though she always referred to their daughter as Anne, while he referred to her as Ann, perhaps out of his affection for his maternal grandmother, Ann Cobb, and his own mother, Ann Hurry.

Letter 3

Edmund Cobb Hurry to Eliza Liddell

Written and delivered by hand, 13 July 1787

12 o' clock, Fryday 13 July 1787

I could not stop after I left you, Eliza, till I had performed a promise made you of endeavouring to acquaint you with the places and times which, thro' God's assistance, I hope to be in the ensuing parts of this year, more particularly as I am perfectly convinced it is not indifferent to you.

From hence I should hope not to be more than eight or ten days at most to Elsinore, where I am obliged to go on shore to clear and from whence a post goes to London twice a week in fourteen days' time.[36] There I am addressed to at Messrs W. Diston Son and Co.; and we will put down, if I may presume to anticipate, the 23rd or 24th July to be about the time I shall arrive there. From thence to Derwinda about seven or eight days may serve here. We'll say the 1 August to be the day.[37] And from thence likewise a post twice a week goes to London, but is four whole weeks. At that place I may stay three or four weeks, say till about the latter part of August, if I should not be under the necessity of staying the whole winter; tho' I do not believe that will be the case. There a letter finds by being only addressed to me, i.e. to Mr Edmund C. Hurry (not to E.C.H. Esq.), at Derwinda, Courland. Should I leave that place I may in all probability return to Elsinore by 14 September and be home by the latter part of that month. But before that time, if E.C.H. breathes, you may depend on hearing more fully what is likely to be the future listing of one who, with great pleasure, subscribes himself your sincerest friend and eternal wellwisher, Edmund Cobb Hurry.[38]

Cover, none. Postmark, none.

---

36 Much of the correspondence reflects the cost and uncertainty of postal deliveries in the late eighteenth century.

37 Derwinda, Windau or Der Windau in the duchy of Courland in the Baltic; now Ventspils in Latvia.

38 The *Fly* sailed early on Wednesday 18 July, having been delayed for several days by adverse winds. Edmund Cobb Hurry had arrived at Rutland five weeks earlier. Counted exactly, this would fix the day of his arrival on Inishcoo as Wednesday 13 June 1787.

Letter 4

Eliza Liddell to Edmund Cobb Hurry
Rutland in the Rosses

Written 23 July 1787; sent from Inishcoo, 27 July;
received at Elsinore, 10 September

Rosses, Monday 23 July 1787

These silent hours of midnight and of melancholy I will devote to you. Would to heaven I could indeed devote them to you that I could see: that I could hold converse with you. Edmund, dear Edmund, great as was my distress, I knew not while I saw you what would be the anguish of my soul when the moment of separation arrived. That moment is past and each succeeding one serves but to remove you to a still greater distance. Stupid, absorbed, I sat for hours after you were gone, unconscious to ought but the pang of parting. Your voice still vibrated on my ear. Every present object receded from my view. And I saw only the form, ever in idea, before me.

This island, once disagreeable, is now become dear to me. Each walk we took, each rock we sat on, all, all memory delights to dwell on. In this room, at this very table I have seen, I have talked, and to you; and how insipid, how tormenting is now the conversation of every other. I avoid it as much as possible, shut up in my own room. I picture to myself my absent friend (that health daily drunk at dinner, said with so much *sang froid*, how vain my attempts to pronounce). I see him shut up in his cabin,[39] incapable as I am of applying to anything, lost in a profound reverie, thinking, perhaps, and surely it is not an improbable hope, thinking of me; while I am denied the happiness of seeing you, even for a moment, and a wide, a terrifick waste of waters rolls between. That thought. Ah, what a dire train of ills does it convey.

Attend, Edmund, my manner of thinking may be an erroneous one. I presume not to be my own judge, tho' to myself I appear not

---

39   Spelt 'cabbin' in the original but modernised here and below.

wrong when I express to you with unrestrained freedom the effusions of tenderness and truth. I should blush to entertain any sentiment that could not stand the test of even an enemy's investigation. Why then conceal from you how very dear you are to me? What a low species of deceit is the affectation of disguise. I cannot adopt what I have been taught to hold in contempt. It would indeed be now too late. You saw what passed in my soul ere I was aware of danger, ere conviction flashed on my mind, that your image was stamped in characters indelible there. Mrs Corbet might well tell me my fancied security was my greatest danger. I laughed at and disregarded what she said. She saw me not happy but serene and unruffled, looking down, if I may be allowed to say so, on the world with indifference; an indifference that I imagined in one instance would never give place to sensibility. Not that my heart was not fully fraught with those dispositions that might lead it to attachment, but it might never meet with the object to rouse what had so long remained dormant.

What a strange revolution has a little time produced. A gleam of happiness shot athwart my way that has left me a prey to doubt, to hope, to anxiety. The 'Ruminating Animal' (as Mrs Corbet used sometimes to call me), when she saw you, ceased to reflect, gave herself up without reserve or consideration to the charm of your society, to the happiness it afforded her; felt an anxious, an ardent desire to be pleasing to you and sighed for the first time in her life at the consciousness of not possessing those brilliant talents that might tend to secure your affections. This was an unworthy thought and I repelled its growth. I did not use to wish for what might inspire vanity, tho' it was not the influence of vanity that suggested the wish.

Mine is a tenderness unutterable – to passion I am a stranger – a tenderness that has your eternal as well as present felicity at heart; that would rather see you in prison and in chains, virtuous and good, than placed on a throne, an apostate from those excellent dispositions God Almighty has implanted in your soul. Yours is a benevolent, a refined, an elegant mind, and you possess many of those softer excellencies which are seldom met with in your sex. That unpersuadableness (for I will not, as you do, term it obstinacy) of temper proceeds, or I am much mistaken, from the general soundness of your judgment, as you seldom form opinions that are not just; and from a degree of feeling that bears down all before it. Why then so heavily complain of a propensity that in some cases, if not carried to excess, is but a proper firmness?

That you have failings I doubt not, but wrong not yourself so much as to suppose them too deeply rooted to be extracted. Yours is a heart capable of every generous, every noble effort and I doubt not if I live to see you, to see you alas, to see you superior to these faults that may have hitherto [*tear*] the lustre of those amiable dispositions you surely possess. When, oh when, should I be tired of writing to you, forgetting that, barren of incident, this has nothing to recommend it but its being a faithful transcript of a heart that is entirely yours? Perhaps it may never meet your eye. What a way, what a long way has it to go. Say, shall I hear from you? Or do you intend to be a pupil of Pompey the Little?[40] Remember you his ungrateful forgetfulness of his friend. One little week and he remembered her no more. And he was but a *dog*. Adieu, adieu. Let me conclude, even my tears blots the paper. Yours ever most truly Eliza A. Liddell.

Mrs Corbet still remains at Mr Olphert's, Mr Corbet in the mountains. And where are you?[41]

Cover, Mr Edmund Cobb Hurry, Messrs John Diston Son and Co., Elsinore. Note, 'No. 1. Received the 10 August 1787'. Postmark, Rutland, 27 July.

---

40   Francis Coventry, *The History of Pompey the Little: or The Life and Adventures of a Lap-Dog* (1750).

41   The Olphert family lived at Ballyconnell House, Falcarragh, Donegal. Robert Corbet (1741-1804), an Irish gentleman from County Wexford, was William Burton Conyngham's principal agent in the development of Rutland Island. The date of receipt is given by Edmund Cobb Hurry incorrectly as 10 August. He, in fact, did not receive the letter until 10 September.

Letter 5

Edmund Cobb Hurry to Eliza Liddell
Stromness

Written 17-26 July 1787; sent from Stromness, 26 July;
received at Inishcoo, 24 August

26 July 1787

Here have I been trying to fold this up so that you might not have any of the previous writing and also to make it look as thin as possible, tho' it's large enough of all reason for a state packet. Well so so much for folding up, and now for compliments etc. First then Mrs Corbet (as I think I shall write Mr Corbet if I have time).[42] My best respects attend her and my sincerest wishes for her speedy recovery to that state alone in which we can enjoy life. To Harriet and the rest of the family whatever you think proper; so in short to Mr Forster, Stewart, Turner, Symes, and all it is proper, suitable remembrance.[43] Nor forget your dear, dear Mrs Lawrence.[44] I should be sorry she should have teased you again, but I fear you have been obliged to go there several times since I left you.

I must now tell how this letter is to travel to you, as I have made particular enquiries about it; and then make all the haste I can to put it in the post office, as the wind is come eights fair, and we must go away immediately. It first goes from hence cross the rapid Pentland

---

42   Edmund Cobb Hurry had brought a cargo, almost certainly of timber from the Baltic, to Rutland.

43   Robert Corbet's daughter Henrietta (or Harriet) was one of Eliza's charges as governess. Nassau Forster, who lived at Lackbeg, opposite Inishcoo on the mainland, was the agent for William Burtom Conyngham in Donegal. His name is given as 'Foster' in the original.

44   Mr Lawrence, whose wife lived a boat trip away from Inishcoo, probably on Rutland Island, had a brig and was a merchant. The Reverend John Stewart had been the vicar of the local parish of Templecrone since 1781. He lived at Maghery, on the coast to the south of Inishcoo. Robert Symes, who lived on Inishcoo, acted as the deputy to Robert Corbet, see below, Letters 9, 10, 14, pp. 66-83, 104-14 and Appendix, A5, A6, pp. 287-90. Turner appears to have been in charge of some of the technical installations on the island.

Firth; then 250 miles to Edinburgh by a foot post all the way, which takes up seven days; from thence to Holyhead;[45] and I fear it will be four from thence to you. So that will make thirteen days. Remember it is now exactly eight times twenty-four hours since I took my leave of Inniscoo, of you, of joy, that is.

It is now Thursday morning 9 a.m. the 26th day of July 1787. I must now conclude by wishing you all that is fit for you in this world and the next, and subscribe myself most truly your sincerest friend and most earnest wellwisher, Edmund Cobb Hurry.

July 1787

Beginning

I could wait no longer than till the ship was round the Staggs,[46] and even that with the greatest impatience, before I sate down to pen a few lines to my dearest Eliza. For I could not forgive myself if, after the sorrow you expressed at my departure, any opportunity should offer, either by ship or otherwise, to have had no letter ready. But even here I have an interested motive to actuate my conduct. For I am truly uneasy. And I do hope after the present conference, for I must hold it as such, to be able to perform some of my neglected duties, which I could not at present tho' my life depended on it. Yet I flatter myself I have omitted nothing essential and that it will only cause my time to be more crowded with occupations and employments than it would otherwise have been. And I trust the necessity of them may be some means of my not suffering so much from the absence of one in whose company the days and weeks have passed away like a dream; and the want of which would otherwise make days months and weeks years.

Even now I am a little easier, tho' Arran is almost lost to view.[47] But I can now pity poor Ives, who has been crying ever since Mr

---

45   Spelt Edingburg and Hollyhead in original.

46   The Stags, three rocks or stacks (called Una, Brian and Teague) just to the north of Rutland Island.

47   Arran or Arranmore Island off Donegal, not the Arran Islands off Galway or Arran off Scotland.

Corbet left us to think he should not have taken leave.[48] And I am sorry I forgot to take him on shore with me this morning, but at his age Inniscoo will soon be forgot; it is now no more than 10 o'clock and Inniscoo is scarce discernible. I must take one more look, and then bid adieu to it for months. Yet if hope could flatter me, or even imagination present one prospect to me, in which I might only doubt or distrust that idea, it would cause a transient joy to cross my mind and make me for a moment easy. I am now called on deck. Adieu.

Now have passed Tory, and I have not been able to do one individual thing more than to think on what I ought do; to resolve to begin about it immediately; to re-resolve; and to be as far from it as ever.[49] The boy has now called me to dinner, and I'll go because it may amuse me. No, I'll go because we'll drink our 'Absent Friends' in a bumper of port, knowing that one who is so dear to me is doing the same, and much about the same time, as for this day we have not varied from the polite hours of the Rosses. But from henceforward about half after twelve o'clock at noon and eight at nights will be the times we shall more particularly think (if it were possible to think more particularly at one moment than another) of those whom if I ever I forget may I myself be amongst the forgotten.

I have now dined and I want your company as much more as I should do my clothes if I had lost them; as the Mind is more endued with sensibility than the Body. It is an odd thought, but I write as free to you as if I thought no mortal eye should ever see it, and I know you'll excuse it. But give me leave to tell you that, if I am as unhappy every day as this, it will be most prudent for me to hasten back to Inniscoo, as I shall be fit for neither company nor business. For the first I care not, as I wish not really to enjoy myself till you make one of it. But I must endeavour to preach to myself that the latter will be to our mutual advantage. And, could I once persuade or rather assure myself of that, I think I should be able to perform wonders in the way of trade and make as hard a bargain as the best of them.

I hope you'll talk in the same way to me as I have done. And, as

---

48   Ives Hurry, the younger brother of Edmund Cobb Hurry.

49   Tory Island, nine miles off the north-west coast of Donegal.

whatever comes into your thoughts or whatever objects you have before you will be always new and interesting to me, if I am not unreasonable, may I entreat you to write me some few lines every day, as I shall do so to you, and always have some letter ready. But I cannot go on at such a rate for every half day as I have done now, for neither your fortune or mine could support that. Let me see: it would be 730 sheets per year, say upon an average 2s. 6d. a sheet, would be near £100 per annum for postage for each of us.[50] But to remedy this, and that you may not pay so dear for such nonsense, I shall continue to write whatever comes into my head and, when an opportunity offers per ship, shall send you several sheets together. Therefore I think it will be best to form them after my journal and therefore I will call the foregoing Thursday till 4 o'clock the afternoon. Tory Island is now SSW eighteen miles from me, so that I am now at least forty miles from my dearest Eliza. Once more adieu.

We have now once more been drinking your health, tho' can scarcely hold either bottles or glasses as it now blows a storm, and I enjoy it, for it suits the temper of my uneasy and troubled mind. I thank God for it. I could not bear a calm, and I am really happier now bustling about than I could be had I nothing to take up my thoughts. And I trust omnipotence will see us safe thro' it. The ship rolls so much that I can scarce sit to write. And yet I must tell you that Ives, young Stewart and a few more have been casting up their account books; whether they balance or not I cannot say.[51] They have paid dear for stuffing too much before they came out; not all the dainties your Florio was invited to would tempt any of them now.[52] I have been attempting to read it since tea, but, alas, reading has now no entertainment for me. So I took and sowed it together and made a book of it. It is now near 11 o'clock and tho', on account of our situation, I shall not go to bed yet, I must bid my Eliza good night.

And may the Almighty watch over and protect her from every danger.

---

50 At this rate the total would have been £91 3s. a year each or £182 6s. together. The cost of postage proved an inhibition on Edmund and Eliza's courtship, as did the uncertainty of delivery.

51 A euphemism for seasickness.

52 Florio, an unidentified fictional character in a book Edmund seems to have been reading.

Land, land, my Eliza, and a good morning to you. Thanks to that God whom the winds and waves obey, we are now running along the western isles of Scotland, the storm not much abated, but fair. And then so smooth I wish Eliza here. What is she now doing? Let me see, just fallen asleep. It's now only four o'clock. May she sleep on to dream of me.

We have this day passed four ships and I could then have wished for fine weather, as I dare say they were bound for some port in Ireland and I would have sent you this letter. But it was impossible in such a storm. Now the storm is over and we are safe past the Isle of Skye. Once more all our sails are spread to catch the falling gale and, thank God, it is still favourable. Now I am sitting two hundred miles from Eliza writing this; and you are dressing for dinner. I wish it was to dine with me, but I have already taken (I may say) my solitary meal; not such as I was wont to enjoy at Inniscoo.

I know not how it is, but if I am two hours without writing something to you I am quite uneasy; and if it is but a line I find myself much relieved. You know, Eliza, I promised you nothing more than nautical observations, such as soundings, winds etc, and you now find I have kept literally to that promise. Our fine wind has at length failed me and a compleat calm hath succeeded it. Indeed it generally verifies the old proverb; but you know I did not agree to write proverbs to you. I can bear the calm better this afternoon than I could have done the last. A settled melancholy (if I may use that expression, for it's rather a perpetual want of something; in short, I know not what to call it other than a gloom over my mind for the want of your company, which if I know myself will be a lasting one) hath succeeded that violent agitation and perturbation which possessed my mind. And nothing can be a better companion for it than the present state of the sea, which I told you yesterday was all violence. Tho' now subsided, [it] is still accompanied by a horrid gloom which spreads over the whole face of the water, and gives a dismal or rather dreadfull appearance to the lands and islands which surround us.

And now I have undertaken to make a sailor of you (without applying my comparison any further, for it has nothing to do with seamanship), I'll endeavour to make you acquainted with this dangerous channel, which is full of hidden tho' not unknown rocks. It lies between the Hebrides (or rather Lewis) and the Isle of Skye and the western coast of Scotland, which are to the eastward of us. It is not much more than a mile broad between the sunken rocks and is full as dangerous for a ship as from Rutland to Mr Stewart's is for a boat.[53]

I was just called away from my writing (by Ives) to look at a fish they had caught, but it was only a poor gurnard and will not make one of us a meal.[54] You must not wonder if I sometimes use the plural number when you might think the single would do as well, but kings and commanders are allowed that priviledge. I ought to have put commanders before kings, for I degrade myself. It is now 6 p.m. Fryday (i.e. 6 o'clock Fryday afternoon) and a.m. before noon is from 12 at night to noon. This is a sea slang which I must learn you, if you are not already acquainted with it, as I may often use it unknowingly. This is no. 1, page 4.

Now I have completely filled four sides, and yet I cannot go to bed without taking leave of my Eliza. It's only 9 o'clock, and we have yet a fine favorable breeze again, but I have not yet been in bed since I left you, forty hours nearly, and I am rather tired. However, now it's fine weather, I'll make up for what I lost last night. So God preserve you and me and defend us this night. And tomorrow you shall have some more lines, as I hope to be able to send this from the Orkneys, if we should go thro'.

Good morning to you Eliza, have you slept sound? This night nine hours has served me, but I find we are very little advanced since I left the deck. And what little wind there is at present is quite against us; the sea smooth as glass. Several vessels to be seen but all a long way from me. Here have I been talking to you and you are fast asleep, but pray get up. It's a fine morning and fit to bathe in, and you need not fear my surprizing you. Often I fancy that rock from which I bathed. Miss Harriet, I suppose this morning you will sit upon it, but not so softly as you did then; so I hope you'll think of your cushion.[55]

What would I give to be still so.

---

53   Mr Stewart's house at Maghery was indeed more hazardous to reach from Inishcoo than Burtonport.

54   Difficult to read, probably gurnard.

55   Henrietta Corbet may have sat on Edmund.

Well, it's now Saturday evening, say 8 o'clock, and we have got a strong breeze against us, which I fear will continue; and numbers of ships are continually passing us with fine fair winds bound home, but [I] have not been able to get on board any of them. This day, but for two three wicked thoughts, I should have employed my time tolerably well, tho' not much to the purpose, as I have been obliged to vary from one thing to another, to keep my attention fixed, as [I] could not continue so to any one thing except thinking of you. However I managed to read a little Latin, a chapter [of] modern history and some problems of geometry, as likewise two whole hours of accounts.[56] Now I should like to know whether you have employed your time better.

We are about ninety-six miles distant from Cape Wrath, the north-western extremity of Scotland, and I question whether we advance much nearer it this night. Pray do not forget to tell Mr Stewart that his son soon conquer'd the sea sickness and I think will be a brisk boy.[57] His companions as well as the mate say he is very proud. You think him conceited. I have not seen enough of him to judge whether he ought to be corrected of either of them. His pride may be nothing more than a proper degree of spirit and, if so, ought rather to be encouraged, tho' I would not wish to encourage conceit. But here it is too late or improper to reprove it. I think it makes a person at every age appear ridiculous and I know [*blank space with y at its end*]. I would sooner endeavour to raise a general laugh than licentiousness. In short I make it a rule never to ridicule any other defects than those which might have been avoided by a person's own care; and which I think may be hunted down as proper game without any offence to good breeding. But here I mean no further than what any person pretends to which he has not but might have had.

Do you know that this is a memorable night on board of all ships, for all these sailors are now employed drinking this Saturday night's toast, 'Sweethearts and Wifes'.[58] Perhaps you were not acquainted

---

56 An eclectic choice of reading by an educated merchant.

57 For other references to William Stewart, see Edmund to Eliza, Letter 6, pp. 52, 55; Letter 10, p. 82; Eliza to Edmund, Letter 14, pp. 112-13.

58 Tactfully, Edmund has omitted the second part of the toast: 'And may they never meet'.

with this before, but all the relations of sailors are, and they generally drink it on the night ashore and receive some satisfaction from being conscious that their friends are employed in the same way and much at the same time. It is now eleven o'clock and I do think you are now praying for my safety and I find a comfort in believing that. And now I'll entreat the Universal Father to shower down the choisest of his blessings on you, and then go to bed and perhaps dream of being with you. So good night again.

Another fine bathing morning. Well how have you rested last night? I've been lazy indeed: was called at 6 and did not get up till after 7. Again fine but tedious weather, at least still thirty miles from Cape Wrath, but I hope we shall get round today. This is Sunday. Do you go to church, or are you reading sermons at home? I have been reading the sixth chapter [of] Mathew. Remember me in your prayers (but as it said in a verse there, 'suffer not vain repetitions').[59] So I shall always think of you in mine, and wish myself better that they might have more weight. For I do not believe that the earnest entreaty of an upright heart will be disregarded by the Father of Mercies, for which reason I doubt not but yours will be to my eternal advantage, as I find your acquaintance has already influenced my conduct towards many good actions already, if I may be allowed to call any of mine such. However, I may with truth say it has caused many good thoughts and intentions, which I hope will not, like many of my former resolutions, vanish in air.

It is 8 at night and rather further off from the cape than we were at noon, so that instead of advancing we have receded this day. It has been a tiresome day to what last Sunday was, and I have no other prospect but that of spending many more such. It is dreadfull to think, but I must endeavour to apply myself diligently if possible, and by that means I shall at last be easier. I have now been reading till 1 a.m. Quite tired and, tho' it is not yet 10 o'clock, I believe I shall go to bed. I would give you all the little I am worth for the sake of your company. I never was such an enemy to the opinions of the world before. I have been reading your three epistles over and over

---

59   Matthew 6:7, 'And when ye pray, use not vain repetitions, as the heathen do: for they think they shall be heard for their much speaking'.

again and, tho' there are some things which give me pain in them, yet upon the whole I receive great satisfaction from them. So they will be my only resource till I have the pleasure of hearing from you. This is Sunday night. A direct contrary wind, but I have still reason to be thankfull to the great first cause of all things that it's moderate, to whose protection I commend you, and hope you will pass the night comfortably. Adieu.

It is now near dinner time and I have not once said good morning to my Eliza, but I thought a few hours ago I should never write to her again. And yet I am not one of those that despair, but I was taken so suddenly and so violently ill this morning that I scarce thought I should have lived an hour. I know not what it was, or to what to attribute it, but I thank God I find myself much better now. And so I just sate down to scribble these few lines, and to tell you we were advanced no further, but are just the same distance from the cape as we were some fifty hours ago. It is already Monday night, and yet we are but little forwarder on our voyage than we were on Friday night.

I hope I am quite recovered from my sudden illness, as I feel nothing like a return of it. I dare say you will be quite tired of reading this long scrawl, for you must know I write so close that it is already near the length of an ordinary sermon. And then it's all about I. But I have neither capacity or inclination to write about anything else. And so good night and God bless you, Eliza, and grant that we may come speedily together again. You are still scarce ever from my thoughts but when I am sleeping, and even then I often dream of being in your company, but awake to solitude again; and then I almost wish I could sleep for ever. Yet I would hope I shall employ my time better, nor have we any need to wish it away, for it flies very swiftly and with you it does indeed. How short these five weeks appear, which I passed so agreeably.[60] It makes the present tiresome and tedious days seem long, very long; nor when they'll end I know not. So we advance very slowly.

It's now 9 o'clock Thursday morning and I suppose you are just getting up, but I have breakfasted. I would hope that this letter

---

60   On this calculation, the *Fly* had arrived at Rutland on Wednesday 13 June 1787.

might reach the Orkney port this day; however, I must prepare some for home, in case it should happen so. Again disappointed. Now near to 10 at night and are at least thirty miles from the Orkneys. I believe no people meet with so many disappointments as the sailors. Continually are they flattered with prospects of speed by finishing their voyage and as often see their hopes blasted. And we are certain it ought not to be as we most eminently wish, or if it was what impression it would have in the world. And therefore I like Pope's line, 'to reason right is to submit';[61] so, trusting that the allwise disposer of events will order all for the best, I'll bid my Eliza once again good night, and, after recommending you, myself and all mankind to the care of Our Father who is in heaven, endeavour to take a few hours of repose.

Now do you know it's almost 12 o'clock Wednesday night and I have not once said good morning to my dearest Belle (no, I meant Eliza, for I do not like the other name); but when you know I did not purpose to spare your pride, I suppose you may possibly not be much pleased.[62] However I solemnly declare it was on no other account whatever. And so do not say I forget you, for I may safely say I have not had you one hour out of my thoughts since I left you (except sleeping).

And at 9 o'clock tomorrow morning it will be eight full days, but it was solely that I thought to get into the Orkneys this day, and to have been able to direct on the back of this sheet, but I could not get on shore this evening. On the contrary we are lying in a very dangerous place for the ship, all amongst rocks. And tho' I cannot go to bed tonight, yet I think we shall get safe off. And so to ease my mind a little I run the risk of another half sheet of nonsense. But if you are displeased at it, and do not like this way of writing, I insist upon it that you inform me of it immediately and I shall alter it to a more epistolatory like letter.

You can't think what pleasure it gives me to imagine that you'll get this letter, rather journal, I should have said, in about eleven days

61   Alexander Pope, *Essay on Man*, i, line 164.

62   Nickname. It is unclear whether this is Belle, Bella or something else. See also Edmund to Eliza, Letter 33, p. 199.

from this time, which will be at least sixteen or eighteen days sooner than I gave you leave to think of hearing from me.[63] And if your esteem or affection, or whatever you please to call it, is in proportion so much greater than mine now, as I thought it was at the Rosses, it will give you some pleasure. And, I assure you, it will be no little satisfaction to me at any time to be able to do that. Have I not made you some amends for not writing this morning? And the other half side must also be filled with compliments, remembrances etc, but I can't write one word more tonight as the tide is come in and we must try to get the ship from this dangerous situation, so God bless you.

Well just so it was. Bump came the ship upon the rocks, and a tiresome night we have had of it; how would you have called out if you had heard the ship thump. But thank God we got off without damage and are now safe riding at Stromness in the Orkneys.[64] 6 o'clock Thursday morning. I'll go to take an hour's nap. Adieu.

Cover, Miss Liddell, Rutland in the Rosses, Ireland. Postmark, Kirkwall, date unclear but 26 July.

---

63   Eleven days would have allowed delivery on 6 August. Due to delays in the post, the letter was only delivered over three weeks later on 24 August.

64   Stromness on Mainland in the Orkneys.

Letter 6

Edmund Cobb Hurry to Eliza Liddell
Elsinore

Written 27-30 July 1787; sent from Elsinore, 30 July;
received at Inishcoo, 19 August

I am happy to inform my dearest Eliza, what I hope she'll know long before she receives this, that is my sending her my first epistle or rather journal containing nine full sides from Stromness in the Orcades, from whence we sailed yesterday evening or rather afternoon as soon as I put it in the post.[65] And I should have already filled another whole side, tho' it's only Fryday morning, had we not such very rough weather that I even now with difficulty can sit to write this. And could I be easy without talking to you (for I think I am doing so), I should have deferred it a little longer.

You are now got down in the parlour to breakfast, I think at this moment. I see you open the tea chest. I wish it were really so, but I often find a pleasure in deceiving myself in that way and perceiving you in imagination. I also wrote to Mr Corbet by the same post to tell him you were going to turn sailor next year; and, for that reason, I had sent you my journal to study. I intend this should only be a single sheet from Elsinore, if please God we have a speedy passage, and I can keep my nonsense to myself. What think you, we are already above a hundred miles from the Orkneys in the middle of the North Sea, rolling and lumbering about in a very tiresome manner, but a fine, fair breeze.

I ought to have told you something of Stromness. It is situated on the south-west end of the island or mainland of the Orkneys, appears to me a full half mile in length, of which alone it consists, as a place cannot be said to have any breadth when there is only one street and more particularly when that street is so extensive as to be eight feet wide and it did not seem to be any larger. And then it is paved with large flagg stones, not like the foot ways in London for they are even, but here you seem as tho' you were continually going

---

65   Orcades, or Orkades, is Latin for the Orkneys.

up and down stairs. Or rather it is not quite so level as the island [of] Inniscoo, where we used to ramble. But because this said street is so narrow, pray do not imagine that it is strait; quite to the contrary, for, by the time you have walked eight or ten yards, you'll find the corner of a house, right bump in your way, and this occurs frequently.

And the reason I know so much about it is because I had to carry my letters to the post office, which was at the farther end from which I landed, and I did not chuse to trust them to anyone else. I was not above three quarters of an hour on shore, so cannot say anything respecting the inhabitants, except that they seemed to be very civil. For many of them entreated me to come to their houses, tho' I never was in the place before, but my own relations are almost all well known there.[66] And they told me, what made me very proud of my family, that my name was enough to introduce me to any house on their island. They supplied me with plenty of eggs and greens, which were very acceptable. But I was obliged to hurry away, the wind being quite fair.

It is Sunday morning and not one word for forty-eight hours. It is too much, I allow, but good reasons, did you know what I have been doing. Travelling 440 miles in so short a time could not be accomplished with much ease. We have had a quick passage thus far, but it has been a rough one. Not one moment could you have sat still, many things flying about our ears. Yet amidst all we did not forget our Saturday night toast, nor have we ever missed a meal without drinking our friends at the Rosses. We are now in a place called the Cattegatt, running along the coast of Sweden, and if the wind was fair might be at Elsinore tonight.[67] But I fear we shall not be able to reach it.

I hope you have before this sent off a letter to me, as I shall earnestly look for one at Derwinda;[68] for I scarce know where to expect

---

66 Hurry is an Orkneys surname, though its origin is probably separate from that of the Norfolk Hurrys.

67 The Cattegatt, Kattegat in Danish, is the sea area between the west of Jutland and Sweden. Elsinore, notoriously in Denmark, is near its narrowest point, called Øresund or the Sound.

68 Derwinda, Windau or Window in Latvia; now Ventspils.

one from you after that, not knowing at present what will be my destination. But of this I shall take care to inform you as soon as it is fixed. Young Stewart wrote home from the Orkneys, and you will please to inform his father he is still in health and behaves very well. I do not think of writing Mr Stewart till I get home.

As I said, so it happened: very little farther than we were yesterday and it's now Monday evening. We had a severe gale right against us all night. Smart trials for patience, after being flattered with the prospect of being in Elsinore in a few hours, to be rather driven farther off. I think any woman must do well to marry a sailor, for they certainly must learn patience. For they are continually experiencing how unavailing impatience is. And yet after all I do not know a set of men less able to endure contradiction, require more attendance, or are less willing to give up any point than they are.

I have been debating all this day whether I should write to you or not, lest I should get my paper full before I reach Elsinore. But, however, I could not put it off any longer, for we have now fine weather again. And I am uneasy when I can sit comfortably if I am not scribbling something to you, tho' it is such nonsense that it would be to my credit, and perhaps to your comfort, if I was to burn it. I might write to you sheets full, or talk to you a month, how much I esteem your friendship, how sincere I am etc, etc, etc; but perhaps I deceive you and myself too. I wish therefore you would give me some occasion or opportunity of convincing you by deeds, for words are not to be regarded always, with what sincerity I can at any time describe myself your 'True Friend'. Nothing in the world could give me so much pleasure, and if I have it in my power to do you any service at any time, by letting me know it you will confer a great obligation on your truest friend, E.C. Hurry.

Great haste to save post.

Cover, Miss Liddell, Rutland in the Rosses, Ireland. Postmark, 14 August 1787.

Letter 7

Eliza Liddell to Edmund Cobb Hurry
Rutland in the Rosses

*Written 1-3 August 1787; sent from Inishcoo, 3 September;
received at Riga*

Rutland in Rosses, Tuesday 1 August 1787

In looking over your paper, where to direct to you, just now I
remarked, dear Edmund, that you tell me a letter to Courland is
four weeks going from London. If that is the case, I judged it
necessary that I should write immediately, since if I do not a letter
would not reach that place before your departure from it; that is
if you leave it the latter end of August, as you proposed. Already I
have written to Elsinour,[69] and once more break through the usual
punctilio of waiting to answer letters received, apprehending that
if I observed that punctilio my letters might never reach you. As I
am not an unsolicited, I flatter myself, I shall not be an unwelcome
obtruder; particularly so as you may depend on this being the last
time I shall thus force myself on your remembrance unless I receive
assurances from your pen that my writing continues to be your wish
and expectation.

I will not, maybe it would be improper I should, dwell on
what the supposition costs me: that perhaps here closes for ever a
correspondence with one that – but on you this depends; on the
continuance of a regard that I think would be of little consequence
to my happiness if it were possible yours was a heart capable only
of such light and transitory impressions as would evaporate the
moment the object that inspired them ceased to be present. It would
betray a disposition more frivolous and contemptable than that,
the light and the vain of our sex testify, when they partially regard
the worthless of yours: the man a monster, the tinsel on his coat
or some other as absurd distinction his highest, his only ornament

---

69   Letter 4, pp. 43-38. Elsinore subsequently spelt correctly.

and recommendation. It would be sporting with the best human affections to gratify a cruel and shameful vanity, for I am well aware there are men who seek to engage our affections from no other motive but to gratify this truly despicable propensity. But Edmund is not one of this odious number; far, far different is he. And what kind of woman must she be that thus circumstanced would not spurn at the base, the ignoble bondage could she wish to be dear to a man so little worthy her regard?

But may it not be that a man of honour, whose heart was replete with every generous, every praiseworthy disposition, may form attachments that may be superseded by others? Alas, I fear so. However, he will be sincere at the time to say he will be immutably the same; he will, he ought not. But then he will not cease to be the friend because 'tis out of his power to be more, unless the person once dear to him should break the bands of friendship by proving herself unworthy his esteem.

Where friendship really subsists, reserve and disguise should be far removed. Each trait of character should be fairly unfolded and even our very foibles we should force ourselves to discover. To acknowledge our foibles to those we value is half to amend them. For I should much rather at any time bear the brunt of the severest and most malicious criticisms bestowed by an enemy than encounter the censure of those I looked up to with deference and esteem.

Thus thinking, you may rest assured that I will not, like the camelion, change my hue but appear as I am without paint or varnish to prove this operation true. Know that I am not, I fear, as disinterested as you may from the above infer. That tho' I would do much to see you happy, that tho' my judgment might approve, my inclinations would revolt at you owing your happiness to an attachment to another. Am I then selfish? Yes, the holding the second place only in your heart I should lament; as I do the insuperable bar my not possessing the gifts of fortune has placed between me and the happiness I should desire from the possibility of seeing you always. And how much do I repine at the uncertainty whether we may ever meet again. What a lesson this, if I am teaching you to despise me. And yet I cannot wish in this particular to be different from what I am.

By this you are at the place of your destination, so other people here say, and the weather has been fine. Have you received my last letter?[70] Have you thought of, have you written to me? Will you laugh at me, when I tell you what no doubt you will term folly, when I inform you that the extreme dejection of my spirits since your departure was increased this day by I trust imaginary ills? Why is it that I should conjure up these chimerical, these fantastic visions to cheat me of all that remains of tranquillity in my breast?

Mr Corbet and the rest of the men at dinner today were ingaged in eager conversation to which I paid no attention, till roused by the sound of war, war immediate with Holland.[71] The stoppage of letters first occurred and then an evil more alarming, dreadful to my imagination. It was that your ship might be stopped. I saw you undaunted and intrepid, seeking by resistance and threats of defiance a death you might avoid. Sick to the soul I left the room to give free indulgence to the tears extorted from me by the hideous phantoms my fancy had created. I ask myself a thousand times why am I thus anxious, thus tremulous about your safety, or why I imagine innumerable lurking dangers where they may not exist. And why I arrogate to the seas and wind a power they can derive from God alone. That they may never have power to destroy, that you may be guarded from their perils, and they may contribute only to your protection and preservation, is the morning and evening aspiration of her who is ever yours, Eliza A. Liddell.

Mr Stewart came to tea.[72] He asked me how long I had been entirely *dumb*. I thought I must say something and said don't you long to hear from your son. I thought where you were. He replied, laughing, I can't say I am as impatient to hear from William as some people are to hear from another on board. Mrs Corbet is not yet come home and I must own that, glad as I should be to see her, I would rather at present be alone. Harriet desires her love to you and your brother. I wish, I wish I could tell you so in person.

---

70   Eliza to Edmund, Letter 4, pp. 36-38.

71   In 1787 the Netherlands were shaken by civil war between the 'Patriots' and the ruling House of Orange, complicated by a Prussian invasion. In the event, this did not lead to war with England.

72   Mr Stewart's son, William, had sailed from Inishcoo with Edmund on the *Fly*.

I thought the precaution of getting Machasy to direct my letters might ensure their arriving safe to your hands.[73] A merchant's letters will be held to be of more importance than a woman's nonsense, as George Liddell said when speaking of his sister's letters.[74] Mr Corbet got a letter from him dated Elsinore, tho' it was impossible I should not hear from you. I felt I will not say what at a letter arriving from that place.[75]

Cover, Mr Edmund Cobb Hurry, Derwinda. Courland. Note, 'No. 2, received at Riga'. Postmark, Rutland, 3 August. Date of receipt unclear.

---

73   Machasy or Makesy acted as Robert Corbet's clerk. See below, Appendix, A5, pp. 287-88.

74   George Liddell was probably Eliza's brother, but he receives little mention in the letters.

75   Eliza received Letter 6 on 19 August but Letter 5 only on 24 August. Edmund's failure to write to her from Elsinore at the same time as he wrote to Mr Corbet caused her great anxiety.

Letter 8

Eliza Liddell to Edmund Cobb Hurry
Rutland in the Rosses

Written 25-28 August 1787; sent from Inishcoo, 13 September,
Received by Edmund at Great Yarmouth

Your lamented, your valuable pacquet, my Edmund, is not lost. 'Tis this moment pressed to my heart. Sunday 19th I received your letter from Elsinore and answered it immediately. Since that period I have not known an easy moment for thinking of your Orkney journal.[76] Yesterday Friday 24th, Mr Machasy sent for me down to the parlour. I had desired him not to deliver letters from you into any other hands than my own. Fool that I am. Was not a Scotch clown for seven days its envied possessor? And yet I dreaded any accident happening between this and Rutland. Just so I used, when you were here, to impatiently watch each moment of your absenting yourself and sigh for your return. That at the same time I fearfully anticipated the future and questioned myself how, if the absence of an hour was so painful, how was I to support my future existence, if doomed to see you no more. God of mercy, grant, if it be thy will, that I may not ever mourn as dead to me a friend so dear. I think, I think, if I was but in the same house with you I would endeavour to be satisfied, tho' denied seeing you.

Oh, when I snatched the pacquet from Machasy yesterday I was provoked by the impossibility of restraining as I read those tears that dimmed my sight and retarded for a long time my knowing all you said. Afterwards, when I sat down to write, my hand trembled too much to permit me. I went to bed at eleven o'clock, but the storm, the frightful storm, allowed not repose. Were you, perhaps a victim to its violence? My heart died within me at the dire apprehension. And I wrapt my head in the bed cloathes, as if to avoid my own reflections.

---

76 Edmund's account of his voyage from Inishcoo to the Orkneys in his letter, Letter 5, pp. 39-49, just delivered to Eliza.

'Tis morning. The winds are lulled and my terror, my distrust, is vanished. I will have confidence in that God who has hitherto protected and preserved you. But you have been ill, dangerously ill, and dangerously encompassed by rocks. The winds have buffeted you about and made you their sport. Altogether, is it any wonder my spirits should for a time be entirely overpowered? I might add you complained of gloom, of melancholy, but I should be a hypocrite if I indeavoured to persuade you that that gloom, that melancholy was a source of uneasiness to me. (Did it proceed from any other cause should I not wish it removed, tho' at the expence of enduring it for you?) Am I not like a malignant giant who with transport views the distress he has occasioned in the victim he has devoted to chains, chains which the amplitude of united tyranny and power must render durable? My simile holds good only as far as what reflects my feelings, with no less joy than the huge giant I have introduced to your notice.

Do I contemplate a heaviness of heart that assures me I am dear to you, you love me Edmund? And should ever if I confess I have the tyranny, tho' not the power, to wish your mind the home of a constant and durable attachment for me and yet the slave. I like not that word. I would substitute another if I could that should at once express that I would have your regard for me the voluntary tribute of esteem, of approbation, of choice, not resulting from a blind necessity. For, if governed by the latter, you might as well feel a penchant for the Witch of Endor as me.[77] (Now I think of it, you neglect your interest in not giving her the preference. You know a sorceress could, at all times, help you to a fair wind and waft you from port to port at pleasure.) And I might, impelled by this blind and rascally necessity, permit poor judgment to sleep and select perhaps some contemptible animal for my friend instead of you. May it not as well proceed from whim or caprice? Certainly not. Have I then no vanity, Edmund? How could you ask me questions so impertinent? And what could induce you to imagine I had not too much politeness to attribute whim or caprice to a Lord of the Creation?[78]

---

77   In the biblical book of Samuel, 28: 3-25, the Witch of Endor summons up the ghost of the prophet Samuel in front of Saul. The ghost prophesies the imminent defeat of Saul, a prophecy soon fulfilled, leading to Saul's suicide.

78   Eliza stands up for the right of women to criticise men.

You know not how highly I am gratified that ideas similar to mine should have occupied your mind: the gloom, the dejection to which I have been a prey, the inability of applying to anything you have felt, while Eliza's image has been no less present to your imagination than Edmund's to hers. You boast indeed of one day's application to business. And shall I tell you I take pleasure in thinking that, could I that day have made my sudden appearance, you would (I am determined to be sure of it) have overturned the table and have flung from you, not me, but the works of those wise antiquaries you were studying.

And now let me tell you, while I think of it, that I have all due respect for those profound treatises of erudition you could name, yet I could wish you to remember you are not writing to or for the world but to a woman, whose limited capacity and defective education would prevent her comprehending the depth or extent of knowledge confined to the head; tho' she is too much interested in the language addressed to the heart not to take the highest happiness that yours should lead you to neglect more important concerns to think of, to write to her. Do not then again ask me shall you alter your style. The spontaneous thought of the moment must ever be more pleasing to me than any other kind of epistle. I know not myself how to write in any other manner, nor ever could form a set speech in my life or dictate a letter till the pen receives motion from my fingers.

My own inclinations it seems coincided with your wishes. Each day I have written something to you. It was the only employment I was capable of; but hitherto, having no means of conveying to you more than a sheet at a time, I regularly burned as I wrote.[79] But I will do so no more. If my scribble can afford you pleasure, I shall not withhold it. I find satisfaction in doing what you desire me; and, tho' it may never meet your eye, I shall devote part of each day to converse with you. But forget not, I annex conditions to my doing so. The first of which is that, the moment you are weary of attending to me, you candidly acknowledge it and forbid my proceeding. Forget not also that we have few neighbours here (fishes excepted), a sad dearth of scandal and that I am cooped up in an island not having to view the scenes of animated nature. There is not anything here to

---

79   The contents of the letters Eliza burnt are of course unknown.

Pupils of a governess. Detail from Richard Redgrave, The Governess (1844)

amuse, enliven or give scope to the imagination. On the contrary, the dull monotony of mere rocks and water must rather tend to blunt the powers of the mind. Expect then not much of incident and less of entertainment, nor be disappointed if forced to exclaim, as a gentleman once did to me, 'Insipidity itself'.

I have yet another condition to make, nay a command to enforce, which is that you have it greatly in your power. I expect you will correct, reprove and consequently be of use to me in any, in every instance which your better judgment condemns. I have ever endeavoured to act, to think right, but to do so always is impossible for a finite being. Mine is the language of sincerity. You may therefore form a just idea in what I am right, in what reprehensible, and I think I may venture to say you will find my faults proceed not from my heart but my head.

This is my first day's journal, though I ought to place to your account the sheets I have burned. A pretty specimen this of what you are to expect. Are you not fatigued? But I will release you. Adieu. In bidding you good night is comprised every dear, every tender remembrance. Past one o'clock, Saturday night, or morning. 25 August 1787.

Sunday morning, 26 August

Not at church, for the weather is deplorable, but I am just returned from the parlour, where Mr Corbet read prayers for us, not at church.[80] Think you I would trust myself in a boat (unless compelled by absolute necessity) with anyone but you? Or rather would anyone but you make allowance for my ridiculous fears or hear them with temper? I have not yet told you: Mrs Corbet and her five daughters came home Tuesday last, 21st.[81] We have been in strange commotion since. Mr Corbet received letters that affronted him. The *Dutchess* was ordered to be ready to sail instantly, this very day I believe, and we were all to go to Corbet Hill. Mrs Corbet is much afraid of the sea and, tho' she was not permitted herself, wished me to go by land. She told me she should be unhappy to involve my fate with hers, for fear of the worst, the weather so tempestuous and uncertain. But she might have talked for ever. I should hate myself if my dread of the sea was to influence me to consult my own preservation only, while not only her and her children were exposed to its dangers, but *you*. How could I think of shrinking from hazards which you are daily encountering? I am angry with myself for being so carried away by fears of an element than cannot destroy but by divine permission. It is a weakness that both my reason and religion condemns, and yet I cannot conquer it. But I have not told you that, after being in a violent bustle for three or four days, we are quiet again.

Mr Corbet, though possessed of some good and praiseworthy dispositions, is the slave of pride, prejudice and passion. Variable, inconstant, he weighs not the chances for or against any scheme he takes in his head. Hence the measures he adopts are all precipitate and too often he has reason to repent having acted in such a rash manner as must hurt himself and those connected with him. He had, however, at present grounds not unjust for considering himself ill used, but last day's post brought him letters from Mr Conyngham and Mr Wade that has refuted the idea.[82] So his family is to remain here two months longer, perhaps the whole winter. As to him, he will

---

80 There was no church on Rutland or the other islands near Inishcoo, so attending church required a boat trip to the mainland.

81 The five daughters were Sarah, Elizabeth, Henrietta, Anne and Ellinor. The Corbets also had three sons, not on Inishcoo, Francis, Robert and Samuel. It is unclear how long the girls had been away, though Anne seems to have been away for two months.

82 William Burton Conyngham (1733-1796), the originator of the scheme to turn Rutland Island into an entrepôt. Mr Wade was his principal agent.

perhaps be a resident of the Rosses till some new pursuit engages his attention.

I am summoned to dinner. A dinner of husks would indeed be with you more acceptable to me than the vain superfluities of the most splendid board. Adieu.

Monday, 27 August

Where are you Edmund? Are you well? Do you soon return to England? I have been thinking of the fate of my three letters.[83] You will not get the first and last till your return to Elsinore. I walked round the island before dinner with the children. They talked, they laughed, they were happy, while my soul was agitated by a contrariety of sensations I cannot describe. Preserve him, heaven, escaped my lips, while gazing on the Staggs which you had passed, too much absorbed in my own reflections.[84] I was unconscious of not being alone till I caught the girls staring at me with a marked surprise.

Well do you observe when speaking of Ives how transient at their age are the impressions of affection or regret. And do we not daily meet with people in the world of no higher order than children who smile on all alike, who are pleased with every passing object, alike forgotten and disregarded when it can no longer contribute to their amusement? And even those who are born with dispositions that are an honour to human nature, exalted sense and keen sensibilities, what pains, what cruel pains does the world take to root out the latter entirely? Yes, even in the cultivation of the first in your sex, and in the female world, how often are our hearts corrupted by those from whom we ought to imbibe an elevated and just turn of thinking. How often, in the words of Miss Hannah Moore, do we find principle for sentiment dethroned.[85]

But hold! What business have I to attempt moralizing? I ought to consider you will have a fortnight to laugh at me and you know I can't bear that. It proceeds from pride, I suppose. But take notice:

---

83   Eliza to Edmund, Letter 4, pp. 36-38; Letter 7, pp. 53-56; the third letter is missing.

84   The Stags, three rocks just north of Rutland Island.

85   Hannah More (1745-1833), playwright and evangelical moralist.

I never am affronted at being laughed at, only when conscious of having said or done something absurd or ridiculous. Then, tho' I deserve it, I am confused and vexed, tho' at the same time I should be grateful for a grave rebuke, nor should feel my temper ruffled, tho' I was treated with undeserved passion.

When, when shall I hear from you again? It is but a few days since I did, but it appears to me a much longer time. The other day after dinner your name was introduced. Each gave their opinion. All were warm in your praise. Langwell, who is vulgar, nay bearish in his manners, whose grovling ideas could not help him but to the most uncouth expressions, put in his word and said you were a very decent young man.[86] Think of the savage. 'Decent', I contemptuously repeated the word after him, which you may be sure caused a general laugh at my expense. I feel the same indignation when I hear any one substitute the word 'hurry' when they mean being in haste. I am ready to ask them how they dare hackney your name.

Last night Mrs Corbet repeatedly urged me to sit up with her. She likes late hours, I do not. She could not prevail till she drew me into conversation about you. Could I then go, or continue drawing? She wishes much to improve her acquaintance with you. She hopes she shall and was disappointed when she found her mistake, for she had taken it into her head that either Mr Corbet or I had told her you were to bring your cargo from Derwinda here. Alas, no![87]

Tuesday, 28 August

My mornings are now filled up by attending to the children's improvements, but what ever avocations I think I ought to mind I may be said to perform mechanically. They read to me, etc, etc, I correct their pronunciation, their blunders, their errors, without knowing I am doing it. The five weeks I spent with you has destroyed my relish for any other society. Alas, in vain do I look at the chairs you sat on; you occupy them no longer. You cannot apply to business,

---

86 Langwell. This is the only mention of him in the letters.

87 There may have been a idea that Edmund should return, as his family's agent on Rutland, but nothing had been agreed.

you wish not to partake in pleasure till I share it with you. Pleasure, happiness and being with you are to me one and the same thing. Reading used to employ all my leisure hours, but I cannot now attend to it. *Emily Montague* is the only book I have touched since your departure.[88] I am not fond of novels, but this I am partial to. There are sentiments in it that confer honour on the author. It was, I am told, written in Canada, which I think not improbable from the spirited and delightful description it gives of that place.

I was sitting at this little desk writing to one of my sisters the day you came into the harbour. Mrs Corbet, who knows I dislike being interrupted from her children to attend to the chit chat of morning visitors, contrary to her usually leaving me to follow my own devices, sent for me down to welcome Mr Hurry; but I was fine lady enough to desire being desired. Would I now do so, would I now sit contented up stairs and know you were below? Impossible!

What an alteration has two months' absence made in Anne.[89] She is much grown, quite a woman, and I suppose she thinks it is a woman's privilege to be conceited and is therefore shaped with a plentiful stock of it. I cannot be attached to this girl, tho' she is mild tempered and on the whole well disposed; but she has no feeling. In the words of I can't remember who, her virtues will be but the absence of vice.[90] People of lively passions and exquisite sensibility are the most liable to indiscretions, particularly early in life. She will be prudent, prudent ever. She will never be led by the enthusiasm of feeling to sacrifice her own ease and comfort on the altar of friendship. She will be a friend, but the gradations of her likings will rise and fall with the rank, prosperity or otherwise of those she honours with her notice. I judge from seeing in her what I have in vain endeavoured to conquer: a strong turn for ridicule; an unfeeling gaiety that satirizes no less the misfortunes than the follies of others. We may talk and

---

88   Frances Brooke (1724-1789), the author of the first novel to be written in Canada, *The History of Emily Montague* (1769).

89   Anne Corbet died unmarried in 1812.

90   According to Cicero, virtue consists of the avoidance of vice. According to Samuel Taylor Coleridge, innocence implies the absence of vice, but virtue the absence of vice from the knowledge of its consequences.

education may effect much, but it can never bestow hearts on those who are born without them. Be afraid that mine will ever think of you with the truest esteem.

I shall not apologize for the enormous length of this, but shall consider, as one proof for my giving you the trouble of reading it, your now sending me a pacquet twice its size. Once more farewell, Eliza Liddell.

I shall not send this till I suppose your return to England will permit me to again hear from you. But when will that be? Whether I have the opportunity or not of sending letters, I shall daily write till you give me reason to think I ought to forbear. 'Ought' – will it ever come to that?

Cover, Mr Edmund Cobb Hurry. Great Yarmouth, England. Postmark, Rutland, date unclear. 2s. 6d. Opened by Samuel Hurry, early October.

Letter 9

Eliza Liddell to Edmund Cobb Hurry
Rutland in the Rosses

Written 29 August to 10 September 1787; sent from Inishcoo, 13 September; received by Edmund at Great Yarmouth

Wednesday, eleven at night, Rosses, 29 August 1787

I have been reading over your Orkney journal and there is one passage in it, Edmund, that hurts me.[91] It appears to me from it that you accuse me in your own mind, or I have mistaken the purport of what you say, of a degree of affectation that I do not possess; tho' from knowing the motives of my conduct I am not surprised you should think as you do. Or rather, as you did when you left this, when you had only read those three papers (which I had no idea you would think it worth your while to preserve).[92] For I should hope, if you have received my three letters, the first and last directed to Elsinore, the second to Derwinda, you will find me a stranger, nay superior, to disguise or affectation.[93]

You say my esteem, my friendship (or whatever I please to call it), now that (whatever I please to call it), and the recollection of a conversation I had with you, makes me think it necessary I should clear myself of an imputation that I should be sorry you should continue to suppose I merit. I did give the name of friendship only to a love (let it go by that appellation) that would lead me to sacrifice my every hope of temporal happiness to promote yours. But, when I called it friendship only, I spoke as I thought. I remained not, however, long in an error. I saw you in situations that opened my eyes to a certainty how extremely dear you were to me. Your dangerous

---

91   Edmund to Eliza, Letter 5, pp. 39-49.

92   Eliza's first three letters, only two of which survive, Letters 1 and 2.

93   Of these later three letters, only two survive (Letters 4 and 7).

boating party to Baliconnell filled me with horror.[94] I wished to go with you. I wished rather to share an unhappy fate with you than live to lament you. The lively joy I experienced when your sudden return ascertained your safety was affection, friendship, love. I could no longer deceive myself and I found it impossible to deceive you. Yes, Edmund, impossible, for I would have done so, I would have left you in ignorance of my sentiments if I could, and that from motives you cannot blame and I hope will approve.

Only consider how very delicately I was circumstanced. It was repugnant to my pride you should know what my refractory heart betrayed, tho' it was never repugnant to either my pride or principles. Could you know me for what I am, could you see the purity, the disinterestedness of my regard, I had nothing to apprehend from your inspection. But you could not see by intuition and had not known me long enough to form an established opinion in my favour. For you to mistake my character was dreadful to me and to prevent your doing so, in growing my friendship for you, I at the same time studiously sought to inform you I was destitute of fortune.

Heavens! What was my disappointment, my consternation, my distress when you first put that paper into my hands, you may remember.[95] I immediately answered it, tho' my tongue seemed parched and my whole frame agitated, almost convulsed with the complicated shock of disappointment, of wounded pride, of insulted delicacy and feeling. My soul was in tumults. It appeared to me that the very means I had made use of to prove my attachment wholly disinterested had had a contrary effect; had turned against me and taught you to despise, to detest me. You, also, I was at the moment disappointed in. Could it be that your heart was so constructed? Could you, who I thought so different, could you adopt the false maxims of the world and confound me, because I had proudly told you I was poor, with the mean, selfish and truly despicable who would grasp at any, at every, opportunity of raising their fortunes? In that bitter moment, perhaps half I felt was owing to the fear of

---

94   Ballyconnell House, Falcarragh, the seat of the Olphert family.

95   See Eliza to Edmund, Letter 1, pp. 31-32. The terms on which Edmund offered to take Eliza with him on the *Fly* are unknown.

finding you thus lost to that true dignity of mind in yourself that could alone teach you to discern it in me.

You hastened to restore peace to my breast. You assured me my fears were groundless. You had not mistaken me. You thought justly of me and were not the narrow-hearted being it had cost me so much, though but for a moment, to suppose you. This *éclaircissement* removed the heavy oppression I knew not how to endure. Certain that you knew me superior to forming any designs that could derogate from the strictest rectitude and propriety, I breathed with freedom and then thought it unnecessary to conceal from you the extent of my regard. To admit the word 'friendship' and reprobate the word 'love', where it really existed, would be disingenuous and affected. 'Love' and 'friendship' in the breast of a woman worthy of esteem are synonymous terms.[96] I will …. Mrs Corbet calls me. Adieu.

Mrs Corbet wanted to tell me Lawrence is supposed to be near this, in his brig. Where, where are you? I am wretched! How can I be otherwise? Are you not exposed to the dangers of the stormy deep? Goodnight. My eyes are heavy. May God protect you ever and, oh, may I be permitted to see you! E.L.

Thursday morning, 30 August

Mr Stewart is just come to pay his first visit to Mrs Corbet since her return home. I sent him down word by one of the children that his son is well. I shall see him at dinner. 'Tis time enough. I remember he and Mr Forster introduced some conversation, one day when you were here, at which I looked grave.[97] When you came upstairs to tea, you told me they had accused me of prudery, of overniceness. I thought you seemed partly of their opinion. To you I wish to be justified (and desire you will retract that opinion). To them I never think it worth my while to reply, to their hackneyed phrases, such as 'overniceness is underniceness', proceeding from prudery or in

---

96   Eliza in a letter, which has not survived, admitted to her friendship with Edmund but denied her love. Here she equates the two. In her first letter she had also told Edmund that she was poor.

97   Nassau Forster of Lackbeg. Given as 'Foster' in the original.

other cases from nasty ideas. Is this, their very elegant and, as they suppose, conclusive argument, the suggestion of their own hearts? How depraved must those hearts be to accuse anyone of being a prude to affix a stigma on their character. At least I think so (as a glowworm that shines not but when surrounded by the dark shades of night; the virtues of a prude fade before the sunshine of truth).

I grant they would be right, could they prove it overniceness. But have they a right to think for others or judge in what light conversation not strictly proper, not to say sometimes indecent, strikes other people? Can they assign no other motive for apparent disgust, or calm disdain, than it being the degrading subterfuge of hypocrisy? To affect a dislike which not to feel would be degrading indeed. Are we then to be censured or laughed at for respecting ourselves; for rebuking with silent contempt the person who, with low ribaldry or light and improper discourse, shall attempt wounding our ears? I should consider as an enemy the person who would seriously dare to instill into my mind ought that could debase me in my own eyes; ought that could lessen the respect we owe ourselves as immortal creatures, as heirs of immortality. And in general conversation is it necessary to promote cheerfulness or display wit that we should depart from truth, from decorum and not only call up blushes in the cheeks of innocence but hazard the corrupting others while debasing ourselves?

The people of this kingdom are satirical. They possess lively dispositions which often gives to their satire a humorous turn. To indulge this their women, no less than their men, often forget what is due to themselves and others. You have not lived as long as I have here, but your superior penetration and knowledge of the world must have made you observe this national characteristic; and will, if you weigh seriously what I have said, acquit me being affected and consequently ridiculously squeamish in this particular.

Stewart is generous to profusion. He is not a bad man, but he aims at wit, or rather buffoonery. People laugh with him and at him, but in so doing cease to value or respect him. He makes me angry, more particularly because he is a clergyman. Forster is a man of more refinement but, shall I say it, it appears to me more the refinement of policy than the native inmate of his breast. He likes to be well with everyone. He studies your disposition, he applauds, he flatters. If you can be caught by it, his manners are wary, elegant, insinuating; or coarse, vulgar etc, etc, according to the company he is in. I love these accommodating tempers, or rather principles. Then he is a philosopher and talks to use his own words scientifically on every subject: scientifically on the formation of the heavens and scientifically on the drawing on of his gloves. He is, however, a prodigious favourite with Mrs Corbet. Nor do I think him destitute of many good qualities. But your 'dabblers' in science, if I may be allowed the expression, they may make us silly women stare at their great learning. Yet they must look very foolish when they meet with an opponent in their own sex more knowing than themselves.

Do not call me ill natured, Edmund. Would it not argue downright stupidity if I were to see people every day without forming some judgment of them, perhaps an erroneous one? But if I do dislike, or think unfavorably of anyone, I do not make a jest of them, or mention publicly my opinion; though to my intimate friends I have no idea of reserve. How, if I hide my sentiments from them, how can they form a true opinion of me, or know how far I am worthy of their estimation? Is it not better I should give you occasion to reprove me than mislead you? Adieu. Mr Stewart, in revenge that I did not go down to him, has found the way up to my room. I must go talk to him.

Friday, 31 August

Mrs Corbet is gone with her daughters to see Mrs Lawrence.[98] I declined going that I might sit down to write you, but I cannot write. I think everybody looks out of humour, but I believe it is myself. The day is gloomy, a thick fog. The atmosphere is not more heavy than is my heart. I thought against probability that I should have had a letter from you today. I have no right to expect one yet, and yet I feel as if you had forgot me. Farewell, I will go and read Miss Seward's *Louisa*.[99] It is a poem, much admired.

---

98   Mrs Lawrence probably lived on Rutland Island.

99   Anna Seward's *Louisa: A Poetical Novel in Four Epistles*, written entirely in verse, was published in 1782.

Saturday, 1 September

On that rock that you honoured with your envy, and your remembrance, I have been sitting these two hours past. The day is fine, the sun quite resplendent. I sat in deep meditation, the children gathering shells in the sand, when I was roused from my reverie by observing very near me a man and a woman, and their three almost naked children, busily employed in search of razorfish to supply their miserable board. Not unuseful was the lesson. I turned my eyes inward and saw not indeed an unthankful heart but a dejected one, too anxious about events that God would direct according to his good pleasure. While I possessed daily blessings, these poor people were denied blessings that would make them supremely happy. Perhaps at this moment I am an object of envy to them. Thus I thought, and bowed in humble acquiescence. Teach me, oh God, teach me resignation to thy will and grant if I must ever, ever in this sad world be parted from Edmund, and my sisters, grant we may meet in glory.

I must away. Dinner, I am told, is near ready. Mr Corbet goes immediately after he has dined on board the *Dutchess*.[100] He is quite an amphibious animal and never so happy as when in, or on, this element. I say 'in', for I believe, rather than give it up entirely, he would gladly descend and remain in a diving bell. He dragged Mrs Corbet and I on board yesterday – we stepped off the quay. But besides being painted all over, I was almost suffocated in his little cabin. Why, it is no larger than a tolerable sized chest. I dread the thought of being shut up in it, for perhaps several days, with such a troop of sick and troublesome brats; and yet I must in about a month or six weeks longer, unless Mrs Corbet remains here the whole winter, which is not yet determined. A summons … Adieu.

---

100 The *Dutchess* was undoubtedly so named in honour of the Duchess of Rutland, the wife of the Lord Lieutenant of Ireland, after whom William Burton Conyngham had renamed Rutland Island.

Sunday 2 September

Another Sunday, Edmund. Good morning to you. How are you to spend this day? On board, on shore, in company or alone? And will you, will you, think of your absent friend who thinks of you incessantly, who envies everyone the happiness of being in your society, a happiness denied to her? Have you written to me again? It would be unreasonable in me to make a request that would take up time you can so much better employ, and perhaps can ill spare; or else how glad I should be you would dedicate a few minutes each day to write to me. I do that myself, because you desired me; because I am never so easy as when writing to you.

Remember, you must not send me *short* letters. I have an aversion to them. They would prevent my answering them. They would seem to say: 'Tormenting creature! I hate to write to you, but I promised I would and must, however disagreeable'. So much for short letters. Now send them, if you are done.

Another injunction you merit, which is: never again, on pain of my displeasure, tease me with apologies for writing *nonsense*.[101] 'Tis time enough when it is so to make these kind of excuses. Besides, how can I think of writing to you if you go at this rate? It will require more temerity than I am mistress of. For, if ready to look for nonsense in yours, nay to criticise them without mercy, what right have I to expect a better fate, who deserve so much more?

I must leave you, Edmund. The boat is waiting to convey me over to Mrs Lawrence. Church is you know almost out of the question here. What a tiresome morning shall I spend. She will talk me to death and scold me too, or I have great good fortune, for I have not been to see her but twice since your departure. Your departure, alas!

Monday, 3 September

This September sets in with charming weather. I wish you at sea now. Perhaps you are. In your letter to Mr Corbet from the Orkneys

---

101   Edmund to Eliza, Letter 5, p. 42; Letter 6, p. 52; Letter 10, p. 79.

you say you shall return the beginning of this month.[102] Yes, you will return to England and I regret, oh so much, my not being there. But what if I was? My wayward fate might order it so that, tho' in England, I might be far distant from you. I will not write any more today. I am alive and well, thank God, but I am too *stupid* to write what would be worthy of a moment's attention from you.

Tuesday, 4 September

A blank.

Wednesday, 5 September

A blank indeed. I could not write yesterday. What variable, what inconsistent creatures we are. These last three days my mind has been a prey to gloom, despondence and unhappiness. I enjoyed not the present and looked forward to the future, if not with dread, without hope – *without hope*! Gracious God! What a perversion of my faculties. Have I not bright hopes, glorious and immortal happiness in view? I will not say why am I not always thus, why not always, as at this moment, content, serene, thankful, fraught with joyful presages of a blessed futurity that shall recompense us amply for what we may endure here. No. To be always susceptive to impressions of unalloyed peace falls not to the lot of fallible beings, fluctuating, irresolute in our best resolves. We must at times sink under the pressure of those contingencies that exclude us from what we consider as present happiness. If raised above worldly considerations for ourselves, would we wish to be divested of humanity and forget to mourn the sufferings of others? Happy those whose lot in life enables them to do more than mourn, to alleviate those distresses that fall within the reach of observation and assistance.

I have sometimes sat for hours wrapt in visionary and delusive dreams of what happiness I should enjoy if rich, immensely so; and,

---

102 See Edmund to Eliza, Letter 6, p. 50.

miser like, I wished to be sole proprietor. My first determination: never to invest another with my right. Hence I was never to marry. This great fortune mine, what a large field for speculation, how judicious in my choice, how delicate in my arrangement of these great donations from which I was to derive such exquisite pleasure. Those reveries or waking dreams would afford me some satisfaction, but for their short duration.

Adieu, dear Edmund. Short indeed was the duration of that more than dream, that reality of happiness your presence created. I could have wished it to endure for ever than to think I could with undaunted firmness meet the severest turns of fortune. Take care of your health, your life. Remember on their preservation depends the peace of E.L.

Thursday, 6 September 1787

Lawrence is this moment come in. His brig lies under Arran. I saw him step on shore and clasp his children to his breast.[103] They, little creatures, had been waiting for him more than an hour and were capering about the rocks as if they were frantic. Poor Lawrence, it was a moment of happiness – many does not fall to thy lot. Symes desired the children to run and tell me Mr Hurry's vessel was coming in![104] How strangely prone to trifle with the feelings of others are the unthinking multitude. Symes is not ill-natured but he is a joker. Mrs Corbet and her daughters are gone to bathe. I chose to remain with you, with you and [*tear*] to dwell on that thought. Now write a line [*tear*] you, till after the post comes in to [*tear*] shall I hear from Edmund.

---

103   Rather than coming to Inishcoo, Lawrence, whose wife's house was a boat trip away from it, almost certainly landed on Rutland Island, immediately opposite Inishcoo.

104   Robert Symes was a practical joker. See the sketch of his character below, Eliza to Edmund, Letter 14, pp. 113-14. Two letters from Symes to Robert Corbet are given below, Appendix, A5, A6, pp. 287-90.

Monday night, 10 September 1787

No better on Friday, nor on Sunday. Tomorrow the post bag again. Shall I, shall I hear from you? I cannot describe the state of my mind. A thousand splendid hopes, and fears, arise to disturb me. Nor will they be dissipated by the remonstrances of reason. What am I saying? Oh yes, they will be put to flight by the remonstrances of reason, but I must seek for it in your letters, not in my own weak head. That head, I will quarrel with it. It is an enemy to the concerns of my heart and has distressed it for some days past with its wicked suggestions. Shall I give you a state of the case? And will you be umpire between the disputants and decide whether the latter is to consider the former only as an apprehensive friend or a base incendiary, when it whispers, poor heart, why so vain, so credulous? Thinkest thou to attach to thee, in bands of indissoluble friendship, a heart whose sincerity may not exceed thy own, but whose superior excellence of understanding may teach it to relinquish the gift of thine as a deposit of no value? Thinkest thou it interests itself in thy welfare or throbs with thee? Responsive tenderness, cruel monitor! Won't you, Edmund, who I delegate sole judge of this affair, won't you convict it of high treason against me, its sovereign mistress?

This is the tenth. I count each day and, ill as I like the sea, follow you with unwearied assiduity through your whole voyage. You are now got back to Elsinore. I think you are, and will soon be in England, rejoicing friends; each dear relation eager to welcome you. Did I think envy an inmate of my breast? And yet it is. At this moment how powerful its influence. I am ready to weep because others are to have the happiness of seeing you, while … But what right have I to talk in this manner, perhaps to you a blank in creation?

Edmund, have I seen you for the last time, the last? Reason, religion strengthens my soul to support an evil I have myself created, and yet not I brought you here. I bid you not appear, to have a feeling, a generous, a good heart to engage my regard, my esteem, my affections, my too anxious interest in your health, your peace, your honour. I have not written a line since Thursday. It is become a too painful task. Need I any memorialist of you, of your absence? Alas! Do I think of anything else?

Good night. I will go to bed, perforce. Oh, who can sleep when agitated by suspense? When, when shall I hear from you? Yours ever, Eliza Liddell.

Cover, Mr Edmund Cobb Hurry, Great Yarmouth, England. Postmark, Rutland, date unclear. Opened by Samuel Hurry.

Letter 10

Edmund Cobb Hurry to Eliza Hurry
Great Yarmouth

Written 8 to 26 September 1787; sent from Great Yarmouth, 29 September; received at Inishcoo, October

8 September 1787

Well I must own I was rather disappointed at being so soon obliged to leave Derwinda on 18 August, as I could not in reason expect to hear from you, knowing it would have been impossible for a letter to travel so quick, if even you wrote immediately after my departure, which I had no reason to suppose you would.[105] I was also uneasy at being so long detained on the sea between Windau and Elsinore, a whole fortnight, and yet in all that time did I not so much as write one single line to my dearest Eliza.[106] Yet you were scarce from my thoughts, and I was almost rejoiced to think you had not ventured this voyage, so disagreeable has this boisterous passage been.

And I realise my passenger would gladly have given the little he was worth to be once more placed on terra firma. I wrote you from Windau ere my departure and informed you of my having a German gentleman passenger; which, least that letter miscarry, I mention again, as he will most likely continue constantly with me whilst I remain in England.[107] And if I do return to that drear country to pass the winter, he will also return with me.

At Elsinore we at last arrived safe the second of this month, and there did I examine all my letters, but could not find one anything like your hand, but immediately recognized that of Mr Corbet's clerk.[108]

---

105 Derwinda, Windau or Windaw in Latvia; now Ventspils.

106 Edmund therefore failed to write anything to Eliza between 18 August and 2 September.

107 This letter from Windaw does not survive and seems never to have reached Eliza. The German gentleman passenger was almost certainly B. Herzwich, anglicised as Hartwick, a Liebau merchant of German origin.

108 Machasy.

Pshaw, said I once or twice, what has he to write about, but perhaps it may enclose one from Eliza. And when I opened it I was overjoyed to find it full of your handwriting.[109] And, but for some exceptionable parts, where you give me undue praise, I should have been better able to express what I feel on reading it. Some parts of it give me great pleasure and others raise my vanity. One thing was very extraordinary: that, if I recollect right, we should both of us much at the same time be writing nearly the same thoughts, and desiring one another's earthly and eternal welfare, I trust earnestly and sincerely. As to those dispositions which you say my Creator formed me with, [they] can reflect no honour on me; on the contrary, if misused, [they] must be the greater blemish. For I cannot but allow that. I believe I know what is right, tho' I do not practise it, and therefore am doubly guilty. But I still say I am determined to endeavour to do whatever I think right. But ill habits are so strong that, in spite of all my resolutions, like law confiders, when most resolute I am nearest suing.

You ask me when you would be tired of writing to me.[110] I believe I may answer when I leave off thanks of you. I have already answered your letter more than a hundred times in my thoughts; and, had I then sate me down, I should have been able to have written you something more to my satisfaction. You complain of your letter being barren of incident. How much more so is mine. Nor have I in my power to make it entertaining to you, but you have Mr Simms to amuse you.[111] I never wish to envy anyone or repine at my situation. On the contrary, I look on mine as the one most suitable to me, and of the vanity of wishes I am fully convinced. And yet, in spite of all this, I dare venture to wish myself in his place, I won't say situation, contrary to all my convictions that it would not be as proper for me as the one I at present occupy. Is it madness or folly?

Such an inconsistent, inconstant, inconsiderate creature is man. And if we look attentively into the best, most virtuous and wisest of them, do we not always see something to pity as well as to envy?

---

109   Eliza to Edmund, Letter 7, pp. 53-56.

110   Eliza to Edmund, Letter 8, p. 59.

111   Simms is Edmund's misspelling of Robert Symes. It seems likely that Symes lived on Inishcoo and therefore saw Eliza on a daily basis, for which Edmund envied him. See Eliza to Edmund, Letter 14, pp. 113-14.

What a deal of confused nonsense have I been writing. I am out of patience with it and, but that I have nothing better, I would burn it. O do you know that I have been hard at work in all these storms translating German sermons?[112] And do you know that I have been vain enough to show them to some people? And do you know that those people have been base enough to praise the translation, tho' I am conscious when I read them myself of a hundred improprieties which I cannot mend? I wish I had an opportunity of sending one or two of them to you and then, if you were wicked enough to add your praise to theirs, O how vain I should be. And now you do know all this and so good night. This is Saturday 8 August 1787 past 7 o'clock and almost dark.[113]

Arrived safe at Hull this 10th instant and was in hopes there to have sold my cargo, but in these, as well as in many others I have been given, likely to be disappointed. However, to make amends for it, I shall now have the pleasure of spending a few days amongst my friends at Yarmouth.[114] How long I know not, nor do I fix on anything in regard to my future destination, but intend to leave it entirely to my father, who I am sure will advise me to what he thinks best for me.[115] I cannot look towards anyone of my proposed schemes, or rather plans, but I find something which makes me wish to relinquish them. For there is not one of them in which either my duty, love or interest do not cross one another. And so perhaps I shall fix on one of them. If I could but find out some sensible way in which I could reconcile them, I think I should be happy; and till then I am almost determined to go to sea. I say almost, for I like it less than ever, as I do not find myself inclined to do my duty there as I ought and used to do.

This I should have put in the post office in Hull, but that I

---

112 Edmund had spent much of the previous five years in Courland, where German was the lingua franca. German-speaking religious groups, including the Pietists and Moravians, had a strong influence on Unitarians and other Dissenters in England.

113 This date is mistaken; it should be 10 September.

114 Edmund had been born and brought up in Great Yarmouth, where his family were leading merchants.

115 Edmund was still dependent on his father at this time, though he established his independence over the following years.

could wish to inform you where you might again direct to me, as nothing could give me greater pleasure than hearing from you. You wish for greater accomplishments or more brilliant talents. I wish for an opportunity to be better acquainted with those you possess, and which I am certain are quite sufficient to make yourself and friends happy. Compliments I know you will not expect from me. If I thought you did, either that or flattery, you would hear seldom from me if ever; and you may depend that whatever I write at the time of writing it I fully believe to be true. However, my opinion may alter after, for it is a thing I cannot myself readily depend on, having been often surprized to find how differently I have both thought and acted at different times under perhaps the same circumstances.

It is now the 26 September and I have been in London visiting my sister and I should have gladly called on yours, if I had but known where to have found them.[116] And I must beg you to allow me that pleasure when I return to London, which I hope will not be much later than the beginning of December, as I am now agoing to visit Riga and not to stay the whole winter there, unless the frost, which often sets in very severely in November, should detain me contrary to my intentions. I have had this letter a long time by me. If you think as you did when you wrote last, I doubt not but that you have already given me up as a reprobate, and in your own mind acknowledge my self-accusations as just. For I dare say you will have heard of my getting here by Mr Corbet, to whom I wrote on arrival, not having heard from him since my departure.[117] Nor even now have I the least intelligence of him and family.

I hope in God nothing ill has befallen any of you, as your letter of the 23 July is the latest news of any kind which I have from the Rosses.[118] From you I could not expect a letter, as I do not think I desired you would write to me at Yarmouth, as first I did not know whether I should go there. Secondly, that you might write treason

---

116   Edmund Cobb Hurry's middle sister, Mary Hurry, had married the merchant David Tolmé in October 1786. They lived in Great Prescott Street, Goodmans Fields, London, near Aldgate.

117   Edmund's note to Mr Corbet caused Eliza great heartache, as she expected one to herself at the same time.

118   Eliza to Edmund, Letter 4, pp. 36-38.

and I knew my letter would be opened by my father or uncle, if I was absent, and I chose rather to inform him of our correspondence myself than that it should come to his knowledge as he might think perhaps by accident.[119]

News from Mr Corbet I begged to hear both verbally and by my letter to him from the Orkades.[120] We had also an account to regulate and two months are more than elapsed since my father wrote him, so that I fear the letters must someway have miscarried, as some of mine did from Rutland. If there is any other cause, I conjure you in the most earnest manner to inform me of it, by writing to me at Elsinore, where I would almost hope, if I darest, to find another of yours to me most interesting letters; but then I dare not expect, without I should suppose you possessed of a spirit of divination. For how were you to know that I intended again to pass the strait, when I knew it not myself?

I find myself necessitated to make this a double letter, as I have a great deal to say to you if I can possibly steal so much time from my present occupations, which are in these troublesome times very numerous, when nearly ready to depart. And I trust we shall depart if the wind suits tomorrow. Think what a parting from friends I scarce dare hope to see again; and but for that I would have staid at home. But it gives me pain to see those to whom I am so nearly connected, even as much so as tho' they were my father and mother, instead of grandfather and mother.[121] I say to see those so near leaving me is one of the chiefest causes for my being determined to leave them, for I do not leave them comfortless. God forbid. They have peace in their own minds and they have grandchildren with them, which may make them dispense the easier with my absence.

Here we hear of nothing but war and destruction. A most violent press has broken out. More than two thousand poor sailors were last week dragged from their wives and families and obliged to serve in

119 Edmund's use of the word 'treason' caused later problems. He explained that it meant the risk of Eliza referring disparagingly to his stepmother, Dorothy Hurry. Edmund to Eliza, Letter 20, pp. 141, 144; Letter 22, pp. 154-56.

120 Edmund had sailed from the Orkneys on the evening of 26 July.

121 Edmund Cobb Hurry's maternal grandparents, the parents of his mother Ann (1741-1779). His grandfather was Edmund Cobb of Great Yarmouth. In the Templehouse Papers, N12, are three earlier letters between Edmund and Ann Cobb, two before their marriage on 1 September 1740.

His Majesty's ships.[122] They talk of fitting out thirty sail of the line. So much for politics, and I should not have mentioned them to you had I not thought it necessary to explain to you what I meant by troublesome times, as this is what gives me so much to do to procure a sufficiency of seamen to get away with. And in general I do not mind trouble, but I find myself very unwell. And if I can but once get to sea I shall then have time to myself. For there I have nothing to amuse or disturb me but my own thoughts; and disturb me much they never shall whilst I have any command over them. I have now been in much bustle since I came here and I have in some measure been obliged to partake of many fashionable amusements. But I am not conscious of having passed I may say a waking hour without thinking of you; without earnestly desiring an occasion to be able to visit you again. I must now leave writing for a while and hope to be able to finish this letter when I go on shore tonight, as I must inform you the ship lays here a considerable distance from the town.[123] And I came on board on purpose that I might have a moment to myself. For, as they all expect my departure soon, I am never left alone on shore.

I am again got on shore and the wind is still contrary, but I hope it will not continue so long so as when I was with you. I then wish'd it not to change, but now I must own I wish myself gone from hence, as a very disagreeable season is fast approaching. Pray do commend me suitably to all with you, and tell Mr Stewart that William is very well. In writing the above sentence I have been called away these ten times and if I do not send it away now I may not have another opportunity. And I would not for the world not hear from you, which I cannot expect to do unless you receive this; and then I hope you'll write immediately.

My dearest Eliza, I must (tho' unwillingly) close this letter with so much paper left, as if I were to go on I should lose the post. And I never know whether you can read this or not, but I know you will

---

122 In anticipation of a possible war with the Netherlands. The press gang was clearly active in Great Yarmouth in the years before the outbreak of the French Revolution in 1789, as well as during the subsequent wars with Revolutionary France after 1793.

123 Great Yarmouth, although very well placed geographically for trade and war with Europe, lacked an easily entered harbour. Ships visiting it usually anchored in its Roads.

excuse it and believe me to be your earnest wellwisher and sincerest friend, Edmund Cobb Hurry.

Do not forget to write immediately.

Cover, Miss Liddell, Rutland in the Rosses, Ireland. Postmark, Yarmouth, 29 September 1787.

Letter 11

Eliza Liddell to Edmund Cobb Hurry
Rutland in the Rosses

Written 11-29 September 1787; sent from Inishcoo, 1 October;
received by Edmund at Great Yarmouth

Tuesday, 11 September 1787

I sealed up my pacquets, or journal to speak in your style, last night, the minute I had filled up the paper. Possibly, if it was again open, if I was to peruse it, I should not have the courage to send it. For to write as I do, the unpremeditated thought of the moment, is to say a thousand silly things that, if confined to one's own breast, would escape censure or criticism. But may not reproof be of use to me? And undeserved censure I fear not meeting from you. The critic I trust will be lost in the indulgent friend. Fairly do I lay myself open to praise or blame, for I know not how to conceal a thought of my heart from one I value as I do you. You will know how to define what I mean and will suspect me of being an indiscreet babbler when I tell you I have an aversion to secrets. Mystery and concealment may in some cases be a duty, but mysterious concealments when unnecessary ought to be avoided. They argue something wrong in the head or heart, and subject us in this bad world to imputations of error that may do injury to the cause of virtue and religion.

This has ever been an established opinion of mine; an opinion that, when but a mere girl, I carried to dangerous excess. Dangerous because I thought all spoke truth, as I did; and, when I found my mistake, felt all the bitterness of disappointment. I bless God I suffered no farther, by the contagion of falsehood; that the love of truth is not eradicated but more firmly grounded in my soul by seeing the want of it in too many others. Yes, Edmund, most devoutly do I bless God when I look back and reflect that my orphan and unprotected youth is passed over. Accustomed, indeed early accustomed, to sorrow, but untraceable to remorse, I speak not this proudly, boastingly, but with gratitude.

Wednesday, 12 September

I always rejoice in a bright and enlivening sun, but now more than ever. Now, when I hope you are on your passage home, I feel its warm rays with uncommon pleasure. What a morning this, tho' enclosed in a gloomy cavern that to the sun's warm and chearing ways was impervious. I met with a thought in some book the other day that pleased me. Here it is for you. Half the world have no souls, at least none but of the vegetable and animal kinds.[124] To this species of being love and sentiment are entirely unnecessary. They were made to travel through life in a state of mind neither quite awake or asleep; and it is perfectly equal to them in what company they pursue or take the journey. Ah, is not this too true? And with people of this cast one may breathe and live, but restless and disquieted. One's soul involuntarily turns to the dear absent friends whose kindred minds beat in unison to ours, with every interesting and social sympathy. Alas, have I not reason, daily, hourly, to lament being separated from you?

How little do they know me here. Their tastes, their pleasures so different from what would afford me satisfaction. Silent, dejected, I shrink into myself and am careless even to blame, whether or not I sink into insignificance with them. Mrs Corbet is the only one I can love here. Her I do sincerely. Though from her unhappiness of mind, which I cannot help participating, from a peevish and unequal temper, I have little pleasure in her society. She possesses some great and good qualities: the most generous disdain of those who have nothing but rank to recommend them; the most exquisite sensibility for the misfortunes of others; and an integrity of heart that thinks no ill. But her temper is soured by frequent disappointments, too many of them brought on by indiscretions that nothing will I fear ever convert. Her attachments are all sudden – ardent to enthusiasm. She dresses out those she regards with more than human excellence. She ceases to approve or reject but as they do. She adopts their opinions, their manners, their tone of voice.

Hence, when she cannot remain blind to imperfections incident to human nature, to errors the best minds may be surprised into

---

124 A theory dating from classical times and held, amongst others, by Aristotle.

and the worst at times feel compunction for, she is inconsolable, accuses with severity her fate, talks of the dreadful deceit of the world with the utmost acrimony and bitterness, and at times is quite a misanthrope. 'Tis a pity, but where shall we find perfection? And much may be said for early wrong impressions; for prejudices few have the strength of mind enough to shake off.

Goodbye. I am called to breakfast and the children are shouting that they see the *Dutchess* off Arran Head.[125] This I disbelieve, for the weather is too fine for Mr Corbet to return so soon.

The children were right. We had scarcely done breakfast when Mr Corbet bounced into the parlour. Nothing would serve him but that we should all go down in a boat to the brig and return in her. Fortunately for me, who trembled at the proposal, the brig was very near the narrows. I had therefore but little boating, which you know I have a great dislike to, for numerous as are the dangerous sunk rocks here. For one there is I apprehend fifty. So now he has taken Mrs Corbet and the children to see Sheenmore.[126] And I must go now and stay with Mrs Lawrence till dinner time. I have always heard of two evils chuse the least, and I had no reasonable excuse for accompanying Mr Corbet through those odious sounds but by saying I would pay this tiresome visit.

But before I go let me, least I forget, communicate a most important piece of intelligence. The Duke of Rutland was three hours on board the brig.[127] The *Duke of Rutland*, eat beef stakes, on board the brig, this at Killala![128] Oh how we love to bow down to the great. For, from Mr Corbet down to the little dirty cabin boy, we are

---

125 Arran Head on Arranmore Island, west of Inishcoo.

126 Sheenmore, a rounded hill about a thousand feet high, in Donegal, to be viewed from the *Dutchess*.

127 Charles Manners, fourth Duke of Rutland (1754-1787), Lord Lieutenant of Ireland, 1784-87, toured midland and northern Ireland in the summer of 1787. His death a few months later, on 24 October 1787, from liver disease, was attributed to an excessive love of claret. Killala is in northern Mayo.

128 In his record of his tour, which lasted from 3 July to 29 September, the duke recorded his visit to Ballina and Killala in Mayo. 'We returned back to Mr King's at Balina. We amused ourselves by shooting at, but missing, seals in the River Moyle. We visited the wretched episcopal town of Killala, supported entirely by fishing; and, in truth, we can make no other remark but that the hospitality of the gentlemen at whose houses we visited made the most inhospitable country on the globe comfortable and pleasant.' *Fourteenth Report of the Royal Commission on Historical Manuscripts* (1896), *The Duke of Rutland*, iii, pp. 419-23.

all elated at this most extraordinary honour. It will be recorded in the newspaper no doubt. Why should it not, since a turtle, travelling after his Grace, was thought an object worthy of public attention? You find, Edmund, folly is not confined to us poor females, and I don't see why the Dutchess of Rutland, or any other lady, has not as good a right to entertain the world, with a history of her fly-caps and band-boxes, as her lord has to record this momentous affair of his cook, and a fat turtle following him, in a tour through the kingdom of Ireland.[129]

William Hamilton (1755-1797), rector of Clondevaddog, Donegal, and a distinguished geologist. He was murdered by a mob at Stratton, County Londonderry, in 1797

129 Lady Mary Isabella Somerset (1756-1831), the daughter the fourth Duke of Beaufort, married the Duke of Rutland in 1775, when he was Marquess of Granby.

13 September 1787, Rosses

This moment I have received your letter.[130] Are you then going back to Derwinda? Your letter I should have told you from that place. Edmund, you are now in England and I am writing to Derwinda. You bid me do so. Your respectable grandmother, long, long may she be continued to you. May you, may you, whatever becomes of me, may you be happy! I have written daily to you and will preserve pacquets till you desire me to send them. Maybe, to use your own language, you will forget to do so. You wish me to write. Why then did you not give me directions where to write to you in England?

Edmund, my heart is full. I know not what I am saying and would wait till I am more composed, but not to wait another post is such a delay. Three letters I have already wrote to you: one at Derwinda, two to Elsinore.[131] Don't you call at the latter place on your return? Where I shall be in the course of a few weeks I know not, for Mr Corbet is urging Mrs Corbet to go either to Dublin or Corbet Hill.[132] We are to go by sea. God preserve us, I dread the thoughts of it. Yet why should I dread dying? Few would lament me and I trust I should be happy. Alas, I cannot be so here while separated from you. Direct here, if you think of me, for letters will be forwarded to me should I leave this. Yours, perhaps too, too much, Eliza Liddell.

No letter today. This is Tuesday 18 September 1787. Your account from Windau was dated the fifteenth – of August, so that I might have received a second by this time.[133] Why did you not write to me? You were to leave Courland you told me in a few hours and might be certain I should remain uneasy till I knew what was become of you.[134] But you have not yet got my letters and tax me with forgetting you. Cruel Edmund! Foolish Eliza!

Tea is over. We were all sitting round the table at our different

---

130   This letter does not survive.

131   Eliza to Edmund, Letter 4, pp. 36-38; Letter 7, pp. 53-56; and another letter which does not survive.

132   Corbet Hill, Robert Corbet's house in Arnestown, County Wexford.

133   This letter does not survive.

134   The duchy of Courland, named after the Curonians, a pagan tribe, is now the western part of Latvia.

works when two letters were brought in to inform Mr and Mrs Corbet that a Mr and Mrs Hamilton were on the way to the Rosses from the Olpherts, at whose house they were on their tour through the north.[135] The night is dismal dark, but Mr Corbet is gone to invite them over. They are at the inn and I am run upstairs to tell you.[136] Do you know I have been so long out of all female company, save Mrs Corbet, that I feel half afraid to encounter this fair lady. I would rather men visitors came here; for from them, if I don't like them, I can run away; but a lady one must talk to sometimes, a formidable chore.

They are come. I must go down. After supper I will introduce them to you. Would to heaven I could, but you are now at home, in the bosom of your family. You will be too happy to bestow a thought on me. Farewell. A pretty train of reflections am I going to meet these strangers with. Alas, it's your presence alone that could make me enjoy any other society.

Wednesday, 19 September

We sat up last night. I could not perform my promise of giving you some account of our new guests. I told you I expected to be frightened at the face of a strange lady. The truth is I behaved very awkwardly and sat, not staring but stupidly silent, with my eyes cast on the floor. After supper I got into a little better humour and surveyed, and talked to, these strangers. (Take notice, my supper was simply milk and that my being more loquacious after supper was not owing to the effects of the bottle.)[137] Mrs Hamilton, then for so much, I like. Her manners are very elegant and her countenance expressive of sense and sweetness.

---

135 William Hamilton (1755-1797), a contributor to the contemporary debate on geology, was the author of *Letters Concerning the Northern Coast of the County of Antrim* (1786). A staunch supporter of the government, in 1790 he became rector of Clondevaddog, Donegal, but was brutally murdered at Stratton, County Londonderry, by a mob on 2 March 1797. His widow and nine children were provided for by a vote from the Irish House of Commons.

136 At Lackbeg.

137 One of a number of light-hearted references to alcohol in the correspondence.

Mr Hamilton is a Fellow of Dublin College.[138] He seems a man of much information and, if I mistake not, of an eccentric turn. I imagine he is a deep researcher into nature and is travelling more for information than pleasure; or rather that he makes the latter subservient to the former. Accompanied by his wife, he has made the tour of England, Ireland and Scotland. They do not make use of a carriage, but she has rode the entire tour on a single horse. If the weather is unfavorable they remain a few days at some gentleman's house or inn. Really I can't but admire the man's wisdom. No panache or expense of carriages; servants all but one footman out of the question. No housekeeping, no expense of cloathes for so many months. Pleasure, information and economy all considered.

And lastly, though of the first consequence to his happiness, he is dayly enlarging the understanding of Mrs Hamilton, who never I believe was out of Dublin before her marriage. And I can't but consider the education of any woman, though carefully attended to, as very defective if confined to a town life. It admits not of reflection, or an intimate acquaintance with a thousand things in nature that will most effectually root out prejudice and give birth to a just and solid turn of mind.

The Hamiltons and Mr Corbet are gone to look at some of the islands. They are to be back for dinner, but I chose not to go with them. I am glad of every opportunity of being alone, which I can seldom be, for the house is so small, and such a number of girls who are always with me, night and day, that I am often weary and wish to be left to my own reflections. What is worse I am under the necessity of bearing the obtrusion of two maids, whenever they chuse to run in and out. You know the door of their room opens into mine. Well there's no help for these things. Patience, and I shall be soon out of the Rosses; for it is almost determined we leave this in a week – by sea. Ah, there's the rub.

I think I shall not be long with Mrs Corbet after she leaves this place. I cannot love her children. They are by nature the very reverse of what I would wish them to be. Their understandings are good, but their tempers bad; and they possess a degree of art or cunning, for it is not penetration, which exceeds what I could have had an

---

138 Trinity College, Dublin, restricted to Protestants, the only university in Ireland.

idea of in creatures of their age; Harriet alas, before I knew her, poor wretched girl. I have done all in my power to check what was wrong in them all and to strengthen what I thought right, but Mrs Corbet, without intending it, counteracts what I do. She holds them at a distance. She is severe for trifles and, though she wishes their confidence, will never gain it, but would not give up her opinions to any other person.

To tell you the truth (though indigence compels me to be in the line of life I am, and though I may be of use to the young people under my care), yet I cannot approve of a mother calling in foreign assistance in order to divest herself of the task of cultivating her children's minds.[139] Few situations can justify it – total ignorance, extreme bad health or some such cause. What respect or gratitude can a child feel for the mother who thinks the bestowing on it any instruction a troublesome employment, who consigns it to another, from whom it may chance to imbibe false notions and bad principles? Oh, ye mothers!

Monday, 20 September

I was right. Mr Hamilton is busily engaged in philosophical digressions. He was out at five o'clock this morning collecting information from the natives. At breakfast he produced some fir cones that were found in a bog and mentioned that some people had offered to shew a plow etc that was found in the same bog – important discoverys there. I have heard Mr Corbet affirm that his plow was the first that had ever been seen in this part of the world, so he thought; and, when he found the people had given Mr Hamilton information they always studiously withheld from him, he was in a furious passion and execrated them at an unmerciful rate.[140] I was wishing to tell him his pride and arrogance made

139   In due course, Eliza took daily control of her own children's education and behaviour.

140   Robert Corbet did contribute, if only minimally, to scientific knowledge. In Edward Wakefield, *An Account of Ireland: Statistical and Political*, 2 vols (London, 1812), i, p. 218, in a list of the mean temperatures of the sea coast of Ireland, the minimum measurement for 'the mean temperature of the island of Enniscoo, one of the Rosses islands on the western coast of Ireland, observed by a covered well in a granite rock, the maximum taken in 1787, the minimum in 1788', the latter measurement is ascribed to Robert Corbet Esq.

them detest him, and considering to what length ignorant minds carry resentment and hatred, he might think himself well off [*tear*] out in some open act of violence [*tear*]. I should like and love Mrs Hamilton were [*tear*] intimately acquainted with. I am almost sure she has a benevolent heart. She talks much, but with such vivacity and good sense that one can't think her tiresome.

I listen, for I don't know how it is I never found myself so totally disinclined to join in conversations in my life. My spirits are bad and I think my temper is grown peevish. I am more ready to find fault than I need to be and less ready to make allowance for the whims of others, perhaps because I am acquiring more of my own. I must seriously take myself to task. Why I suffer what is wrong to grow on me, the cause I am not at a loss to seek for; but to you I will not tell it. It would gratify your vanity too much to know the unhappiness your absence creates in the breast of her who begs of the Almighty to protect and bless you ever. Eliza Liddell.

Edmund, if you ever see these papers, I intreat you to burn them when perused. Think how mortified I should be that you should have it in your power to bestow a second reading on them. Consider that I write, at any time and in any humour, surrounded by five noisy children.

Cover: Mr Edmund Cobb Hurry[141]

22 September 1787

Suspense, thou fever of the mind,
No rest from care thy victims find.
Terrors vain, an imaginary numerous host,
Prone of trifles to make the most.
Cameleon like, oft change their hue
And picture ills imaginary as true.
How steered by hope our little bark
The port of joy at distance mark.
The port of joy – delusive sight –

---

141 Sent inside Letter 11.

No sooner seen when lo, 'tis night.
Night horrible, tempestuous, dark;
Hope no coast doth now remark.
Despair commands, no longer now he steers,
His post resigns to sighs and fears;
Fears that drown the mental sight
And dawning peace, inhuman slight.
Driven on affliction's coast by adverse winds
Our care-worn bark no safety finds.
Now pierced by rocks, sharp-pointed, through,
Or plunged in waves till lost in view.

The tardy morn arising, resignation takes her stand
And points to a remote and happy land.
Religion steers, the port is gained
And perfect bliss at length obtained.
Preserve thou fever of the mind.
Then rest from care thy victim's mind.

Where did I find those lines?[142] 'Tis no matter the poetry is bad, but applicable to the present state of my mind. One minute tortured with anxiety and torn, on your account; and again I am in hopes you are safe in some port; or, if out at sea, the Almighty is sufficient to save and preserve you. Oh, 'tis a fearful storm.

It is now five in the morning, Saturday 22 September, and it has raged with unabated violence these four and twenty last hours. I will go to bed. May heaven guard you. That I were asleep!

Saturday, ten o'clock. The storm is over. I am endeavouring to compose myself by reflection that you, perhaps, were safe in some port and not exposed to its violence. Tomorrow I shall get a letter, I hope. The Hamiltons are still here. We shall miss them. They are really pleasant, agreeable people. We leave when it ought to have been them. For, as to myself, society without you is solitude to me.

---

142 Poem untraced, possibly by Eliza herself.

To you, who so well know sweet friendship's power
I dedicate the feelings of a lonely hour.
Tho' unadorned with legendary art,
They yet may please the tender social heart.
Say, why does absence so severely prove
Our warm attachment to the friends we love?
Why does each virtue steal upon the mind
And paint the object only good and kind?
In fond oblivion enjoy foibles lost.
Een what we have censured then becomes our boast.
Alas, the labyrinth of Crete in art
How trivial to the windings of the heart![143]

Sunday evening, 23 September

After enduring some hours all the bitterness of wounded pride, of tenderness insulted, I am again calm. My tears no longer flow, nor my heart beats as it did with violence, as if ready to burst its prison. I will try to bow, in humble submission, to my Creator's will. I will say to my soul, be at peace. This scene of suffering will quickly pass away and I shall be at rest. Vain heart! The tears I bid cease to flow again obtrude. I must lay down my pen.

Edmund, may you never experience the sorrow you have this day occasioned me. What if you did not receive my letters? Was it not more reasonable to suppose that was owing to your quick removal from place to place than to my neglect of writing? Recollect. Oh how could you so soon forget how much I regretted your departure? Regret. How incompetent that word to express what passed in my soul! If you had regarded me, would you have written to Mr Corbet to tell him of your arrival in England (he who, though he regards you, comparatively speaking it was of no consequence to) in your letter from Windau?[144]

You say you could have written ten sheets to me, if opportunity

---

143 Poem untraced, possibly also by Eliza herself.

144 See Edmund to Eliza, Letter 10, pp. 80-81. Eliza to Edmund, Letter 13, p. 101.

had offered of sending them; and the moment you got to Yarmouth from whence you might write twice ten sheets, you neglect *one*. You write a formal letter of business to Mr Corbet (he gave it to me to read) and you coldly desire your respects to the family. Well, and have you not a right to do as you please? And you did not chuse to write. When I think of this, my pride revolts at the idea of my folly in suffering so much on your account. Then again, I consider you are piqued at my seeming neglect, not having received any of my letters. Then I excuse you and am hurt at the notions that you have set me down as a weak, contemptible being, incapable of a solid or permanent attachment, and that you are distressed at my silence. Good God! What would I not give but to see you for a few moments that I might omit nothing to convince you how regularly I have written. I dispatched two letters to you the moment I had read yours to Mr Corbet.[145]

Two letters to Yarmouth, and in a woman's hand, subject of alarm I suppose to your family.[146] Their affection for you will rouse their curiosity. Who is this unknown? It is evident she is me, who fears not their inspection or she would not openly address you at the very abode of your friends. But I presume they will not interfere with your friendships, nor think themselves authorised to pry into your correspondances or reprobate them, if known. If they do, why let them. They would not if they knew the heart of Eliza and that she would be the last person in the world to sway you to ought that should derogate from the respect and duty to the honoured name of parent. (She knows their value by their loss.) She is your friend and that word, when not abused, comprises every wish for your honour and happiness, both temporal and eternal.

But on second thoughts, on further consideration, your family may be alarmed at finding you correspond with a *female* they are unacquainted with; may be alarmed without any impeachment of the liberality of their minds. So much depends on the disposition of the woman a young man considers with esteem. If he mistakes that disposition, it may be a dangerous acquaintance. I shall not blame them or complain if they are unjust to me, not knowing me. I am prepared for that. They will be apt to be so, the higher they regard you.

---

145   Eliza to Edmund, Letters 8 and 9, pp. 57-76.

146   Edmund Hurry's father and uncle, William and Samuel Hurry, both lived in Great Yarmouth.

And shall I blame this tender anxiety – when that tenderness must constitute in a great measure the happiness of Edmund? Oh, no!

I am the child of misfortune but I will never be the child of prejudice. At the same time, I might avoid their notice by not addressing my letters to you at their house. I might and would, if in fact I was an improper acquaintance for you. It appears to me a ridiculous form that I am to avoid writing what I would say if you were present. If our principles are right, why disguise them? What then have I to fear? Had I parents, I certainly should decline a correspondence that was not perfectly agreeable to them; or, if a mere girl, would conform to the opinions of those who had a right to judge for me. But at five and twenty, when I flatter myself the character is established, I can see no impropriety in adopting the only means heaven permits of conversing with my friends. Whatever I would say in conversation, why not transmit to paper?

24 September 1787

Thursday morning, seven o'clock. Yesterday I wrote the above to divert, how impossible, the uneasiness I feel. We got up this morning before day to give the Hamiltons their breakfast before their departure. It was the same thing to me when I was to get up, for sleep thus the wretched. Be not confused at the strength of that expression. I cannot help marking myself of the number. Misfortunes, what the world terms them, I can support, nay scarcely feel. Adversity in any shape, when the heart is uninterested in what it is, how trifling, how little to be regarded. But to centre in a dear friend the tenderest affections of one's soul, and for that friend to aim the shafts of unkindness or neglect, there I am vulnerable indeed!

But though I feel no less than I did yesterday, and though I shall remain unhappy till I hear from you, yet I am more reasonable than I was, or rather wish to sooth myself with hopes that you will write immediately. And though, till you have received my letters, I cannot be at rest, yet the certainty that your neglect only proceeded from pique would mitigate in some degree my uneasiness. Do not expect me to continue my journal. Under the uneasiness of sadness and disquiet, I cannot arrange my thoughts sufficiently to know what I am saying. Whatever may be the fate of your friend, may the God of mercy be your guide and protect you ever is the never ceasing aspiration of Eliza Liddell.

Rosses, 29 September

Tuesday this. I have waited till our post came in. Foolish creature. I flattered myself I should have heard from you. I have consulted Mrs Corbet whether I ought to send this. She urges me – but I will write no more unless I hear from you. I owe this to myself. May you, Edmund, be happy ever. Farewell.

Mrs Corbet says that it is probable your father may open my letters to you, as thinking they are on business. Can I wish he should not or ought this consideration to deter my writing? No.

You then, sir, father of Edmund Cobb Hurry, I address and dare entreat you will forward to him these letters, two sent by the last post and two by this.[147] If you think he can any way suffer by my correspondence, I shall abide by your determination, nor will in future trouble him or you. For me to relinquish his friendship I now depend on himself alone.

Cover, Mr Edmund Cobb Hurry, Great Yarmouth, England. Postmark, Rutland, 1 October 1787. Opened by Samuel Hurry in early October.

---

147 Eliza to Edmund, Letters 8, 9, 11, 12, pp. 57-76, 84-99. Eliza addressed this covering note to Edmund's father, mistakenly thinking that this was Samuel Hurry, who was his uncle, not William Hurry, his father.

Letter 12

Eliza Liddell to Edmund Cobb Hurry
Rutland in the Rosses

Written 23 September to 1 October 1787; sent from Inishcoo, 1 October; received by Edmund at Great Yarmouth

Rosses, 23 September, 1787

While I have been alarmed to death concerning your safety, you are safe in England, thank God, and have escaped the fearful storm of last Friday. Four letters have I written you, who chid me without answering them. Why did you not give me direction where to find you in England, and then there would have been no fear of their being lost, as I suppose mine are? Two went to Courland, two to Elsinore.[148] Wonder not at this second. This moment Mr Corbet received a letter from you *and none for me*. What am I to think? In compliance with your request I have been writing daily to you. One pacquet I send. Perhaps the next I must retain. Perhaps I am to learn that you are like the rest of the world, incapable of remembering an absent friend. Be it so, may you be happy. I received your letters. Do they say I am to be so soon forgot? 'Tis well. Eliza Liddell.

Perhaps this is a last adieu. I am soon to go by sea, *sea at this time of year, either to Dublin or Corbet Hill.

I send openly to your father's house my letters. Perhaps you disapprove of this. It may be you like not my doing so. For many reasons, any of which I can't agree to, if I was worthy of being your friend (you called me such), I am worthy to be so in the eye of all. I disdain concealments of any kind. Tell them all. Tell them not to fear me. Tell them I am *poor* and *proud*; that I have no view of drawing you from your duty; that I am not a giddy girl, but

---

148 Eliza to Edmund, Letter 4, pp. 36-38; Letter 7, pp. 53-56; and two others which are lost.

have learned to respect myself too much to suffer a clandestine correspondence – tho' ought but friendship may be thought of.

Cover, Mr Edmund Cobb Hurry, Great Yarmouth, England. Postmark, Rutland, 28 September. Opened by Samuel Hurry, early October.

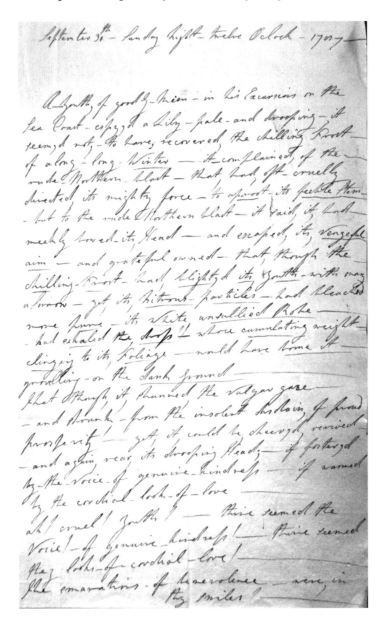

Eliza Liddell to Edmund Cobb Hurry, Letter 13 (below, p. 100), September 1787

Letter 13

Eliza Liddell to Edmund Cobb Hurry
Rutland in the Rosses

Written 30 September to 3 October 1787; sent from Inishcoo, 3 October;
received at Elsinore, 26 October

30 September, Sunday night, twelve o'clock, 1787

A youth of goodly mien, in his excursion on the sea coast, espied a lily, pale and drooping. It seemed not to have recovered the chilling frost of a long, long winter. It complained of the northern blast that had oft cruelly directed its mighty force to uproot its feeble stem. But to the rude northern blast, it said, it had meekly bowed its head and escaped its vengeful aim, and grateful owned that, though the chilling frost had blighted its youth with many a sorrow, yet its nitrous particles had bleached more pure its white unsullied rose, had exhaled the dross whose cumulating weight, clinging to its foliage, would have borne it grovelling on the dank ground.

That though it shunned the vulgar gaze, and shrunk from the insolent disdain of proud prosperity, yet it could be cheered, revived and again rear its drooping head if fostered by the voice of genuine kindness, if warmed by the cordial look of love.

Ah, cruel youth! Thine seemed the voice of genuine kindness! Thine seemed the looks of cordial love! The emanations of benevolence were in thy smiles and thy mild eyes seemed illumined with understanding and with truth. Those eyes rest on the diffident and unassuming lily. Ah, why did they *rest* on it? Why assure it of tenderness and sincerity? Nurtured by the vivifying warmth of thy soothing attentions, the poor flower revives its pristine form of placid ease, of innate peace.

Soon, too soon, torn from thy bosom, reluctantly torn, it mourns thy absence and fondly dwells on recollected hours of happiness spent with thee – while memory paints thee good and kind – deceitful sunshine, dangerous delusion.

The damp dews of unkindness and neglect succeed. Ah, what was the rude northern blast, what the chilling frost, to thy damp dews of unkindness and neglect! The lily hangs its head. It droops. It dies.

Tuesday, 2 October 1787

This is post day. Well, what is that to me? I shall get no letters, at least from him. What taught me to expect a far different story? Oh, why can't I too forget? Why is each moment of my life embittered by the recollection of his delusive tenderness? Why does my heart throb with anxiety for his safety, who thinks not of me? Inhuman! Why delude me with the dear hope of being dear to thee?

Thy letters, I dare not trust myself to look them over. (They shake my resolutions of sincere obedience and resignation to the will of that God in whom is no shadow of turning.) They almost tempt me to ask why, why is this? I wish I could forget you entirely. I wish I could forget those passages in your letters that memory has too faithfully treasured up. What right had [I] to suppose you would rank me in the number of your friends? Am I not *poor*? But does that lessen me in my own esteem? No. Nor would in yours, if you thought rightly; but you don't. You are a son of the world. You bow down to its degrading opinions.

I will not be your friend. How can I? We think so differently. My soul is incapable of weighing the circumstances of those I think worthy of my esteem. Afflicted, distressed and unprotected by the whole world, they would become tenfold dearer to my heart. This would be to render indissoluble my friendship.

To what purpose am I writing? You bid me write every day, but it seems our correspondence has closed for ever. Four times I wrote to you.[149] You remained not long enough in any place to receive my letters, you know you did not, and you lay hold of this poor excuse to neglect me entirely, and to mortify me. To render the neglect more pointed, you write to Mr Corbet the minute you get to England. No longer was Eliza's acquaintance or friendship of any consequence to

---

149 Edmund to Eliza, Letters 4, pp. 36-38; 7, pp. 53-56; 8 and 9, pp. 57-76.

you.[150] When shut up in the solitary island of Inniscoo, her company might serve to amuse you. When cooped up at sea to write to her preserved you from idleness. But when returned to your own family, oh, she was forgot entirely. No, not entirely, but you wished her to know she must not consider herself of any consequence to your happiness. Oh, how my heart rises at my folly!

Wednesday, 3 October 1787

Eighteen days ago you wrote to Mr Corbet.[151] I imagine perhaps you had written to me, perhaps your letter was lost, and therefore sent off two letters to your father's house in hopes you would get them before your departure; and two I sent the post following.[152] I wish I had them back. Nine days ago my first two went, so I may reasonably conclude they are arrived. Where you are I can't conjecture, but your father, tho' he will be certain they are not letters of business, will open them. Do you know that, though I am too proud to wish he should not on my own account, I am uneasy at the apprehension that yet those letters may be productive of something disagreeable to you? Your father will take you to task, perhaps be displeased with you. God knows I would not wish that, or the smallest measure of uneasiness, to dwell on your mind. But no, he need not, you will answer carelessly. I was a 'Bath' acquaintance (you know Bath acquaintants are not worth remembering), and he will be satisfied.[153]

Sometimes a ray of hope darts across my mind: that Mrs Corbet is right; that your silence is solely owing to your being hurt at not getting letters from me. But this is a dangerous supposition. It revives all that tenderness that destroys my peace. It makes you appear interested about me. Ah, I must not dwell on that. Feeble as I am, I must fortify my mind against the worst. It cannot be. You regard me not. Nor would I leave anything I loved to the torturing doubt that they were disregarded, forgot.

---

150 A main cause of Eliza's despair.

151 15 September.

152 Eliza to Edmund, Letters 8, 9, 11, 12, pp. 57-76, 84-99.

153 Bath acquaintances were holiday friends, forgotten on the return home.

Farewell, a long farewell. May you be as good and as happy as I wish you to be. I will go look at that sea I am soon to rest upon; rest, yes it may be an everlasting rest. Edmund, if Eliza were dead, would you not feel some compunction that you had contributed to make her wretched while alive? Wretched, what a word. I am *not* so and I am *not* fast hastening to immortality.

This letter from its date you will find was written several days ago. Rash, precipitate, you find I am unworthy of your friendship. I have sent several letters to your father's house on a supposition that perhaps you were uneasy at not receiving letters from me. 5 September 1787.

This I ought not to have done: me involve you in a quarrel with your friends. Good God, how I am distressed. You cannot but think of me with resentment and hatred. E. Liddell.

Cover, Mr Edmund Cobb Hurry, Messrs John Diston and Co., Elsinore. Note, 'No. 4, received at Elsinore. Received the 26 October 1787'. Postmark, Rutland, date unclear.

Letter 14

Eliza Liddell to Edmund Cobb Hurry
Rutland in the Rosses

*Written 7 to 10 October 1787; sent from Inishcoo, 10 October;
received at Elsinore, 29 October*

Sunday evening, nine o'clock, 7 October 1787

I have left the drawing room that I may converse with you. Perhaps
you will tell me I ought rather to take up a book of sermons; perhaps
I ought, and I don't know but it would be better for me to do so. For
sermons might tend to inspire me with content and cheerfulness;
and writing to you has always a quite contrary effect on my mind.

When I sit down to write, I sigh over the necessity for so doing
and repeat: why can't I see him? Why am I denied a happiness I
should be so grateful for? He may never get my letters. He may never
know how tenderly I remember him, how dear he is to me. And
this particular letter you may never receive, or indeed any other
from me. Your family, who now know of our correspondence from
the letters I sent to you to Yarmouth, may be displeased with you
on my account; and Eliza may be the sacrifice no less to duty than
inclination. 'Inclination', I repeat, for you may feel resentment to me
for involving you in even a trifling quarrel or dispute with those you
must highly value. When I think this, but patience, a little time will
relieve me from this most painful state of suspense. I will indeavour
to forget how I am circumstanced and talk to you as usual. I can
burn it, if indeed I am to write no more.

Your letter was dated the 26th September.[154] I wish I knew
whether you left Yarmouth immediately after you wrote to me.[155] I
wish I knew. If you did, you are probably past Elsinore. The weather
is good at present and I hope it may remain so, no less for your safety
than to preserve my peace, for I shall be miserable if the weather

---

154 Edmund to Eliza, Letter 10, p. 77.

155 Edmund left Great Yarmouth before Eliza's four letters, Letters 8, 9, 11 and 12, reached there.

should be bad while I think you are at sea. May God Almighty, infinite in power and in goodness, preserve you. But why did Mr Hurry, for you said you would leave it to his determination,[156] why did he permit you to go to sea at this time of year, and the probability too that you may be detained all winter, should the frost set in early? Alas! Alas! Shall I ever again see you?

The observation you made in your last letter of the similarity of thoughts in each of our first letters recurred to me while I was reading your Orkney journal for the first time. It appeared to me extraordinary, and afforded me the most sensible pleasure, that your ideas should be consonant to mine on a subject I was so highly interested in. It seemed to me an assurance I was so dear to you, since your language has assumed the garb my heart had taught me to clothe my expressions in. You answered it in thought a hundred times, dear Edmund. How my vanity would be raised by your saying so, but that you take care to humble me again by telling me of exceptionable passages.[157]

I cannot at this distance of time recollect all I said, and now feel half afraid to write to you, least I should expose myself to your criticisms. What did I say that was so very exceptionable? I felt when I read your letter ashamed and confounded, as if you were present, and that I had said or done some foolish thing, and was nearly going to hide my face with my hands. Remember, I expect from your friendship advice, and reproof when you think me wrong; and, though I may be ashamed to deserve censure or reproof, I shall not be ungrateful for it. Indeed I think it requires some temerity on my part to correspond with you, but I trust your regard for me will sometimes step in to blind your judgment. Or else what business have I to write?

But hold! The thought this moment suggests that perhaps you may mistake me and imagine I am seeking, by assumed humility, for compliments. But no, you cannot think so meanly of me. That would be to suppose me artful, despicable and deserving only of your contempt. Away with the humiliating idea. But sure that woman must be a downright fool who does not feel most truly

156 Edmund was still working for his father, William Hurry.

157 Edmund to Eliza, Letter 10, p. 78.

her inferiority when writing to one of your sex, whose superior advantages of education (to say nothing of the greater depths of your understandings, and greater knowledge of the world) must point out to you defects we ourselves are not sensible of. Those of you who I will not say condescend (I like not abject expressions when the female part of the world are in question); no, well then, those of you who please to think us of sufficient consequence to ingage your attention, may be of essential service to us; nay enlighten and enlarge our minds, if instead of degrading yourselves and insulting us by the poison of flattery, you treat us as rational creatures, companions, friends.[158]

I always feel indignant when anyone considers me as a mere puppet, and annoys me with ridiculous compliments. I once very gravely, when I was in wicked humour, turned to a gentleman who had exhausted himself in making what he thought such fine speeches as to deserve my most serious attention, and desired him to repeat all that over again (for 'it was really very pretty and I wished to remember it'). I was not, however, ill natured enough to join in his confusion, and since think that everyone has a right to indulgence and pity when weak enough to deserve our scorn.

Supper on the table. Good night. I must attend. A thousand times good night.

Monday, 8 October 1787

We are all in commotion. All going in the brig to Dublin, it is said, if the wind is fair, by Saturday next. I wish the wind may continue contrary this fortnight to come, for by that time I may get a letter from you; and, if it comes, it would be a delay of more than a week, though we should have a quick passage, to forward it to Dublin; and a week, when you are in question, is an age.

All places, unless I could be with or near my sisters, are alike to me where you are not; and I think I would rather continue here some time longer. I dread the bustle of Dublin. I would rather go

---

158 This is the strongest statement in the letters of Eliza's demand that women should be treated by men on some sort of equal footing.

to Corbet Hill. Is it any wonder that I should be scared and like a frightened bird at the multitudes a great town contains, after being confined on a solitary island in the great Atlantic for two years? Dear island, here I saw *you*. I never saw you in Dublin and I can't return there without recalling the bitter sorrow I experienced there.[159] My mother, my dear and honoured mother, it was there, brought by my brother-in-law's means, it was there the finishing stroke was added that concluded a life of calamity.[160] And there was I left alone, unprotected, unprovided for, a stranger, with a frame feeble, delicate, ill able to encounter and endure the distress or difficulty, from both of which I was preserved by the abundant mercy of a bountiful God. May my soul ever bless and praise his holy name, who endued me with such firmness of mind at the time that now I think of with astonishment.

Rosses, 8 October 1787

What a state of spirits must I be in when I could scarcely preserve myself from fainting, when Mrs Corbet flew up stairs with your letter to me.[161] It was a considerable time before I could read it. This was Friday last. The post was immediately going out. It was impossible for me at that moment to write with any degree of coherency. And it was necessary I should not delay or you might miss my letter.

I had several sheets ready written. The last one I took up, added a few lines to it and sent it off. This from the nature, the folly, of its contents, I cannot forgive myself for so doing or deserve that you should either. How unseasonable, how unjust must I appear to you! Shall I deface the impressions you must have conceived to my disadvantage by attempting not my justification but apology?

I should not tease you so soon after my last. I should not till you favoured me with another letter, but that I should remain unhappy till I at least explain why my last to Elsinore was so very absurd. It was not when wrote *intended for your eye*, but much intended

159 Eliza's mother, Elizabeth Liddell, had died in Dublin.

160 Eliza's estranged brother-in-law, Mr Collier, had invited Eliza and her mother to Dublin.

161 Edmund to Eliza, Letter 10, pp. 77-83.

to ease the oppression of my heart, and I certainly should have destroyed it.[162] You *never* should have *seen* it, but when your letter so unexpectedly came from Yarmouth (for I had taken it into my head I was neglected, forgotten),[163] I was too much agitated to recollect what in that paper I had said, and was glad, since I found myself unequal to hold the pen at the time, that I had a letter ready to send. I wish it may be lost. I hope you will never see it.

For several days before Mr Corbet received your letter from England, I had been wretched on your account, in consequence of several dreadful storms, and I awaited with the most anxious impatience to hear from you. You wrote to Mr Corbet and my first sensations were those of joy, that you were safe. But why did I not get a letter also instantly occurred. You had not, I supposed, got any of mine.[164] Perhaps you were piqued at my seeming silence. You thought I had forgot you. Desirous to justify myself in your esteem, while under this impression, I wrote to Yarmouth in hopes you would not leave that place before my letters arrived. And how rapid the transition from this idea to one less flattering to me than that you were piqued by my silence: to me painful indeed, infinitely so to me, and injurious to you. That was that you wrote to Mr Corbet purposely that I might know you were in England and that I might know that, when you were with your friends and family, I was of too little consequence to you to hold a place in your thoughts – and not sufficiently punished by what this reflection has for so many days cost me. And will you, Edmund, will you think me worthy of a continuance of your esteem, me who so hastily condemned you and thought you would act like the rest of the world?

What contributed to give rise to this notion, and confirm it, was my remembering that you never desired me to write to you to Yarmouth. My pride was roused and a thousand vague conjectures disturbed me. I would have given much to recall the letters I had sent off to Yarmouth.[165] How little on this occasion do I thank your pride. You should have remained neuter till time had proved whether I

162 Eliza to Edmund, Letter 13, pp. 100-3.

163 Edmund to Eliza, Letter 10, pp. 77-83.

164 Letters that either were lost or have not survived.

165 Eliza to Edmund, Letters 8, 9, 11 and 12, 57-76, 84-99.

ought to make choice of you as a necessary and proper auxiliary. There was no occasion for her forward advances till the tormenting memories that haunted and tormented me were realized.

I bless God they are not. Your letter, I feel conscious of not deserving it. Such an outrage against friendship, so contrary to my general character (rash condemnation). I can't think what bewitched me! But why did you not write to me as well as Mr Corbet on your arrival in England? Had you done so, it would have spared me much uneasiness and I neither should have hazarded your esteem or had so many self reproaches to bestow on myself. And more, I should have escaped the dire apprehension of having done wrong in writing to Yarmouth.

You say your father will open your letters addressed to you in your absence and I may write treason.[166] Is it then treason to write to you? I own to you I am hurt in more ways than one at that expression. On my own account, I cannot repent though your father should open my letters, I having sent them to his house. And though they should undergo the scrutiny of perhaps his severe and unkind criticisms, pride again; but in this respect it interferes not with what is due to friendship.

And here I owe it to myself. On my own account, observe I do not repent. On yours, I think very differently and am shocked and grieved least I should be the unhappy occasion of even a trifling misunderstanding between you and Mr Hurry.[167] Better, better you had never known me rather than this should happen. Hesitate not to give up my acquaintance entirely. And am I constrained to say this? Yes, I ought, I must, though my heart revolts at what I say. And you are going to Riga at this time of year. Great God preserve you! But every storm till you return will be a dagger to my heart. You will find, if not lost, two letters to Elsinore from me and two I sent to Derwinda.[168]

Mr Corbet did write to you, either to one or the other place; he got directions from me. He is almost determined to send his family

---

166 See Edmund to Eliza, Letter 10, pp. 80-81; Letter 20, pp. 141-42, 144.

167 William Hurry.

168 See Eliza to Edmund, Letters 13 and 14. The other two letters were either not received or have not survived.

from this place immediately, though he remains here another year. We go to Dublin, if a proper house can be procured time enough, or else to Corbet Hill. But, if you write again, direct to me here, as letters will be [sent] to me till we are settled. We I say. I often determine to go to England, but I fancy that till spring the superscription to Corbet Hill requires only the addition of Rosses, Ireland.

I wish we were to remain quietly here till spring and perhaps shall, for Mr Corbet is very wavering and uncertain. As to going by sea, I no longer dread it, nor ought, while a friend whose preservation is of infinitely more consequence to me than my own is daily exposed to its dangers. You were ill when you wrote. I trust you are no longer so. Surely you ought not to go to sea when so. I wish most ardently you may quit it for ever. It is dreadful: a social and liberal mind to be eternally cooped up in a ship when a being who had but half a grain of sense would answer the purpose as well and be no loss to society. You do be but [*tear*] do not expect compliments from you. I have [*tear*] detestation of every species of flattery and near [*tear*] point out a fault in myself, not to extort what can [*tear*] no shape afford me any pleasure and must lessen you in my opinion if you were inclined to bestow it. But though I disclaim flattery, I must say I experience the most gratifying joy when I meet with the real approbation of those whose good opinion I value.

I know not whether my sister will be in London or not, when you return to it, and should have been happy I had given you her address. She is not at present in London. But if my sister Barbara, whose other name is Collier, should be in London, if you will do me the favour of calling at No. 21 Crown Court, Westminster, you will give my cousin, John Barnes, great pleasure, and he will either send for Barbara or tell you where she lives.[169] That dear, unfortunate sister. Her marriage, though from many circumstances she cannot have the shadow of blame cast on her, has cost her and her sister many subsequent misfortunes from her unworthy husband. I hope she is eternally separated. She complains not even to me. I have said to Barnes, and I repeat it, I should cease to respect her if she did. A mistaken choice cannot justify or authorise either party, I think, from suffering in silence.

---

169 John Barnes, a wine merchant, was in partnership with Eliza's host in Chester, Mr Eltoft. Crown Court was near Covent Garden.

Barnes, in a letter to me the other day, says 'in an evil hour your sister listened to a man so totally deficient in the qualifications necessary to make her happy'. For added to the defects of understanding, I fear something beyond that is wanting: natural good principle, an innate sense of honour, which will shew itself where the mind is but poorly informed. His conduct from first to last has been a scene of extravagance and duplicity. Truth scarce ever proceeded from his lips; and, if he could but find the nearest way to enjoy the present moment, he cared not at whose cost. Alas, I wanted not this confirmation to make me sigh over the fate of my sister. I cannot conceive a lot more dreadful than for a woman of sensibility and real worth to have linked her destiny to such a man as this odious Collier. Are you not glad the paper is not filled up, but that I can't write more? Yours most truly Eliza Liddell.

[continues]

And which was highly necessary to preserve me from despair, so numerous and so complicated were the ills that surrounded me and from which nothing but the Almighty hand could have extricated me.[170] It was not till after they were past I thought them distressing. At the time of endurance I shrunk not from the evils that threatened me, or those I felt. I looked down on the world, if I may use the expression, with a mixture of contempt and indifference. The peace and resignation I implored was not denied. I seemed to tread in air and my soul longed for its enlargement.

I have often thought, when I have been tempted to compare my lot with many others, how contrary to the usual plan of providence such very early afflictions. I have often thought they were designed to prepare me for an early death and that, by this means, I should acquire betimes just notions, both of a present and future state. But why do I repeat these kind of things to you? Why, because I find it impossible to restrain my pen from saying what it pleases. Do not, however, from my dwelling on this subject imagine I indulge a gloomy disposition. Far otherwise. Considerations like these must

---

170 This is the beginning of a new sheet, in the correct date order, but does not run on from the previous sheet.

have a very different effect. My spirits were never violent but they are good and perhaps better from the cause that might seem to depress them. But I shall release you and go walk with the children. Adieu.

Tuesday 9 October

A letter is just come from a person Mr Corbet employed to take a house for him in Dublin. A house is taken, No. 6 Hamilton Row.[171] This row is immediately at the back of Merrion Square, where you told me you dined with a Mr Shelton, but why do I tell you this?[172] It seems as if you were near and that I expected to see you. I wish I did – but you justly observe how unavailing our wishes. But I am not a philosopher and so shall wish on.

It is now evening. Mr Stewart came in while we were at dinner.[173] He had just received a letter from his son, William, dated 29 September. I was pleased when I heard you had not then sailed: in two or three days after that date, my letters, at least the first, would be in Yarmouth and I am in hopes you were not gone when they arrived, because you were averse to their falling into your father's hands.[174] Nor am I less so. And, because I flatter myself you would be glad to hear from me, I think you would write the minute you received those letters. So, if you were not gone, I may expect an answer by Friday or Sunday next.[175] On which account I trust we shall not be ready to sail till after that period, or that the wind may prove contrary, which it is not at present.

It is a sad thing my happiness should be in the keeping of post boys – depend on the uncertain receipt of letters and such like wayward contingencies.

---

171 The house in Hamilton Row fell through.

172 Merrion Square, laid out in the 1760s, was an elegant Georgian square. Edmund had clearly been to Dublin, though Mr Shelton is unidentified and the name is difficult to read.

173 Stewart's son, William, had sailed from Inishcoo on the *Fly* in July 1787.

174 Eliza to Edmund, Letters 8, 9, 11, 12, pp. 57-76, 84-99.

175 This gives an indication of the possibility of an exchange of letters between Dublin and Great Yarmouth in not much more than a week.

Wednesday 10 October

Everyone here seems much in the dumps at our departure. Some because they like us and others because our decampment will break up a large family where they were always welcome (and sometimes not pleasant) society. A very material loss this in a country so much a desart.

But I forgot to tell you, William Stewart spoke with gratitude to his father: that you were very good to him. He need not have told us that. We were sufficiently inclined to believe you would be so. But, if you are in a quarrelsome humour, I had better forbear. You will affront me by such words as undue praise. Must I then be constrained when writing to you to meditate what I am going to say, least I should write what appears to you exceptionable? No. I must hazard that. I must say what I think, if I do write. Nor am I quite certain that it is in every instance necessary (when yourself is the subject) to be of your opinion to think justly of you.

I have you observe Mr Symes.[176] To amuse me – and you envy him being in the house with me so continually – I vainly, saucily, told him you said so. And what was his answer? 'Faith, if Mr Hurry knew but all. Your company? Why I would give up your company at any time to follow a hare or dance at a pattern.' This is an Irish wakes, and most true was that declaration. I believe he has a sincere esteem and, I may add, respect for me, and would do anything to oblige or serve me; but I am not the kind of woman he would be much interested about (and you know how female vanity will naturally attribute this to total want of taste). Nor is he the kind of man whose absence I ever regret, or even mark, or whose presence can contribute to my amusement. You will think this odd, when I tell you he possesses a world of original humour, but I will explain why his company does not amuse me when I have indeavoured to define his character.

He has a sweet temper. Few things I believe could ruffle it, but that even, that sweet temper proceeds from a uniform flow of spirits that can extract a laugh from those things a mind of sensibility

---

176 Robert Symes, see Eliza to Edmund, Letter 5, p. 113; Letter 9, p. 74; Edmund to Eliza, Letter 10, p. 78; Appendix, A5, A6, pp. 287-90.

contemplates with pain and uneasiness. Without deep feeling, he possesses good nature and wit, though his understanding is but of the common order. He is a man of strict honour, though his notions are confined. He has no liberality of sentiment. He would say with Sir Somebody in *The School for Scandal*, 'Damn sentiment!'[177] Can I better illustrate this than by telling you (a mortification to conceit) that when Mrs Corbet and I have been in the clouds, and have talked our very best in the midst of our fine speeches, Symes has jumped up, not in ecstacy, not to admire some fine woman passing by, not even to admire himself in the glass, but to examine his *rat traps*. And if his devices, to entrap the unwary rats, have succeeded, with strings fastened to their legs or tail, whatever number he has caught, he marches before him into the room we are sitting in and enjoys the confusion, and screaming, he occasions, the tumbling over tables and clang, much more than the conversation or company of any woman in the world.

Cover, Mr Edmund Cobb Hurry. Messrs Diston Son and Co., Elsinore. Note, 'No 5: Received at Elsinore, 1 December and answered immediately'. Postmark, Rutland, post paid 1s. 10d., received 29 October 1787.

---

177 Sir Peter Teazle, in R.B. Sheridan's *The School for Scandal* (1777), act 4, last line, 'Damn your sentiments!'.

Letter 15

Eliza Liddell to Edmund Cobb Hurry
Rutland in the Rosses

Written 17 October 1787; sent from Inishcoo, 17 October;
received at Elsinore, 6 November

Rosses. 17 October 1787

The wind is fair. We were to have gone to sea this morning at five
o'clock, but that Mr Corbet, contrary to his wishes, was obliged to
wait for the return of Mr Symes from Ballyshannon.[178] If he returns,
we shall go this evening or tomorrow morning. What a coward.
What a foolish coward am I. Why cannot I be more composed, more
satisfied to go this voyage? God is all sufficient to protect us. If I was
with you, I think I would not fear any thing.

I have been debating whether or not to write. I asked myself,
had I a dear friend at the point of death, would I not wish to receive
their last remembrances? Would I not wish to know their genuine
sentiments respecting me (and that I am a friend dear to you I could
not at present bear to think otherwise)? 'Tis true I am not at the
point of death by sickness, but the inexpressible horror I have of the
sea makes me look forward to the worst.

Edmund, dear Edmund, now in this to me solemn moment
receive my perhaps not last farewell, though it may be such. Now in
this solemn moment I can think of you and of my tender affection
for you without the shadow of self-reproach; but to give language to
sentiments less pure, less profound is impossible. I trust your heart
beats in unison to mine. If so, you can form an idea how much I am
interested in your happiness and honour.

I wrote to Elsinore twice and, but for the voyage I am now taking,
I should wait till I heard from you. If you had left Yarmouth before

---

178 Ballyshannon, Donegal, twenty miles from Rutland and the nearest port to it of any size. Ships
arriving at Rutland had to clear at Ballyshannon until William Burton Conyngham belatedly acquired
port status for Rutland.

my letters arrived there, I beg you will demand my four letters from your family. If, on my account, they are one or more displeased with you, pardon me for being the unhappy occasion of it.

If we get safe to Dublin, letters will find me [at] No. 6 Hamilton Row, Dublin, but if it should be my lot to go, think of me sometimes, but regret me not.[179] I dare hope, through the mercy of my Saviour, a blessed immortality. May it be the portion of both. Edmund, friend of my heart, dearest of men, farewell. I pray Almighty God to bless you and he may grant you divine grace. Think, oh think of the shortness of life, of a never-ending eternity. May we meet in glory.

I would yet say more, but am half stupid, incapable of writing coherently. Quite stupid must I be when I cease to think of you, Eliza Liddell.

If we should not sail to night or in the morning, I will not send [this].

Cover, Mr Edmund Cobb Hurry, Messrs Diston Son etc, Elsinore. Note, 'No. 6. Received at Elsinore'. Postmark, Rutland, cost paid 1s. 10d. Received the [6] November 1787.

---

179 Intriguingly, another English governess had been living in Dublin, at 15 Merrion Square, between February and the summer of 1787, shortly before Eliza's arrival in nearby Holles Street (the house in Hamilton Row fell through). This was Mary Wollstonecraft, who had taken a position as governess to the children of Lord and Lady Kingsborough of Mitchelstown Castle, county Cork, in 1786. She too found her pupils trying: 'wild Irish, unformed' and spoiled by their mother's combination of overindulgence and excessive restraint.

Wollstonecraft had already written a collection of short essays, *Thoughts on the Education of Daughters*. She drew on her experience as a governess in Ireland in her *Original Stories from Real Life with Conversations to Regulate the Affections and Form the Mind to Truth and Goodness* (1788, with illustrations by William Blake) and in her *A Vindication of the Rights of Women* (1792). See Jenny McAuley, 'From the Education of Daughters to the Rights of Women: Mary Wollstonecraft in Ireland, 1786-87', *History Ireland* (January-February 2016), pp. 22-25.

Dublin

Dublin Bay, seen from Clontarf, by John Laporte, c. 1800

3

Dublin

Despite her fear of the sea, Eliza's voyage with the Corbets and their children to Dublin was accomplished without incident, other than in her being teased by Mr Corbet and by the ship being blown in the Irish Sea over towards the Isle of Man. After leaving Inishcoo at dawn on Tuesday 17 October, the party reached Dublin in the evening three days later. Following two uncomfortable nights in a hotel, Eliza settled with the family into a house in Holles Street, where she lived a quiet life with Mrs Corbet and the children:

> Living here is an expence they are very unequal to. And, as they came here solely to procure masters for their children, they mean to live in the utmost retirement, which gives me great pleasure, as I detest crowds and mixing with the gay world. I need not have said *they*, but Mrs Corbet, for Mr Corbet is to live mostly at Inniscoo. [1]

This suited Eliza, who found the bustle of Dublin stressful and its fashionable women artificial:

> How I hate Dublin. I hate going out. Every face I meet is so busy and yet so vacant. And the women, women of quality, I mean, are so highly painted, have such a confident stare, they put me out of humour. Could I chuse for myself, I never would live in a great town. I detest the parade and state of fine houses, fine carriages and fine people. They annoy me. In the vortex of fashion, every

1   Eliza Liddell to Edmund Cobb Hurry, Letter 16, p. 129.

emanation of goodness is obscured or lost. The retirement of the country admits of affection, calls forth and confirms each virtue of the heart: retirement, friendship, books are indeed real blessings … but here in Dublin I will not live.[2]

As well as praising the country above the city, Eliza was nostalgic for Inishcoo:

after living two years in Inniscoo you will not wonder at my being much annoyed by finding myself out of that quiet retreat. Dear Inniscoo. The morning we came away I took a last view of the spot where your vessel lay; of the little room where we so often sat together.[3]

Such society as was on offer was not to Eliza's taste. She had no wish to renew her acquaintance with Mrs Ashworth, the sister of Susannah Corbet and Eliza's previous employer. Two Mr Stokes, who called, though 'very learned, very sensible men', talked above her head; while Sir Jerome Fitzpatrick, 'who is Mrs Corbet's physician and dines with us very often, is desperately in love with me. 'Tis a pity he has a wife, for Lady Fitzpatrick is a high sounding title'.[4]

Nor could Eliza avoid calls from her sister Barbara's husband:

I am interrupted – my brother in law. This is another source of disquiet, my sister. What a pity I lament not his bad circumstances. Pecuniary considerations are not to be put in competition with the disposition of the man a woman is united with for life. Cunning with him supplies the place of understanding, the defect of which is rendered more insupportable by a thorough assurance that he is ever attempting to deceive you. I cannot see him, and think whose husband he is, without the deepest distress, heightened by

2   Eliza to Edmund, Letter 16., p. 131.

3   Eliza to Edmund, Letter 16, p. 129.

4   Edmund's response to this news, sent in Letter 23, p. 163, shows his confidence in the strength of their relationship: 'You have acted a very impolitick, nay a very imprudent part, in not listening to the attentions of that great gentleman in Dublin. As to his having a wife was a mighty ridiculous reason: for I doubt not, if you had given him any encouragement, he would have found means to have been rid of her'. See Letter 30, pp. 192-193.

the necessity there is that, for her sake, I am obliged to disguise my sentiments and receive him at least with civility, though his sight is odious to me.[5]

In a more sinister development, Mr Turner, who had carried out engineering works on Rutland Island, appeared twice in Holles Street:

The malady I informed you of has again seized him. He came to Dublin immediately after us, by land, shocked Mrs Corbet and I excessively by his sudden appearance, or rather by the evident disorder of his mind. I feared some disaster would befall him during his stay in Dublin, for it was plain he was not capable of taking care of himself, but he suddenly took it into his head to return to Liverpool. Poor man. I feel much for his unhappy lot. A mind in his deplorable situation is of all the calamities incident to human nature the most dreadful.[6]

Turner's derangement may even have been partly due to William Burton Conyngham's failure to pay his bills. A second visit by Turner is described by Eliza:

I was so frightened at his strange and shocking gestures, and conversation, that I whispered one of the maids to come and stay in the parlour with me. What a pity to see such a mind so woefully overturned. He was at Barnes, when in London, and abuses him to me for not lending him five hundred pounds, he says he asked him for.[7] He has been in a number of shops and he speaks things to a vast amount and desires them to come to Mr Conyngham for payment.[8]

The failure of the Rutland Island project itself is also evident in Robert Corbet's inability to pay the Hurrys' account. 'Mr Corbet delayed answering that letter, nor intended acknowledging the having received it for some weeks, from mean, prudential motives respecting a present want of cash.'

---

5 Eliza to Edmund, Letter 19, pp. 139-40.

6 Eliza to Edmund, Letter 16, p. 131.

7 John Barnes, Eliza's cousin.

8 Eliza to Edmund, Letter 24, p. 167.

Any question of further dealings with Conyngham or his agent must have vanished: 'I am surprized Mr Corbet should never settle his account with me ... My father, who is rather suspicious, as most are who have long been hackneyed in the ways of men, generally thinks the worst of those things'.[9] Although Conyngham himself is mentioned as being in Great Yarmouth, all that was now in prospect was a law suit.

Although still separated, with Edmund taking twenty-six days to arrive in Riga, the couple's relationship, following the delayed but safe receipt of letters which assured them of each other's affection, now entered into a calmer stage, where concern for the other's welfare, health and safety replaced anxiety about their mutual commitment. The relationship was also now not simply between themselves, as it become known to Edmund's family in Great Yarmouth after Eliza wrote to him there. He told her:

> You made a great mistake in directing your letter to Mr Samuel Hurry, as he is not my father but my uncle, and could not possibly understand your letter. He told my father he had a letter from an 'Irishwoman' whom by its contents he supposed had a son on board the *Fly*. Yet he could in that light make no sense of it without making great allowances for blunders natural to people of that country. However, my father soon comprehended the whole affair and by this means it became quite publick; and from what I may judge has done no harm to our cause. I would not have you suppose my uncle published it intentionally but, as he could not guess at the intent of the letter, he gave it to his son-in-law and it was read openly.[10]

The result of this announcement was:

> My father said what family, what fortune, what religion; but I can tell you my sisters said fortune is of no consequence. And I think so too. I despise her gifts any further than as they are absolutely necessary to our subsistence and comfort. Indeed nothing could give me greater happiness than to have it in my power to show you how little

---

9   Edmund to Eliza, Letter 20, p. 148.

10   Edmund to Eliza, Letter 21, p. 151.

I regard the acquirement of riches, had I but a decent sufficiency, and which I flatter myself perhaps may not be far distant should it please God to bless my honest endeavours.[11]

With their relationship now in the open, the couple renewed their long-term commitment to one another. Edmund asked Eliza for her assurance that she would continue to love him after their marriage:

Now suppose I do all in my power to amend my errors, to use you with the utmost tenderness, nay as far as is consistent, do all you would wish me to do. In this case, can you positively assure me you would esteem me as much after a nearer connection as you do at present? This is a serious question: our future happiness in this world, I had almost said in both worlds, depends entirely on this. Nay, I know I should be wretched indeed were I afterwards to find any abatement in that esteem and affection which you at present have for me.[12]

Eliza was very willing to return to him her conviction as to their future happiness:

How can I more fully prove the extent of my esteem for you than by assuring you that, till I knew you, I held it impossible for a woman to have any chance of happiness in marriage, either if possessed of a very large fortune herself or totally destitute of any. It matters not the many reasons that induced me to think this. Suffice it to say, when I knew you, I thought differently. I saw in your disposition the certainty of happiness for the woman you might value that the destitution of fortune on her part could not have power to destroy. Yes, Edmund, it would be a matter of indifference to me whether I had thousands to bestow on you or whether I consented unportioned to unite my destiny with yours, certain that you would not connect yourself with one you could not regard for herself alone.[13]

---

11   Edmund to Eliza, Letter 21, p. 142.

12   Edmund to Eliza, Letter 20, p. 146.

13   Eliza to Edmund, Letter 23, pp. 162-63.

All that still needed to be resolved was what they should live on. Edmund painted an unpromising picture:

> I will now discover to you my real situation in that respect and leave you to judge whether it would be prudent in me at present to alter my situation. If I were to live on shore, I could not promise myself more than £70 to £80 per annum, and that in so precarious a stock as to proceed solely from shipping.[14]

Eliza's response to this was to rule out early marriage on his behalf, as she refused to impoverish him. Fortunately, Edmund came from a wealthy family and his prospects were good.

In practical terms, Edmund and Eliza planned how and where they should next meet. At one point it seemed likely that Edmund would be able to come to Dublin in December. In the end, Eliza determined to make her own way to England. Having given notice to Mrs Corbet, she sailed from Dublin on 5 January 1788.

---

14   Edmund to Eliza, Letter 20, pp. 142-43.

Letter 16

Eliza Liddell to Edmund Cobb Hurry
Dublin

*Written 25-30 October 1787; sent from Dublin, 30 October;
received at Elsinore, I December*

Dublin, Sunday evening, 25 October 1787

Some days are gone by without my writing a single line to you. But does a single *hour* pass by that I do not think of you? Alas, too intently for my peace; too intently to think of ought else. Mrs Corbet some times asks me why I sigh. 'Why?' I repeat and she understands me, but she cannot fully enter into my feelings; they are too complicated for foreign inspection and too profound for me to express or define.

I took your letters out of my pocket (where they always remain) and broke the seal of the paper, in which they were inclosed, with an intention of reading them. What of tenderness, of melancholy, of agitation, of suspense did I not suffer at the moment. I did not, I could not peruse those dear evidences of your thoughts and remembrance, but returned them to their sanctuary and busily employed myself in playing with the children, merely that I might fly my own thoughts and regain sufficient composure to appear at dinner.

This was yesterday, but why should I dwell on the feelings of one hour or day? For the last three months of my life, has not each hour, each week, each day been uniformly filled with regrets at your absence, anxieties for your preservation, and a thousand nameless apprehensions? Sometimes I resolve to disregard the vain cares of this world and literally take no thought for the morrow. Weak and fleeting resolutions, no sooner formed than broken. A look, a word, a sentence in a book that has any reference to the state of my mind instantly banishes every impression from it but the one. That is, I fear, stamped in indelible characters there. But whatever may be the regard I entertain for you, whatever the weakness of heart or understanding that leads me to sigh for this or that earthly good, yet

I do from the very bottom of my soul say God's will be done, and may his grace enable me cheerfully and contentedly to submit to the dispensations of his providence as most just and righteous.

I have been this whole day alone. Mr and Mrs Corbet and their two eldest daughters went yesterday five miles out of Dublin to Mr Ashworth's.[15] He is married to a sister of Mrs Corbet's.[16] With them I spent three years before I went down to Corbet Hill, and every hour I lived in their house confirmed my unhappiness, disgust and aversion. Mrs Ashworth is indeed a very different being from her sister, Mrs Corbet: selfish, narrow-minded and implacable in her resentments; her heart never expands to pity, benevolence or friendship. Mr Ashworth is our countryman and came here thirty years ago, destitute of every thing but good dispositions, which he might have retained had not a variety of lucky circumstances (not extraordinary talents) enabled him to realize a fortune of more than £60,000. He is a good husband and father, but pride, avarice and meanness are the leading features of his character.

They have but one daughter. I undertook to form her mind – preposterous task. They wished to see her amiable, because they wished to see her admired. They had no higher views for enlarging her mind but because it might promote her worldly interests. And daily did her mother counteract my indeavours, to inspire her with right dispositions, by the most absurd indulgence and by her own example of a total want of humility, charity etc, etc.

They treated me with respect, nay with a deference that they both, I have reason to think, wondered they felt for me (considering I was poor; and to be without money with them was to be poor indeed). A deference that I certainly owed to the superiority of my sentiments over theirs: that taught me to look down on my own destitute circumstances without an idea of shame or humiliation; and also to contemplate their great wealth with indifference, not to say contempt, since it could not dignify them with a single virtue and perhaps took from them many. Despising them both, unhappy and unable through the influence of example (it would have been

15 Mr Ashworth's estate unidentified.

16 Mrs Ashworth and Mrs Corbet came from Drumbarrow, County Meath.

improper in me to point out as wrong in her parents) to be of any use to their child.

I highly offended them by chusing to leave them and live with Mrs Corbet. That I did so I have no cause to repent, though my situation is in some respects insupportable, but I shall soon return to England. I love Mrs Corbet, but her children I cannot. I will not write any more to night. I have a dreadful cold, which I increased this morning by wetting my feet, and my head aches so violently I can hardly discern what I write. Again unwelcome thought, why suggest, perhaps, I must never send this. Good night. Good night.

Thursday, 26 October 1787

Let me not forget to inform you that I am writing this from Holles Street, Dublin.[17] Last Tuesday week we left the Rosses and my poor head is yet in such a state of distraction that, if it were not to you, I would not attempt writing till more capable of doing so. This day month your last letter to me was dated, and I feel as if it was a year since I heard from you.[18] You were going to Elsinore, to Riga.[19] Did you go? Did you get my letters? And did you write to me?

Those letters that I sent to Yarmouth, what of evil may they not have been productive of. Oh, Edmund, when I think of this, when I think your father may forbid our correspondance, or that perhaps you forget Eliza! What is to become of my pride? I weep incessantly. I lose all fortitude of mind. The world appears a dreary desert and I am wretched.

On Tuesday 17 October at six o'clock in the morning we left Inniscoo. The day before, I wrote to you what I considered a farewell letter, a last one.[20] Your firm and undaunted mind can ill conceive the horror I entertain of the sea. I seem when in a ship as if entombed alive, and each squall of wind, each rising billow, my scared imagination represents as threatening instant destruction.

17   Holles Street runs north from Merrion Square, see below, p. 157.

18   This letter has not survived.

19   Edmund had reached Riga by 26 October, after a passage of twenty-six days. See Letter 17, p. 133.

20   Eliza to Edmund, Letter 16, pp. 125-26.

Thanks to the Almighty our passage was not tedious and the weather was good. On Friday evening we landed and remained till Sunday evening at the Marine Hotel on George's Quay, where I got a most unmerciful cold by a damp bed.[21] The house in Hamilton Row, that Mr Corbet expected to get, he was disappointed of; but fortunately the house we are now in was ready furnished and to be let. It is at the back of Merrion Square, entirely out of the town, and commands a fine view of the bay and ships; but, tho' it is a retired situation, yet after living two years in Inniscoo you will not wonder at my being much annoyed by finding myself out of that quiet retreat. Dear Inniscoo. The morning we came away I took a last view of the spot where your vessel lay; of the little room where we so often sat together. I would have given much to remain there, for there I [shared] short hours of happiness with you. Will such hours ever return? Whether or not, may God Almighty guide and protect you.

It is an odd thing to say, and yet most true, that, though I detest the sea, I felt a degree of satisfaction at being in the same element with you. The second day of our voyage Mr Corbet came down to the cabin, where I was lying stupid as a log of wood, and said he saw two sail; that one of them was a ship so very like yours he did not doubt it was you, as that was the course you must steer to the Baltic. I was on the deck in a moment, and when I saw the ship, about a league from us, I would have given worlds to have been along side of her. I pictured you on the deck and my soul sickened at the impossibility of flying to you.

Mr Corbet remarked my anxiety and perturbation, when I tottered back to my cabin; and then, laughing, told me he knew at first it was not you. Gracious God, what cruel sport to trifle with the feelings of a fellow creature. It was not out of curiosity to discover my sentiments, for he knew full well how tenderly I regard you; or, perhaps because I never mention your name, he thinks I have forgot you. What a false method of judging is this, methinks. If you were more indifferent to me, I could talk more about you. But when I would speak of you, your absence, the uncertainty whether I ever shall see you again, the state of suspense I am in respecting your safety, exposed as you are to the dangers of the dreadful ocean, all,

---

21   George's Quay is on the south bank of the River Liffey near the centre of Dublin.

all press heavily on my heart; and of any thing or of any person can I speak with more ease than of you.

I have since thought that, for my reputation's sake, it was happy for me that it perhaps was not your ship we saw; that it did not come near us. For I am much afraid that, in that critical moment, satisfied with my own innate rectitude, rejoiced at the sight of you, if from you I received a cordial welcome, I much fear the world and its opinions would have been totally forgot, and Eliza would have become the companion of your voyage, the sharer of your dangers.

Nothing else should, or could, have prevented my doing so, when you left Inniscoo, but that I feared being misjudged and condemned by the world; and, more, I feared God might punish me by a presumptuous reliance on my own purity of heart. But when you were at Inniscoo, I had time to reflect and to determine. But had I met you at sea, I had time for neither. In my first transport of surprise and joy, I should most undoubtedly have placed myself under your protection; and, though condemned by the multitude, I think I should, my peculiar situation considered, have been fully acquitted to you, myself, and I may add to my Creator, for the seeming rashness and impropriety of my conduct. Nor would Edmund, I am satisfied, have given me cause to repent the unbounded confidence I placed in his honour.

We were within nine miles of the Isle of Man, and the wind was ever driving us to England. I wished it might, for I certainly would have remained there, but it was ordered otherwise. And now I think I shall continue with Mrs Corbet till spring and then return to England. I certainly, for various reasons, never will go again to the country with her, and she remains but six months in Dublin. Living here is an expence they are very unequal to. And, as they came here solely to procure masters for their children, they mean to live in the utmost retirement, which gives me great pleasure, as I detest crowds and mixing with the gay world. I need not have said they, but Mrs Corbet, for Mr Corbet is to live mostly at Inniscoo.

My mornings, which as we don't dine till five o'clock are tolerable long, I shall spend in my own room, writing, reading, working and instructing the children, sometimes walking when the weather permits. We shall have some odd people, now and then, to partake of a family dinner, but no formal company. Of this I am glad. For Dublin fine ladies are my aversion. They are so much alike, mere automatons. They walk, they talk and dress, all in the same style. Their faces are enamelled and their hearts, if they have any, envelop it from sight, by affectation, pride 'and self-plumed vanity, with fancied consequence elate'.[22]

Only I think of a little girl about eleven years of age telling me yesterday that really she saw no harm in painting; that every person of fashion did it; that when she was a little older she would certainly make use of it. For that she once applied it to her cheeks, and every body told her she was much handsomer for it. Poor child! I could not help pitying her, and told her so, at which she looked at me with surprise, for she knows she is to have twenty thousand pounds; a counterpoise this, in the eyes of her mistaken parents and self, for every good quality.[23]

Do you know, Edmund, I some times rejoice at my poverty? It has taught me many useful lessons, but pray do not mistake me and, because I speak freely my sentiments, of my description of women, suppose I am not ready to praise and admire the truly estimable of my sex. I speak only of a certain set, that are to be met with more or less everywhere, who have no laudable pursuits, who alike neglect to improve their minds, or perform the respective duties of their station, who pride themselves not in indeavouring to attain the applause of conscious worth, but because they can look with scorn on those who are not like them, the envied possessors of rank and wealth: rank, which they cannot adorn; and wealth they neglect to make a right use of.

Sunday 30 October

This day dined with us two Mr Stokes, very learned, very sensible men, both in the college, but their learning, their sense – true

---

22   Edmund Cartwright, *Armine and Elvira: A Legendary Tale* (1784), 'No self-plumed vanity was there, with fancied consequence elate'.

23   As none of the Corbet girls could hope for such a dowry, it is likely that the girl in question was Mr Ashworth's daughter, Mrs Corbet's niece and Eliza's one-time charge. See above, p. 126.

female! – were both thrown away upon me.[24] I have left them in the midst of a very elaborate disquisition I did not understand and am come up to my room to converse with you, to tell you if I could but see you for one hour I would give up, most cheerfully, all other society for six months.

How I hate Dublin. I hate going out. Every face I meet is so busy and yet so vacant. And the women, women of quality, I mean, are so highly painted, have such a confident stare, they put me out of humour. Could I chuse for my self, I never would live in a great town. I detest the parade and state of fine houses, fine carriages and fine people. They annoy me. In the vortex of fashion, every emanation of goodness is obscured or lost. The retirement of the country admits of affection, calls forth and confirms each virtue of the heart: retirement, friendship, books are indeed real blessings, but let me learn content for more than a [seal] if health but smiles on me [seal] it murmur, but here in Dublin [I] will not live.

Poor Turner. The malady I informed you of has again seized him.[25] He came to Dublin immediately after us, by land, shocked Mrs Corbet and I excessively by his sudden appearance, or rather by the evident disorder of his mind. I feared some disaster would befall him during his stay in Dublin, for it was plain he was not capable of taking care of himself, but he suddenly took it into his head to return to Liverpool. Poor man. I feel much for his unhappy lot. A mind in his deplorable situation is of all the calamities incident to human nature the most dreadful. Adieu, Edmund. May you be preserved from every evil is the constant prayer of Eliza Liddell.

Cover, Mr Edmund Cobb Hurry. Postmark, none. Received, Elsinore, 1 December.

---

24   Descended from the surveyor and cartographer Gabriel Stokes (1682-1768), two branches of the Stokes family produced a series of outstanding mathematicians and scientists over at least four generations, culminating in the world-famous scientist Sir George Gabriel Stokes (1819-1903). The two members of the Stokes family Eliza met were probably Whitley Stokes (1763-1845), later Professor of Physics at Trinity College, Dublin, and his cousin Gabriel Stokes (1761-1834), a Trinity College mathematician. The father of Whitley Stokes, the Reverend Gabriel Stokes (1731-1806), was also a fellow of Trinity College. It is not surprising that their conversation passed above Eliza's head.

25   See also Letter 24, p. 167. There is no previous mention of Turner's illness in Eliza's surviving letters.

Letter 17

Edmund Cobb Hurry to Eliza Liddell
Riga

Written 26 October 1787; sent from Riga, 26 October;
received at Dublin, November

26 October 1787

O Eliza, Eliza, when shall I see you again? When shall I hear from you again? How long does it seem since I had your first, and is it to be also your last? But I have no right to expect one. For if you did send one it must be at Derwinda, and if it is there I shall get it next Saturday. And I am almost sure it is, for Eliza said she would never forget me, and I never had reason to disbelieve what she said and pray God I never may. For I trust she will be as sincere in every respect towards me as I shall be towards her. What do I say I trust? I *know* she will. I suppose you thought me distracted when I so abruptly finished mine of about the 26th of last month.[26] It would appear to you I doubt not a very confused affair. To excuse it I need not, for I know *you* excuse me.

But still let me tell you it was the cause of indisposition, of languor, of disappointment, but they are all causes which have but little effect upon me. But they will touch at times and those are times I would never chuse to write to one whom I esteem so highly, for whom I have such an affection as I trust she is fully sensible of, measuring it by her own towards me. Those are times I would never chuse to correspond with my dearest Eliza, but choice was not to be obtained, I mean choice of times, for I had already postponed it so long that I was not certain of having another hour in England at my own disposal. And I should have been exceedingly mortified to have left it without giving you the least information that there was still such a being existing as myself. But I was not uneasy about you. For, tho' I have not been so fortunate as to fall in the way of your letters,

---

26   Edmund to Eliza, Letter 10, pp. 82-83.

yet I heard very lately of your welfare, even so late as the middle of last month. For I received Mr Corbet's letter a few days since, when I was in Elsinore, and I shall take that liberty with him of enclosing this in his.[27] If it is improper, or you do not wish to have it so, pray mention it in your next.

Here am I now safe arrived at Riga after one of the most tiresome passages that you can almost possibly conceive, and so exceedingly tedious as to have been twenty-six days on it, tho' frequently made in six or nine. But to such disappointments as these I have been regularly trained from my earliest youth, and I flatter myself I should not sink even under much greater ones. I am determined never to repine, as far as is possible, at any of them. For I never met with anyone, that did not absolutely proceed from some fault of mine, that was not in the end productive of some real benefit. I now expect to be soon supplied here with a full and valuable cargo, with which I must proceed to our metropolis, and where I think I am not unreasonable if I say I expect to arrive on or about the middle of December. At which nothing could give me greater pleasure than to meet some little narrative from and of my Eliza. If directed to me at Anthony Brough Esq., Batson's Coffee House, I doubt not but I shall receive it safe.[28]

I have just been up at the city of Riga (for the ships lie here near eight miles from it). I feel myself overjoyed at being thus far distant from it. You cannot think how melancholy it makes me when I contemplate that once flourishing city, of whose merchants it might truly be said that they were princes, now wanting only the name to be slaves. Indeed they are truly so without the name, their trade spoiled by enormous duties, and their own persons and properties every moment in jeopardy.[29] Figure to yourself the same persons only a few years past enjoying every liberty that any European whatever could enjoy. And then say what they must feel if they have any feeling, and how much every son of liberty must be shocked

---

27 This explains why this letter is addressed simply to Miss Liddell, without an address.

28 Batson's Coffee House was in Cornhill. Established since the 1690s, it was a well-known venue for art auctions. Thomas Clarkson, the leading slave abolitionist, was living there in the late 1780s when he set up his campaign. Anthony Brough was a Russia merchant.

29 Riga's former independence had been undermined by Russian control.

at the sight, knowing that it is possible to be his own case. How ought it not to warn him of his danger and to make him sensible of the real value of his superior priviledges. How thankfull ought all Englishmen to be for theirs, and how exceeding carefull of them.[30]

I have already finished my sheets and have scarce said one half of what I had to say, but indeed I find such a pleasure in writing to you that I could keep scribbling all the day long some nonsense or another. But you have already sufficient to tire your patience, for I was unfortunately [led], by what I felt for the miserable people here, to say something about liberty, a thing you know you women never make any pretension to.[31] With most suitable remembrances to all acquaintances in your neighbourhood and particularly to Mrs Corbet, I subscribe myself with the sincerest wishes for your welfare, yours most truly, E.C. Hurry.

Cover, Miss Liddell. Postmark, none.

---

30   An expression of pride in English freedom, contrasted with subjection in Russia.

31   Edmund shows an awareness of the nascent demands by women for independence.

Letter 18

Eliza Liddell to Edmund Cobb Hurry
Dublin

Written 11 November 1787; sent from Dublin, 11 November;
received at Elsinore, 1 December

Sunday, 11 November 1787

I have weighed in my own mind what would be the effects on yours of your father's opening the letters I sent to his house for you. (It was hard you did not remain one day or two longer in Yarmouth. If you had, I should have been saved the uneasiness I feel on different accounts, respecting your father receiving those letters.)[32] Why did I send them? Why? And yet, Edmund, how could I act otherwise? Must I not have been entirely indifferent to you if I could have been collected enough to consider that it was imprudent to address you where I did? I was not capable of cool deliberation at the time. The weather had been dreadfully strong. You were at sea for three weeks or a month. I had remained in the most torturing anxiety for your safety.

The moment your safety was ascertained by your writing from England to Mr Corbet, my anxieties were not diminished, they were added to tenfold, though they had changed their object. I was pained to the very soul. What, Edmund in England and not tell me so, me who was so highly interested in his welfare! What a return this for my tenderness, so deep, so sincere, that to shield him from harm I would joyfully bare my bosom to the assassin's most vengeful aim. What, was I to think not that I was forgot? I could not suppose you were so deficient in the common regard due to my sex as to acquaint me of the change in your sentiments through any other medium than your own declaration. To write to Mr Corbet for the purpose of acquainting me that you no longer wished to continue our correspondence would have been treating me with a rudeness

---

32   Eliza to Edmund, Letters 8, 9, 11, 12, pp. 57-76, 84-99.

Customs House and Essex Bridge, Dublin, late eighteenth century, by Joseph Tudor, 1751

and disrespect I was not entitled to. It appeared to me most probable that you had not received any of my letters and proudly neglected writing to a being you began to consider as unworthy of your friendship, since of so capricious a disposition.[33]

What an idea was this. You thought meanly of *me*. It was insupportable. Impatient to be restored to your esteem, I wrote. I had no other way of convincing you I had done so before, if my former letters had never reached. You were in Yarmouth, and in Yarmouth I addressed you, and hoped my letters would arrive before you left it.[34] Indeed I must own that a contrariety of distressing suggestions impelled me to write. Sometimes I imagined you disdained my acquaintance and did not chuse to have it known to your family that you thought it worth your while to write to me.

My pride was roused. You continued silent and I again wrote, guided by resentment. It occurred to me that my doing so might lead to an explanation with your father that we had corresponded. But what of that? The integrity of my heart taught me to be fearless, to despise concealment. Edmund, pardon me. What the consequence might be to you was unthought of till your letter arrived some days after, in which you observed (and acknowledged the receipt of one

---

33   Eliza's explanation of why she had sent her four letters to Great Yarmouth.

34   Edmund left Great Yarmouth on 26 September.

of my letters) that you had reasons for wishing me not to write to Yarmouth.[35] You had reasons that must be right, though I was unacquainted with them.

So I thought, when I read your so long wished for letter. I was not forgot. I was dear to you and I had doubted our truth. I had injured you perhaps with your family. What a revolution did not your letter occasion. My pride no longer piqued, I saw a thousand reasons myself why I ought to have been cautious for your sake of writing. I have said I have weighed what will be the effect on your mind, if my having done so should be productive of uneasiness to you, and think you will not be severe to condemn. You will make allowances for the state of my mind and you will not hate me; for indeed I have felt uneasiness enough without your added displeasure or resentment.

A week ago came a letter from your father to Mr Corbet, to beg to know what he should do with the letters, he supposed from him to you, that did not arrive till you were gone. Think how I was embarrassed at this information. Mr Corbet delayed answering that letter, nor intended acknowledging the having received it for some weeks, from mean, prudential motives respecting a present want of cash.[36]

What was to be done? Mrs Corbet, as well as myself, was vexed at his conduct and shared the uneasiness and perturbation of my mind. She advised me to write a concise letter to Mr Hurry; acknowledge my having sent these letters; and beg they might be kept for you. I delayed some days but at last ventured. Perhaps this also was a wrong though an unavoidable step.

Cover, none. Postmark, none. Received Elsinore, 1 December.

---

35 Edmund to Eliza, Letter 10, pp. 80-81.

36 Robert Corbet's failure to answer William Hurry's letter delayed the clarification of the source of the letters.

Letter 19

Eliza Liddell to Edmund Cobb Hurry
Dublin

Written 26 November to 5 December 1787; sent from Dublin, 5 December; received in London, December

Dublin, Monday 26 November 1787

Am I not a weak creature? A few nights ago I dreamed you wrote to me. I remembered part of the contents of that letter; and from this shadow of hope received comfort. My expectations were raised and, every time the postman rapped at the door, I was certain of receiving a letter; but each day's disappointment more than any effort of reason has convinced me of my folly. I am ill and I am unhappy. The latter too well accounts for the former. For the state of my heath generally depends on the state of my mind.[37]

November is just over and you are either returned to England or must remain all winter at Riga. Perhaps at this moment, the merciless ocean! Edmund, my heart is agonized and tortured with being thus left to form the most direful conjectures. The least part of the calamity I can picture to myself is your being returned and Eliza being forgot. But my pride at the moment should most fervently return thanks to heaven. For your preservation would assist me to think of you, if not with indifference, with tranquillity. But if I am to mourn you dead, dead, Edmund dead! But I have not heard it yet. O what signifies what passes in this poor heart? What are its concerns to anyone here? Unfeeling creatures. They perhaps attribute to singularity of disposition, nay it may be to a fault in my temper, the distraction of mind but too evident.

I am interrupted – my brother in law.[38] This is another source of disquiet, my sister. What a pity I lament not his bad circumstances. Pecuniary considerations are not to be put in competition with the

---

37 See Eliza to Edmund, Letter 23, p. 159.

38 Mr Collier, the estranged husband of Eliza's sister Barbara.

disposition of the man a woman is united with for life. Cunning with him supplies the place of understanding, the defect of which is rendered more insupportable by a thorough assurance that he is ever attempting to deceive you. I cannot see him, and think whose husband he is, without the deepest distress, heightened by the necessity there is that, for her sake, I am obliged to disguise my sentiments and receive him at least with civility, though his sight is odious to me. But I shall soon be from him; soon in the bosom of friendship.

Please the Almighty repose my sorrows and indeavour to forget them. Yes, Edmund, though you may forget (perhaps, I was going to say, scorn) the poor Eliza. But though I will not erase the word, it ought not to have dropped from my pen. I merit not scorn from mortal. But though you may forget me, I have yet a friend, humble as are my fortunes, a dear, a tried one, who would stoop from a throne to fold Eliza to her heart, tho' the child of poverty and misfortune.

Ah, doubt not of the worth of a female heart, its pure, its exalted, its disinterested propensities. Do you remember my mentioning to you a friend I had in Chester? Mr Eltoft, I may add his valuable wife, are my friends; but Miss Eltoft, their eldest daughter, is more immediately so.[39] She conjures me to go to their house. It will be my asylum till God provides another. I will go. I will tell Mrs Corbet tomorrow that I will.

Cover, none. Postmark, none. Received, Elsinore, 1 December.

---

39   Mr Eltoft's wife was called Anne. Their daughter was Mary. Eliza's mother's, Elizabeth Sharples, came from Neston in the Wirral. The Liddell family had previously lived in Liverpool and in Chester.

Letter 20

Edmund Cobb Hurry to Eliza Liddell
Elsinore

Written 1-10 December 1787; sent from Great Yarmouth, 11 December;
received Dublin, December

Elsinore, 1 December 1787

I anticipated the pleasure which I should here receive from a letter
or letters of my dearest Eliza. And absolutely my impatience was so
great that I left the ship near twenty English miles from hence, it
being calm, that I might no longer be disappointed of the happiness
which I had promised myself. Accordingly three letters did I secure
with a joyous heart, and opened them with an eagerness which had
almost torn one of them to pieces.[40] The first I read happened to be
the last you wrote, and on one account gave me inexpressible pleasure
to find that by assistance of unbounded goodness we should in all
probability be situated within a few days' post of each of other.[41]
And so near that it shall not be my fault if I have not a still greater
pleasure than ever I darest hope for: I mean that of seeing you. Yet
in this I would not have either you or myself raise our expectations
too high, least we should meet with a disappointment. For you must
know that in some cases I look upon myself as entirely dependant.

You know I never could praise you for your great courage upon
the waters. At the same time I think you wrong, nay I know you
think yourself very wrong, in being so, I would not say, distrustfull
in Providence. I know you are conscious that there is an Almighty
arm can save when even to all human appearance there is not the
most distant possibility. Why then should you fear when I think you
have not the least reason, nay I dare almost aver, not the most distant
prospect of danger? I am well acquainted with every foot of your
route and know you have harbours the whole way situated at very

---

40   Eliza to Edmund, Letters 13, 14, 15, pp. 100-16.

41   Eliza to Edmund, Letter 14, p. 106.

small distances where, in case of bad weather, you will undoubtedly take shelter. In short, except on account of your fear, I must own I have not the least anxiety nor doubt but that your voyage will terminate happily if not speedily. I thought you did not mind a ship, and surely the one you go on in I look on to be much safer than a larger one.

But why I am writing all this? It ought to have been before. And if I had thought you would have been so uneasy at the voyage, and could have supposed that my writing would have lessened your anxiety, I would have written you a sheet from Yarmouth describing every port you pass, all of which I am pretty well acquainted with.[42] But thank God you are now safe in Dublin and that I shall be safe in London by Christmas.

And now for your scolding letter (if you'll allow me to call it so), for that came next under my inspection and made me resolve to sit down immediately to justify myself.[43] For you have reason, as the Frenchman says, and you are wrong. First, you have reason after the account I gave you of myself to suspect me of everything that was base and dishonourable. Yet surely, was I to behave as you supposed, it ought not to cost you a moment's uneasiness. Mr Corbet's letter was the sole ground on which you had to go on. Might it not have been possible for a letter to have miscarried, tho' it had been sent a post before that? But it was not so and you had still reason, reason to accuse me of neglect, of forgetfulness, if indisposition both of body and mind will not mitigate the crime.[44] Add to that a continual hurry from Hull to Yarmouth, from thence to London, which with the discharge of the ship and many vexations and disappointments all in the short space of a fortnight. Yet all these are nothing. I was wrong and acknowledge it. I am vexed for the uneasiness it caused you. I ought to have written the moment I arrived.

But you accuse me wrongfully of being ashamed to acknowledge my acquaintance with you to my friends, and still do not seem to be convinced of it even in your last. The word 'treason' seems to hurt

---

42 Edmund, who knew the coast between Donegal and Dublin well, must clearly have been to Ireland more than once before coming to Inishcoo.

43 Eliza to Edmund, Letter 14, pp. 105-6.

44 Edmund's apology and explanation for not writing.

you,[45] but if you only recollect what I told you at the Rosses (that I had promised my father never to commence any such a correspondence without informing him of it, which for good reasons I did not chuse to do by letter), I flatter myself you will immediately see the propriety of my wishing that none of your letters should come to his hand before I had acquainted him that such I did expect.

I did inform him of it, and from your knowledge of the world, and from what you had reason to expect from me, I do not wonder at your supposing it would give my friends uneasiness that I should wish to be connected to a person not possessed of the good things of this world (tho' I trust with a heart superior to them all); and that I should likewise repent of having formed such a connection. That you should thus think I am not surprized, for prone to anticipate sorrow as you are. And which I heartily wish you would endeavour to conquer; or it will cause you many uneasy moments, if not entirely destroy your health. And therefore you should look on it as your duty to surpress it as much as possible. I wonder not that you should thus indulge your thoughts, but why not rather flatter yourself that things are not so, and look on the best and most pleasant side? For it would make you easy for a time and, if you deceived yourself, you would have but one sorrow and it will always be found to come soon enough when you are certain of it. Whereas, if you do not anticipate grief, perhaps it may never come.

In some respects you guessed right. My father said what family, what fortune, what religion; but I can tell you my sisters said fortune is of no consequence. And I think so too.[46] I despise her gifts any further than as they are absolutely necessary to our subsistence and comfort. Indeed nothing could give me greater happiness than to have it in my power to show you how little I regard the acquirement of riches, had I but a decent sufficiency, and which I flatter myself perhaps may not be far distant should it please God to bless my honest endeavours.

I will now discover to you my real situation in that respect and leave you to judge whether it would be prudent in me at present to

---

45   Edmund to Eliza, Letter 10, pp. 80-81; Eliza to Edmund, Letter 14, p. 109.

46   His father was William Hurry (1734-1807). His two sisters living in Great Yarmouth at the time were Elizabeth (known as Betsy) and Priscilla.

alter my situation. If I were to live on shore, I could not promise myself more than £70 to £80 per annum, and that in so precarious a stock as to proceed solely from shipping.[47] From my father I know I have nothing to expect, as it has been an invariable rule in our family for the elder branches never to part with anything till death; which God forbid should happen this many years. Besides there are seven of us all equally entitled to their share. If a good business could be found out in England, I doubt not but he would lend me money sufficient to undertake it. In a foreign country he did not chuse I should reside, or there I was fixed in my own mind, and with your company, could have lived as happy as an angel.

We must hope for the best. No one knows what the ensuing winter may produce. I have many irons in the fire and, tho' some should burn, it would be hard but that others may be properly heated so as to produce what they were designed for. I have now explained to you my sentiments on those parts of your letters which struck me most forcibly, with the openness of heart which I flatter myself will always continue to be evident in yours. And it would be unjust were I not to read again the third and conciliatory letter, if any had been necessary, tho' I should certainly have attributed the former one to its just cause, your anxiety for me; and have equally been desirous of answering it had I not received the latter one.[48]

At sea, Monday 3 December 1787

Well, I just got time to send you a long letter from Elsinore, tho' I was obliged to finish it before I had said one half of what your letters would have induced me to say, for to suppose *that* should give you uneasiness, which made me easy about sending my letter from Yarmouth.[49] For I well remember thinking at that time: it is of no consequence sending this letter off till I know whether I leave England or not. For Eliza will be perfectly satisfied by hearing that I

---

47   Even if this was an accurate figure for his current income, Edmund here was certainly playing down the very considerable wealth of his family.

48   Eliza to Edmund, Letter 15, p. 115.

49   This letter has not survived.

am safe and well thro' the means of a letter which business obliged me to write. At the same time you will know from my letter that great parts of it was already written even before my arrival. And had it once occurred to me (which at any other time it certainly would have done) that you would be distressed on that account, I certainly would have sent it when I was at Hull.

For I would rather have written twenty letters than you should suffer what you certainly have done on that account. But I must tell you it was disagreeable at that time even to write to my Eliza, for it must have been composed of formal, forced expressions, nay unconnected ones, in such a frame of mind was I at that time, so out of temper myself and everything around me.[50] Your company might indeed have alleviated it, nay even your letters would have been some refuge, but at that time only one was in my possession. But I should not, as you conjectured, out of pique have done any such a thing, for I know not what pique is towards anyone, much less so dear a friend, without one is determined to affront me. I never will take one from any supposed injury; for why may not I as well construe any action which appears as an offence into an unintended one rather than one on purpose to affront me, till it is made evident and beyond dispute so. I shall certainly be happier and avoid many broils which a hastier temper might entangle me in. At the same time a designed affront, tho' I might on proper concession forgive, yet I would never silently suffer, without I must despise the person that had designed it, and could visibly show them they were beyond anger, being beneath my notice.

In regard to the word 'treason', does my letter imply that your writing to me is treason? Certainly not. But suppose you had written to me at Yarmouth; that your letter had gotten there before my arrival; and that it contained, which it certainly might have done, some hints respecting my mother-in-law. I say had that been the case, which surely was possible, and had that come to my father's inspection, I leave you to judge whether it would not have been treason. Treason which nothing hereafter could have possibly done away. For I would not have my father know what I think of Mrs Hurry for the world; it would make him miserable and you know is

---

50   Edmund's excuse for not having written to Eliza.

the chief reason of my being so little at home.[51] It was what drove my sister and her husband from Yarmouth.[52] For there is no living there without being a studied hypocrite or making my father miserable.

But as to hypocrisy, that you know is my forte. I have been obliged to act the hypocrite to duty to hide my own faith from the world, and then I own I think it is excusable. For, as nothing corrupts as soon as bad examples, there is scarce a better action which a wicked person can perform than to hide his vices from the sight of those who surround him. Perhaps in a few days I shall be able to put this letter in an English post office, and then you will be sure of having the first intelligence of my arrival this time.

I must not omit to tell you I enclosed you a letter in one to Mr Corbet from Riga about the latter part of October;[53] and I also sent a very long one from Elsinore.[54] Yours I have all received, except the Yarmouth ones, from whence I sailed in September and therefore could not get them.[55] I should not imagine that they will be opened; but, if they should, provided they contain no treason, it cannot be of any consequence, tho' I shall not be pleased at it. I hope a few days and they will be safe in my hands.

Monday 10 December

Thanks be to unbounded goodness for the best passage, considering the time of year, that it was possible to have and that I am once more safe landed amongst my friends. And this morning my father deposited your to me most agreeable and affectionate letters, but I was under the necessity of keeping them in my pocket almost this whole day without being able to get through them.[56] For tho'

---

51 William Hurry's first wife was Elizabeth Cobb (1741-1779). He had recently married a second wife, Dorothy Coldham, a widow and the mother of George and Wright Coldham. Edmund did not like his stepmother.

52 Edmund's sister Mary and his brother-in-law George Morgan.

53 Edmund to Eliza, Letter 17, pp. 132-34.

54 This letter has not survived and may not have reached Eliza.

55 Eliza to Edmund, Letters 8, 9, 11 and 12, pp. 57-76, 84-99.

56 Ibid.

several times of the day I did make the attempt, yet I was continually interrupted. And when all the family were at supper I made another beginning, yet I never could get one of them finished before some one or other had something to say to me.

But now at midnight that I am got up in my own room at my grandfather's, I have received the greatest pleasure which, excepting your company, it would be possible for me to enjoy in this world.[57] And I am fully sensible how undeserving I am of your tenderness, how every way undeserving of you. I would not have you think I say this with any views whatever of lessen[ing] your esteem for me, for I must own that would make me as unhappy as it is possible for anything to make me. At the same time I would wish to be as open and sincere to you in every respect as you have been to me. And I doubt not but you will do me the justice to say that the moment I durst conceive you had conceived a good opinion of me, without having a greater degree of vanity than I hope will ever fall to my lot, that I informed you how unworthy I was of your esteem.

You then thought I did it because you were poor, as you say, or thought myself above you.[58] No, I think far otherwise. I think myself above no one, no not the meanest. At the same time, I think no one above myself but as they exceed me in virtue, which I hope is the case of millions or this world is bad indeed. Now suppose I do all in my power to amend my errors, to use you with the utmost tenderness, nay as far as is consistent, do all you would wish me to do. In this case, can you positively assure me you would esteem me as much after a nearer connection as you do at present?[59] This is a serious question: our future happiness in this world, I had almost said in both worlds, depends entirely on this. Nay, I know I should be wretched indeed were I afterwards to find any abatement in that esteem and affection which you at present have for me. You must be equally miserable, and from what I know of myself I see nothing

---

57   While in Great Yarmouth, Edmund usually stayed with his grandparents, whose house was immediately next to that of his father.

58   Eliza had admitted her poverty to Edmund on Inishcoo. Eliza to Edmund, Letter 1, p. 31.

59   This is the nearest thing in the letters to an explicit proposal, though Edmund and Eliza seem to have had a clear understanding of their intention, if possible, to marry. See also, Eliza to Edmund, Letter 23, pp. 162-63.

that could enforce (if I may use the word) the continuation of them, but many things which I think must, when they come to lay more open to your inspection, cause at least a great diminution if not a total suppression of your tenderness towards me. How willing would I give the half of the little I possess for one single opportunity of showing you how sensibly I feel that tenderness, that affection which runs thro' all your letters, *even those I have most reason to dislike.* But I know you think otherwise of me now than you did when you wrote them, and that makes them lose half their weight. For they would have made me very unhappy had I received them at the time I might have done, and at a time that I own I really deserved them.

Without you are well convinced that what I have mentioned above will not be the case, it were much better we had never seen each other. Without you can entirely shut your eyes to all my follies and weaknesses, how can I, who possess such a number of them, expect you should continue the same with your eyes open? No, you will say, you are not the same man; you did not use to do or act so. And such a sentence would make us wretched for ever. Could I discover in myself anything to counterbalance these failings (if I may be allowed to give them so soft a name), I might then hope. But I have nothing to offer you but good nature, which (if I do not flatter myself) I do possess abundantly, with a willing desire to do my fellow creatures all the good that lies in my power, and which I hope will ever be my study as far as is consistent with my other ties and connections.

I may really say with Young the clock strikes one, and I dedicate this night, at least all of it that I can, to my conference with my dearest Eliza.[60] It blows a storm of wind and the ship not in safety, but I hope she will receive no damage. You know we have to proceed to London, but this place lies in our way thither from the Baltick. Would to God Dublin was so. It is impossible for me to express how much I desire to see you. And, depend on it, I will do all in my power not to be three months longer without it. Great opposition I know will be made to it, not on any account which you might suppose, but merely as my stay is likely to be so short in this country.

---

60   Edward Young (1683-1765), *Night Thoughts*, i, 'The bell strikes one. We take no thought of time'.

The beginning of March I again set sail for the Baltick, if it pleases God to spare me as long. I shall only go out passenger and shall be under the necessity of staying some time there in different parts. Perhaps, if I have my earnest desire fulfilled by visiting you this winter, you may make it convenient to accompany me on this side of the water either to Chester or London. Surely there will be nothing improper in it, and I know you will do it if there is not. If you could make London your abode, you will then have my company till I leave this country again. And if there is any obstacle prevents you which I can remove, if you do not desire me to do it you will act very unkindly.

My father also goes to London this week, as my mother-in-law is fixing her eldest son as a lawyer in London.[61] I should have said settling, for she is fitting up his house. He is a very good natur'd, worthy young man as any I know. I wish I could say as much for his mother. You see I am writing treason every line, and I would as soon lose my life as that my father should read this letter. I hope I shall not be above two days on my passage from hence to London, tho' I may be detained here some time by contrary winds which blow very hard at present. Mr Conyngham has been here.[62]

I am surprized Mr Corbet should never settle his account with me. I would hope it was on account of that quarrel. My father, who is rather suspicious, as most are who have long been hackneyed in the ways of men, generally thinks the worst of those things. For in the past I never distrusted a man till he has deceived me and I may sometimes suffer for it, yet I generally find those who find we place a confidence in them most willing to do us justice. Whether it proceeds from a wish to preserve that good opinion they already think you have of them or from an innate good principle, I will not presume, but I suppose sometimes for one and sometimes the other. I would not have you mention a word to him about it. Only if [he] says anything of it, in letting me know you may enable me to prevent my father doing something disagreeable to Mr Corbet

---

61   George Coldham, Edmund Cobb Hurry's stepbrother, born in 1766. His father, also George Coldham, was a linen draper in Norwich. When first married, Edmund and Eliza lived with him at No. 11 Leman Street, Goodmans Fields, London.

62   Conyngham was the driving force behind the development of the Rutland Island fishery. 'William Burton Conyngham, 1733-1796', *Oxford Dictionary of National Biography*. See above, pp. 4-17.

and to me likewise. You see my paper is full and at four o'clock I must go on board, so I shall throw myself on the bed for an hour or two. And now let me beg of you as you value my peace to quash all apprehension in regard to my affection or my love. And rest assured that I am sincere when I subscribe myself most truly yours, Edmund Cobb Hurry.

P.S. I wrote you where to direct to me at London both from Riga and Elsinore,[63] but, least they should not come to hand so soon as this, you will direct to me at Batson's Coffee House. Adieu. If I did not finish this letter to night, I know I should not have been able to have done it tomorrow, for they all appear here so glad to see me that one or other are continually coming in.

Cover, Miss Liddell, Robert Corbet Esq., No. 21 Hamilton Row, Dublin.

---

63   Edmund to Eliza, Letter 17, pp. 132-34. His letter from Elsinore has not survived and may not have been delivered.

Letter 21

Edmund Cobb Hurry to Eliza Liddell
London

Written 13-14 December 1787; sent from London, 21 December; received in Dublin, December

Thursday, 13 December 1787

Two days ago I sent my dearest Eliza a tolerable long account of my safe arrival at Yarmouth, but I have great reason to fear that I made such a capital blunder in the direction that it may not have come to your hands without being enquired for at the post office at Dublin. For not having your last letter on shore with me, I addressed it at No. 21 Hamilton Row instead of No. 6; but should Mr Corbet have some letters by the same post it may still come in course.[64] I have one more fear least the one I enclosed from Riga in Mr Corbet's may likewise be long ere it comes to hand, should he be situated at any distance from you.

And now for good tidings. And may God preserve me and I will see you at Dublin this winter. I have hinted to my friends and, I can with pleasure tell you, they made no other objection than that my stay was to be so very short in England: they should have none of my company themselves. But nothing but ill health shall prevent me. I told them I would endeavour to divide the short space into as equal portions as I possibly could: that one part would be in Ireland; one part with my sisters; and one with them.

As to the time that I shall be able to leave London will be very uncertain; for, till this cargo is entirely disposed of, I shall be chained. However, nothing shall be omitted by me to make all the dispatch I can, and [I] most sincerely wish it were consistent with your peace and happiness to accompany me back to London. And, you may depend on it, I will take all the care I possibly can of you. At the same time, should Chester be more agreeable, I will see you

---

64   Neither address in Hamilton Row was correct, as Eliza was living in Holles Street.

safe to that place. You will be something nearer me. And, tho' there is no probability of its being possible to be next summer in the same place, yet, should it please God to preserve us, your being in England may be the means of our meeting sooner in the next autumn.

You made a great mistake in directing your letter to Mr Samuel Hurry, as he is not my father but my uncle and could not possibly understand your letter.[65] He told my father he had a letter from an 'Irishwoman' whom by its contents he supposed had a son on board the *Fly*.[66] Yet he could in that light make no sense of it without making great allowances for blunders natural to people of that country. However, my father soon comprehended the whole affair and by this means it became quite publick; and from what I may judge has done no harm to our cause. I would not have you suppose my uncle published it intentionally but, as he could not guess at the intent of the letter, he gave it to his son-in-law and it was read openly.[67] And then my father found himself necessitated to clear up the mystery, and all who heard it were very warm in your praises; and, to my grandparents, laid me under the necessity of reading some parts of your letters which I received at Yarmouth and at which they were highly delighted; and announced to me what I little expected from them. As tho' they are far from possessing the illiberal notions which many of their age do, yet they being at a time of life when the passion of avarice is most predominant, I must own I did them the injustice to suppose it would not meet their approbation. They seem all to be fully satisfied (I say all, for none but them and my father has anything to do with it) at our *nearer alliance*. I should rather have said *nearer residence*, for I hope it would be doing us both injustice to suppose that a nearer alliance could take place.

Yet I must own that I find my affection and my love, at least I think so, daily increasing and for that reason would again conjure you, on my account as well as your own, not to expect too much from me, but

---

65   Samuel Hurry (1727-1800), fifth son of Thomas Hurry (1719-1801) and Anne Hall. He married Isabella Hall, who died in 1754. His two children were Samuel Hurry junior, who died in 1788, see below, Edmund to Eliza, Letter 40, p. 236; see also below, p. 278; and Elizabeth, who married Robert Alderson. Samuel Hurry senior lived at No. 133 King Street, Great Yarmouth.

66   The *Fly*, Edmund's ship on his visit to Inishcoo.

67   Samuel Hurry's son-in-law, the husband of his daughter Elizabeth (1751-1791), was Robert Alderson, a barrister and later Recorder of Norwich.

to make yourself fully acquainted with my character and my foibles. For should you afterwards find you have allied yourself to a blockhead, with few if any good qualifications, you must at least possess hypocrysy enough to hide it from me. For if you are not, we never shall be able to live together. One house will be far too small for us.

We are now nearly half way betwixt Yarmouth and London and I hope it will not be long before I can forward this to you, as I dare say you will have to enquire for my last at the post office.[68] I should have told you my father's name was William Hurry, in case you should again have occasion to address him. I believe he did not write to you, tho' from my grandmother I understand he had talked of it. I offered him the perusal of your letters, as I thought myself justified in so doing. He refused it, saying he could have read them before. I replied I well knew they had been long in his possession and that he certainly might have done as he thought proper with them. Yes, he said, he had also your leave. This surprized me till he produced your letter to my uncle.[69] However, he said he did not read them. I much wished that he had two of them, as I am sure they would have given him much pleasure. I have been lazy enough to write the above in bed, and I know not how short a time I may be allowed to sleep. Recommending you to the particular care of an all sufficient being, I bid you good night.

Friday, 14 December

Since I wrote the above, we have been much detained on our passage to London, but thank God, this day (i.e. Thursday 20th) got the ship safe here, but I was not able to send this away this post. However it shall go tomorrow, tho' I own I am much disappointed at not finding any news from my dearest girl. I might now torture myself with hideous ideas. I might suppose many things, which I trust are not, and spend many an anxious hour with imagining things which to me would be the most dreadfull that could happen to disturb my peace here. But I will not.

---

68 Sailing on his ship, the *Fly*.

69 Eliza sent a note addressed to Samuel Hurry to explain her letters for Edmund.

I will only suppose you have not yet received my letter to inform you where I might be found. I can urge to myself many good reasons to support that idea. It was enclosed in one to Mr Corbet. He is a long way distant from you, perhaps where no letter can reach him for some time, and yours is consequently detained in it; but I will not be guilty of the like simplicity any more. But at that time I had not the most distant idea of your removal to Dublin. Now I will suffer no other fancy whatever than the above to occupy my thoughts, tho' I must confess I shall be very uneasy if I have not soon a sight of your handwriting. Pray suffer me likewise to recommend the utmost attention to your health, for without it this life is most certainly a burthen,

Cover, none; postmark, none.

Letter 22

Edmund Cobb Hurry to Eliza Liddell
Riga

Written December 1787; forwarded from Elsinore, December;
received in Dublin, December

I have now again examined your third or rather second letter, tho' I happened to open it last.[70] You there again aggravate your own uneasiness by endeavouring to find something very mysterious in my not wishing you to write to Yarmouth. But a moment's consideration of my former letter (if I am not mistaken) would surely have been at least a lenient if not an absolute cure. For I think I there said (but perhaps I only intended to say) that I was uncertain of my destination, which you know was really the case.

For I first went to Hull and then Yarmouth, tho' I might have staid wholly at the latter till I again proceeded to the Baltick, which would then in all probability not have been above eight days. And I thought it was very uncertain whether a letter could come in answer to mine, had I met with a speedy passage. I would not have multiplied these reasons, but that in case any accident of the like should again occur they may then serve as a palliative to that uneasiness which I know foreboded misfortunes (if I may call them so) are always attended with. For in that they must certainly exceed real ones and have no other difference whatever as long as they are not discovered to be fictitious. Indeed our joy may then be somewhat uncommon, tho' it but poorly rewards us for the many anxious moments the thoughts of their being real has cost us.

But perhaps I did not tell you. I knew not my destined port. For we often think we write our friends what we are conscious we know very well ourselves and indeed from that very reason neglect it. For the failings which things of that sort, which are constantly in our minds, excite make us suppose that we must already have acquainted our friends with them. Yet from their obviousness they are forgot.

---

70   Eliza to Edmund, letters 15, 16 and 18; pp. 115-16, 125-31, 135-37.

And it is exactly the same with respect to observations which we make on things which fall within our notice, many which we think ourselves to be well acquainted with and for that very reason take the least notice of. Yet it often occurs that to have examined them more minutely would have been of the utmost advantage to us.

Your sister's situation I sincerely pity, and do most feelingly condole with you and her upon the occasion. It is a situation most truly lamentable, as it admits of no remedy; yet it surely may be made supportable. I wish it were in my power to be of any service to her. If it is so, and you do not desire me to do it, I shall be much displeased with you. But to suppose that either she or your cousin Barnes should accept of my acquaintance without an introductory letter from you shews you to be but little acquainted with the general suspicious temper of Englishmen towards strangers. And more particularly so are the Londoners. I hope therefore you will indulge me with one either to her or him, enclosed in yours to me, and you may either direct to me at Batson's Coffee House, London, or at Anthony Brough Esq., London.[71]

And now I have drawn my breath a little since the flutter your letters first put me in. I have collected time enough to be able to inform you that your two letters to Derwinda were safely forwarded to me at Riga and there afforded me great satisfaction and pleasure.[72] Only I am sorry to be so much behind hand in regard to the number of letters, yet I am determined the length of this shall in some measure make up for that deficiency. I have not those letters here on shore and, tho' they have been my evening meditations for some time past, yet do not recollect anything particular which you would wish answered in them.

As to your giving me leave to relinquish your correspondence, rather than incur the displeasure of my family, [it] is a permission, if I thought it in your power to grant it me with comfort to yourself, whatever uneasiness it might cost me, yet I should certainly regard it as no longer worthy my continuance. But to suppose that would, I am fully convinced, be doing you the highest injustice [*blot*] to you

---

71   Anthony Brough is listed, under Batson's Coffee House, as a merchant in *Kent's Directory for the Year 1794: Cities of London and Westminster and Borough of Southwark*.

72   Probably Letter 7, pp. 53-56.

and likewise torment myself with ideas. But I am determined to look towards the bright side of an object if there is even improbability in it. Much more as where, if my vanity does not flatter me, there is not the least reason to doubt. I do not wonder at your spirit, for I don't call it pride, having taken the alarm; but I should have been very sorry to have placed my affections where there was any reason for shame, if that were possible. But in these things I think very differently from many people. For was there what my friends might with some degree of plausibility think shamefull, yet, if I know myself, where I had once fixed I should never give it up on that account, tho' I might not have it in my power to draw the connection nearer without their consent.

Now I doubt not but you will say those who would hinder me following my inclinations in that way would not be my friends, but in that I cannot agree. For that they think for my good I doubt not. And the uneasiness that it would cause those that had done, and still continue to do, all in their power to make me happy and comfortable would be an insuperable bar to any undertaking of that kind. At the same time I have no reason to suppose my father would be much against it; without I should fancy he thought it more necessary for me to marry a fortune than my eldest sister. There he declared fortune to be no object, and the unexceptionable character of the man he was sure would make his Nancy happy. And had they £500 a year, I do not suppose there could be a happier couple in the world. Indeed, situated as they are, still happier than most.[73]

I have been writing this in a counting house and have been frequently interrupted, so that I suppose it is not very connected. It was just what occurred at the moment and, as the wind is fair, I have scarce time to look it over. My best respects to Mrs Corbet and family. To her I am under great obligations for her good opinion of

---

73   Ann Hurry, known as Nancy, had married the Reverend George Cadogan Morgan (1754-1798) in 1783. Morgan was the nephew of the celebrated dissenting minister Dr Richard Price (1723-1791). Morgan, after an early appointment as a preacher at the Octagon Chapel in Norwich, was briefly a minister in Great Yarmouth, but moved to Hackney in 1786 to assist at his uncle's Meeting. He taught at New College, a dissenting academy in Hackney, and also took in personal pupils. In July 1789 Morgan went on a continental tour and was in Paris at the fall of the Bastille. He was an enthusiastic and radical supporter of the Revolution and in 1792 published *An Address to the Jacobine and Other Patriotic Societies: Urging the Establishment of a Republican Form of Government*. Apart from his political writings, he was an expert on electricity, publishing his *Lectures in Electricity* in two volumes in 1794. He died, supposedly after inhaling poison during a chemical experiment, on 17 November 1798. See 'George Cadogan Morgan, 1754-1798', *Oxford Dictionary of National Biography*.

me, which I will endeavour never to forfeit. And now for England and may God ever bless you prays your Edmund Cobb Hurry.

Cover, Miss Liddell, Robert Corbet Esq., No. 6 Hamilton Row, Dublin. Note, 'Forwarded by, madam, your most obedient servant John Diston Son Ltd.' Postmark, 15 December, 1787.[74]

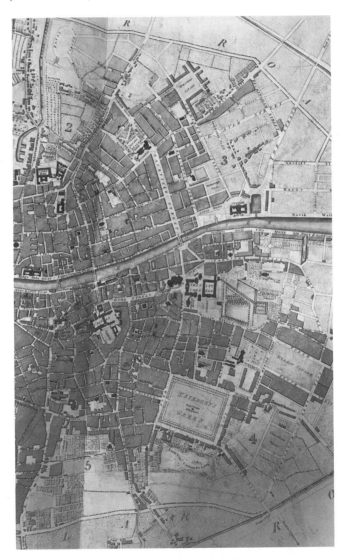

St Stephen's Green and Merion Square, Dublin, 1797, by William Faden

---

74   The agents specified by Edmund Cobb Hurry to Eliza Liddell in his initial instructions as where to send letters.

Letter 23

Eliza Liddell to Edmund Cobb Hurry
Dublin, 23 to 30 December 1787

*Written 23-30 December 1787; sent from Dublin, 30 December;
received in London, 8 January 1788*

Dublin, 23 December 1787

On Friday your letter from Elsinore arrived.[75] I wish I had waited its arrival ere I wrote to you, for your letter from Yarmouth, as well as this last, demands a more rational answer than I was then capable of writing. I was not sufficiently collected to arrange my ideas, and have scarcely any recollection of what I said. I am now sate quietly and will attempt refuting a mistake of yours by faithfully unfolding to you my sentiments on what was partly the subject of your two last letters.

But first, let me ask you, was it well done, Edmund, to venture twenty miles at this time of year in a little cockleshell of a boat? Was it well done to risk a valuable life for my worthless letters? Indeed, I am angry with you. And were you more prudent in sitting up the night you landed, when you must be fatigued and required repose, sitting up, for what? To read my letters, some of them, too, did they not well reward you for the trouble, unjust and unreasonable as they were? You did well to enumerate your catalogue of reasons for not writing. I feel my folly the more forcibly: indisposition of body, of mind, business, etc, etc. Why did I not apprehend all this and spare myself the mortification of appearing to you so very, very absurd.

Alas, I appear so to you on more accounts than one. *Burn* those moments of my folly, I beseech you. Yes, I am arrived safe in Dublin, notwithstanding my ridiculous fears. Not a single argument can I urge in my own defence. I am wrong, very weak. 'Tis a shameful imbecility of mind, particularly so as I never entertain a doubt of

---

75 This letter has not survived.

the power or the mercy of the Almighty. Am I also apt to anticipate misfortunes? This is another charge against me, and I deny stoutly that it is my natural temper, though I will admit you have every reason to suppose the contrary. However, I could tell you some circumstances in the past that would convince you that I am not always inclined to contemplate the gloomy side. My spirits, though never violent, have mostly been good and have helped to support me through real and many sorrows.

But I must own I think am much altered. The fortitude I once flattered myself I possessed seems to have deserted me entirely. I am conscious of the alteration and I am, I know not why, perhaps in this particular less worthy of your friendship than I formerly was. But I will indeavour to correct myself: when my spirits are dejected, I will read you advice and that will animate me to think and act as I ought.

I thank you, most sincerely, for your desire to serve my sister.[76] Your acquaintance may contribute to her happiness, but to serve her otherwise than by your good wishes I think you cannot. I am sure she would be grateful to you for your intentions, but a married woman has no alternative: if not supported by her husband, she must earn her own bread. 'Tis a delicate situation and my Barbara would be pained to the soul to receive obligations from anyone.

Her husband is in Dublin. He could to my knowledge support her comfortably, if he had a mind. He calls on me sometimes. He makes me large promises, but I must not believe him. Time only will discover whether he really feels the compunction he pretends. He talks of bringing Barbara to Dublin, but I am thoroughly persuaded she would think it an act of mercy in him, and bless him for it, if he will permit her to remain where she is. She is lately ingaged in the millinery business. Her success I consider as very uncertain, as she was not brought up to any. Collier says he will send her thirty guineas next week, but here again I must distrust him.

I thought to have been possessed of a sum of money, though not very great, that would have been of use to her. (She does not, however, materially want it at present.) In a letter I wrote to Barnes, I mentioned that I should have it in my power to be of use to her.

---

76   Barbara Collier. For her husband, from whom she was separated, see Eliza to Edmund, Letter 15, pp. 110-11; Letter 19, pp. 138-39.

I mentioned this to him with a view that he should tell his wife; and hoped it would insure her civil treatment from that lady, who is much carried away by money and its concomitant advantages (and I feared her narrow soul would fear my sister would be indebted to her for more than civility). But I was disappointed. My little sum is not, nor ever will, be mine, and I am inclined to think Barbara would not have accepted it from me. But she has no one to support but herself, and I cannot say I am half so unhappy on her account as while she lived with Collier, whose inattention to business, and expensive turn, kept her mind in a continued state of anxiety.

I ought to apologise to you for not thinking of an introductory letter, which I now inclose, least Barnes should not get my letter to him. If he does, I think you will not have occasion for this, as you will tell me whether you like him or not, as I should if he was your relation. For I have no idea of regarding people merely on that account. I have not seen him for years and, if the world has not altered him, he is a very amiable character. Barbara lives five miles out of London, but Barnes will I am sure send for her and not give you the trouble of going so far.[77]

And now let me, as I said I would, attempt refuting an opinion of yours respecting my sentiments. You say you doubt not I will say that who will hinder you from following your own inclinations cannot be your friends. You doubt not, and do you so little know me? Do you think so meanly of me? Shall I own to you all the pleasure I received from your two letters vanished when I came to this sentence.

I know not ought on earth could so sensibly distress me as your harbouring a mean opinion of me. And that you do in this one sentence in two places, else why would such a thought have occurred to you? Learn to know me better. And, believe me, so far from thinking those who would oppose your inclinations respecting me as not your friends, I should consider them as wanting in regard to you if their sentiments coincided with yours. A good father, who has every right to expect his sons marrying well (according to the world's acceptation of the word), who sees that son on the brink of forfeiting every worldly advantage, attached to a woman whose

---

77 Barbara Collier, who had no children, lived in Putney.

disposition may not be amiable, a blind partiality may influence the son's judgment to think too favourably of her; his father knows her not; his father, his true and tender friend, must be averse, anxious, perhaps displeased.

Who is there that would not wish honours, wealth and every earthly good for a deserving child? And who shall be so unjust as to condemn a parent for disapproving what he considers as injurious to his child's interest, perhaps happiness? Unknown as I am to your father, may he not be distressed with an apprehension that, swayed by mercenary motives, I may be ready to bestow my hand without the consent of my heart? (That most women are ready to do so, I have been told, is a general received opinion among men. My indigence gives room for the surmise, and your father's ignorance of my heart and character would justify him, even to me, were he to think in that manner of me divested of prejudice. And my resentment would not be excited, though I might lament not being in a situation to convince him of my disinterestedness.)

No one has higher notions of the relative duties of parent and child than I have. A good parent must ever be to me an object of the highest reverence and respect. I would not, now that I have lost my valuable mother, have to reproach myself for the slightest omission of gratitude, respect or duty for all the world could offer me.

Judge then, would I wish you to deviate from duties I hold sacred? And would you accept as a proof of my regard that I should say 'they could not be your friends who would hinder you following your own inclinations'? Selfish and low-minded must I be if I did. No, Edmund, no. My soul is superior to my situation, and I trust in God will never seek to purchase any temporal advantage by transgressing its duties, or by misleading others for my sake to forfeit their own approbation. As well might we hope for pardon at the throne of mercy through the intercession of the demons as seek to derive happiness from any source that would render us unworthy to deserve it. Ease then the heart of your father. Inform him, if he speaks of me (that independent of what I owe myself); assure him that I will not be the means of embittering his days with sorrow and yours with remorse. Assure him that, without his consent and approbation, I never will be yours.

More is not in my power; it would be barbarity to expect it. Let him not seek to deprive me of your regard. That would be to render life an unsupportable burden. Surely it is infringing on no duty that I should be dear to you. Ah, may I ever be so. I will not say my existence depends on a continuance of your regard, but my more than existence: my peace, my all of happiness in this life. And even your father has no right to interfere so far or attempt indeavouring to deprive me of a happiness to me inestimable.

The above would at present be unnecessary, but that I wished you to be satisfied you wronged me in supposing that I should condemn your friends, or consider them as not such, if they wished to thwart your inclinations. For another, no less formidable, objection remains that would compel me to reject you. A father and other friends out of the question, would you credit any other than myself, were she to tell you, I would refuse to be yours because you are not *more* wealthy?[78]

Beware of misconceiving the purport of my assertion when I inform you it is certainly the case that, because you are not *more* wealthy, I cannot be yours. And that if you were more so, my hand would be freely bestowed. Oh, what gives rise to this declaration? Does it prove me a mercenary, underserving of your regard? Does it teach you to despise me? Or, on the contrary, will you with your usual generosity enter into my feelings, my situation, and acquit me of being guided by any other motive but what has your future welfare for its object?

How can I pay you a higher compliment? How can I more fully prove the extent of my esteem for you than by assuring you that, till I knew you, I held it impossible for a woman to have any chance of happiness in marriage, either if possessed of a very large fortune herself or totally destitute of any. It matters not the many reasons that induced me to think this. Suffice it to say, when I knew you, I thought differently. I saw in your disposition the certainty of happiness for the woman you might value that the destitution of fortune on her part could not have power to destroy. Yes, Edmund, it would be a matter of indifference to me whether I had thousands

---

78 Another example of Eliza's anxiety to avoid any thought that she was marrying for money. See also Eliza to Edmund, Letter 7, p. 54; Letter 9, p. 67.

to bestow on you or whether I consented unportioned to unite my destiny with yours, certain that you would not connect yourself with one you could not regard for herself alone.

I should only rejoice in having a fortune for your acceptance, only as the means of empowering you to follow the bent of a benevolent heart, a heart that if deserving of its esteem I would, without a shadow of apprehension, though unportioned, venture most implicitly to depend on. For such treatment as would almost reconcile me to, nay teach me to forget, that I had brought you no fortune. This, if you were more independent than you are as it is.

I must not be yours, at least at present. Your income is much too small at least for more than yourself. I will not lessen it. I will not have to reproach myself hereafter for plunging you into difficulties, for involving you in ruin. Me ruin you, me who would die to promote your happiness? I could not bear it, Edmund. It cannot be. With you I would share the most deplorable fate; a dangerous gloom would have no horrors for me with you. But no horrors, no melancholy, no despair, could equal mine if a connection with me was the fatal cause that brought misfortune in any shape to visit you. You must not think of it.

I hope you have got my letters safe. I directed them to Batson's Coffee House. I will seal this before your answer arrives, for fear, no matter what. I shall go the moment I receive your answer. That is, if you tell me you don't come here, if the wind serves. Surely, surely I shall see you in Chester. If I thought not, I should be careless about where I am. Mrs Corbet desires to be affectionately remembered to you. Adieu. God bless you ever. E. Liddell.

I have had the above written some days, as you may see by the date, so I won't do more at present than fill the cover.[79] You do not come to Ireland. Nay, more, you shall not. No, my dear Edmund, I am not so selfish as to wish you to take a voyage at present so highly inconvenient. To prevent you doing so, I will, please God, take the opportunity of the first ship that sails for Parkgate.[80] You

---

79   23 December 1787.

80   Parkgate in the Wirral was the main port for travellers from Dublin to England until it silted up, being then replaced by Holyhead.

know Chester is but twelve miles from thence. And be assured that I have not the smallest apprehension about the sea. As to male or female friends, I shall take my chance; and, since you are not to be of my party, care very little about who is. For I do not in these calm times times expect being run away with. Perhaps I might if I staid here much longer, for Sir Jerome Fitzpatrick, who is Mrs Corbet's physician and dines with us very often, is desperately in love with me.[81] 'Tis a pity he has a wife, for Lady Fitzpatrick is a high sounding title.

Remember, your next letter must be directed to Mr Eltoft's, Chester, and remember I expect to see you there, as does Mrs Eltoft. And the minute I arrive there I shall write you word. Perhaps I may sail the middle of next week. Mrs Corbet sends her most affectionate remembrance. When I see you in Chester, we will talk over my going to London. I am truly grateful to your sister, but I think at present I must not accept her invitation. Pray return her my best acknowledgements. If any letters arrive here from you, Mrs Corbet will forward them to Chester. Mr Corbet sent me your letter from Riga.[82] Yours ever, Eliza Liddell.

Mr Conyngham is supposed to be dying – a dreadful fever.[83]

Cover, Mr Edmund Cobb Hurry, Batson's Coffee House, London. Postmark, Dublin.

---

81   Sir Jerome Fitzpatrick MD (1740-1810), later Inspector General of His Majesty's Land Forces.

82   Edmund to Eliza, Letter 17, pp. 132-34.

83   Conyngham survived the fever. He died in 1796.

Letter 24

Eliza Liddell to Edmund Cobb Hurry
Dublin

Written 2-3 January 1788; sent from Chester, 7 January;
received in London, January

Wednesday, 2 January 1788

Do you not deserve a scolding letter?[84] You know I am famous for those kind of productions. You do, for not content that I should be well at the fire side, you must desire me to go out. And here am I returned from a walk, a pair of shoes the worse and swimming in mud, and so excessively fatigued that I have been deliberating whether I should go lounge on the bed or write to you.

Let me see. I have some doubts whether I can elude your penetration, so must confess that not in Stephen's Green nor in the Mall, where alone you desired me to walk, did I encounter mud cakes and such a mud as almost frightened me, who have so long been used to retirement. To Mr Eltoft's account then must I place my fatigue, my fright and my dirt, for he desired me to bring him over some Irish garters and I was obliged to go to the liberty for them, through fifty odious streets.[85]

Edmund, this is Wednesday and I was in hopes to have been at sea, but the captain has deceived me and does not go till Saturday. Oh, I hope he will not defer it longer, for every step that draws me nearer to you must be happiness to me. But I remember you said you thought it but right to wait patiently for a wind, etc, etc; so I indeavour to restrain my impatience by thinking you would be angry with me if you saw me uneasy. And yet how can I be otherwise? Nanny Eltoft says she shall count the

---

84   See Edmund to Eliza, Letter 14, pp. 105-6.

85   St Stephen's Green is a small park in central Dublin. The liberty or liberties of St Thomas were next to Dublin Castle. The Mall, unidentified. The letter in which Edmund advised her where to go in Dublin has not survived.

hours till I arrive, and about the middle of this month I shall see you, God grant.

Beside, my situation is very, very unpleasant here. Mrs Corbet is distressed much at our separation. She looks at me so pitifully that she makes my heart ache, independent of her attachment for me. There is one fatal circumstance that has already wounded her to the soul, that may again when I am gone, and that I have hitherto happily had it in my power to prevent, at least for some time past; and yet that very circumstance would, if I had no other inducement, oblige me to leave her.[86] She will write to you to inform you when I am gone.

Have you seen my Barbara? I have also another sister near her, a sister who I have often wished in heaven.[87] Her health has been very bad for some years past; and she has such a melancholy turn of mind that she enjoys not anything. I am very little acquainted with her. I believe her heart an excellent one, but her temper is, I understand, much soured by misfortune and she has contracted many oddities.

I charge you, if you regard me at all (if you do – what a speech from me, who would not for the world it were possible to doubt what is so necessary to my peace), well then write not to me at midnight hours. I would rather receive but one line from you than that you should destroy your health. And what can more effectually do it that sitting up late?

I could not help laughing at my mistake respecting your uncle.[88] It was so ridiculous. And yet I am vexed. What business have you to tell me your father's name, me write to him. No, no. I have got enough of that. I wish I could see you this moment. Perhaps, involved in business, you would not get time to speak to me. Oh, how I should flounce away if you did not.

Did I thank you in my last, or rather your sister, for her kind, her obliging offer of making her house my home for some time?[89] But, Edmund, what, though on your account she invited me, what would

---

86   The nature of this problem is unknown.

87   Mary Lawrence.

88   Edmund's father was William Hurry (1734-1806); his uncle was Samuel Hurry (1727-1800).

89   Mary Tolmé, who lived in Great Prescott Street, Goodmans Fields, London, near Aldgate. When she came to London, Eliza accepted this invitation. Edmund's letter with this invitation has not survived.

she think of my assurance, if I could bring myself to take advantage of her offer? Me an entire stranger, unknown to her, unregarded by her, her only inducement must be to oblige you. And if my pride could permit me to go to her, only think if she should happen to dislike me; only consider how disagreeable my company would be to her.

I am called to dinner, but must stay to tell you. Turner surprised Mrs Corbet and I very unpleasantly the other morning by his sudden appearance, quite out of his reason.[90] We had hoped his friends would have detained and confined him in England. Mrs Corbet dined out and he returned in the evening. I was so frightened at his strange and shocking gestures, and conversation, that I whispered one of the maids to come and stay in the parlour with me. What a pity to see such a mind so woefully overturned. He was at Barnes, when in London, and abuses him to me for not lending him five hundred pounds, he says he asked him for. He has been in a number of shops and he speaks things to a vast amount and desires them to come to Mr Conyngham for payment.[91] He has shocked me [*tear*] excessively. I much fear Barnes and their friends attribute his wild and mad conduct when in England to a bad heart. He says they all think ill of him, but says, while his every feature is convulsed with his unhappy malady, 'I never was mad'.

Conyngham continues dangerously ill. Mr Corbet is down at the Rosses and I know is at this moment in a very distressing situation, for Mr Wade has stopped paying any of his bills till Conyngham's fate is determined.[92] He said, in a letter to Mrs Corbet, he would write to you directly. Adieu, Edmund, and excuse this scrawl. Consider my state of mind, waiting for you to reply. E. Liddell.

---

90   For Turner, see also, Eliza to Edmund, Letter 16, p. 131; Letter 24, p. 167; Appendix, A5, p. 289.

91   Given as 'Mr C.' in the original and more likely to stand for William Burton Conyngham than Robert Corbet.

92   For the problems at the Rosses, see Appendix, A1, A2, A5, A6, pp. 281-84, 287-90.

2 January 1788, Wednesday

Don't expect to hear from me again while here, and remember I told you to write to Mr Eltoft, Chester.[93] He bids me tell you, through his Mary, that he shall expect to see you at his house. Mary says also much about you. She is angry with you for [hastening] to take me up to London from her; and, worse, she threatens me she shall indeavour to supplant her friend in your regard (she had letters not).

Thursday, 3 January

The frost is gone and the wind against us. I guessed it would be, but Brown has promised to sail if possible on Saturday. Perhaps this day may bring me a letter from you. Now don't be making yourself uneasy about my foolish fears, for I assure you they have entirely forsaken me, so that I am ready to climb the masts, if my assistance should be necessary. God bless you ever.

Cover, Mr Edmund Cobb Hurry, Batson's Coffee House. Postmark, 7 January 1788. Sent from Chester.

---

93   Mr Eltoft's wife was Anne (or Nanny); his daughter was Mary.

Chester

tenets are nearly the same, but you are *an* Hypocrite
Deny it, if you can, nay I have positive proof of it;
For you profess a religion whose tenets you do not
believe, that is you give your consent to what you
have told me you think unjust and honied I suppose
you know what I allude to; but I would have you
consider my dearest Eliza, that not only in the eyes
of men but in the eye of God, when we go constantly
to a church, it is taken for granted, nay we profess
we firmly believe what is held in that Church to
be the true religion of the Gospel, therefore if we do
not believe it, we cannot deceive God, but we certainly
are Hypocrites to our Fellow Creatures; we are neither
bound in Nature or in Reason to follow the Code laid
down to us by any particular Church or any particular set of men; But as each of us must one day
find Sense enough to Answer for ourselves, so it would
appear unjust if we were not endued with powers
sufficient to Judge for ourselves; and this is my Creed
that if any one has used proper means to instruct themselves;
or to take it more largely, whatever any one can firmly persuade themselves, is to them apparently the
true Religion, to them it sufficeth; and is to them the
best; For if they act up to it, whether Jew, Grecian, or
Mahometan, it will certainly be found to them the

Edmund Cobb Hurry to Eliza Liddell, Letter 28 (below, pp. 186-87), January 1788

4

Chester

Delayed in Ireland by an adverse wind, Eliza did her best to suppress her excitement at the thought of being closer to Edmund:

> Edmund, this is Wednesday and I was in hopes to have been at sea, but the captain has deceived me and does not go till Saturday. Oh, I hope he will not defer it longer, for every step that draws me nearer to you must be happiness to me. But I remember you said you thought it but right to wait patiently for a wind, etc, etc; so I indeavour to restrain my impatience by thinking you would be angry with me if you saw me uneasy. And yet how can I be otherwise?[1]

At last, with the wind shifting, Eliza sailed from Dublin on Saturday 5 January 1788, landing at Parkgate in the Wirral two days later. As she wrote the same day, 'We landed here at ten o'clock. Two tedious days were pent up in that delectable thing called a ship. Edmund, I am now in the same kingdom with you, thank God.'[2]

In Chester Eliza stayed with the Eltoft family, with whom she was connected through her cousin, John Barnes, who was in partnership with Mr Eltoft. She knew them from before her years in Ireland and was particularly friendly with the Eltofts' daughter, Mary. Eliza was, however, in Chester for less than a month, while plans for her onward journey to London and her lodging there were being settled.

---

1   Eliza Liddell to Edmund Cobb Hurry, Letter 24, p. 165.

2   Eliza to Edmund, Letter 26, p. 180.

Having so recently left them behind, there are mentions of the Corbets, as well as affairs on Rutland Island in her letters. According to Eliza, 'Conyngham continues dangerously ill. Mr Corbet is down at the Rosses and I know is at this moment in a very distressing situation, for Mr Wade has stopped paying any of his bills till Conyngham's fate is determined'.[3] In response, Edmund wrote gloomily:

> at present things appear darker to me than they have for some time. Murray has proved a rogue and I am afraid Corbet is not much better. I have written them both two such letters that, if they have either shame or honour left (for honesty they certainly have none), they must do me justice.[4]

Much more of the correspondence, however, is about their hopes for their future together. After Edmund arranged for her to stay with his married sister, Mary Tolmé, in Goodmans Fields, near Aldgate, Eliza had expressed scruples:

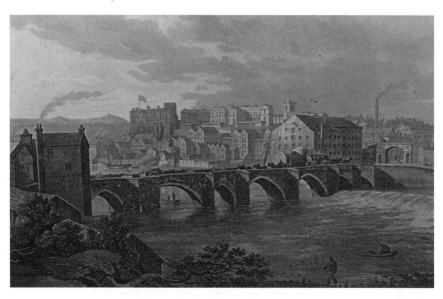

Handbridge, Chester, 1817, by George Pickering

---

3   Eliza to Edmund, Letter 24, p. 167.

4   Edmund to Eliza, Letter 31, p. 195.

Did I thank you in my last, or rather your sister, for her kind, her obliging offer of making her house my home for some time?[5] But, Edmund, what, though on your account she invited me, what would she think of my assurance, if I could bring myself to take advantage of her offer? Me, an entire stranger, unknown to her, unregarded by her, her only inducement must be to oblige you. And if my pride could permit me to go to her, only think if she should happen to dislike me; only consider how disagreeable my company would be to her.

In the event, she did stay with her future sister-in-law on her arrival in London.

Edmund was naturally keen to come to Chester as soon as he could. As he expressed it, 'You say you hope you shall see me in Chester. If I can crawl there you certainly shall …'; causing Eliza anxiety about his state of mind. 'If you can *crawl*, you will come to Chester. Are you then so bad? Edmund, I am on the rack of anxiety. Oh, write tell me you are well'.[6]

Others, too, were worrying about Edmund:

I cannot say that I have done more than exist ever since I came to London; and, whenever I have been with my sisters and family, I have been as low and dejected, as sour and peevish, as the greatest misanthrope that ever exists. I would not advise you ever to come to London again, at least whilst any of this part of the family are in it, for it's doubtfull with me what they might do with you. For they one and all declare you to be the sole cause: that my unhappiness is entirely on your account; and that I am so strangely altered of late that they know me not for the same person. But, as a lawyer makes up one part of the family, you may depend upon proceedings being legal and that no steps will be taken irregularly against you.[7]

Even his own father, William Hurry, was concerned: 'For my own father

---

5   Eliza to Edmund, Letter 24, pp. 166-67. Mary Tolmé, who lived in Great Prescott Street, Goodmans Fields, London, near Aldgate. Edmund's letter with this invitation has not survived.

6   Edmund to Eliza, Letter 25, p. 178. Eliza to Edmund, Letter 27, p. 182.

7   Edmund to Eliza, Letter 28, p. 184. They would proceed only by the law, not by violence.

says in letters to my sister that Edmund's letters are not such as they used to be. "I fear his intellects are a little disordered".[8]

On a more positive note, Edmund had finally managed to meet Eliza's two sisters, Barbara and Mary, giving Eliza a full account of his trip to Putney and Hammersmith, and of his meeting with them, in both cases suffering problems to do with their addresses and identity. With Barbara, 'This little mistake rather disconcerted me, and I think we rather passed two or three formal hours than friendly ones; but, be that as it may, it might be from the newness of our acquaintance rather than any other cause, and I am a strange person where I am not known'.[9] With Mary he had more success, once an initial misunderstanding was resolved:

> I was consequently ushered in; and, as I immediately knew her, I concluded she must know me by the message I had sent. However, we had talked together near five minutes before I perceived myself to be a stranger. Then, making myself known, I spent a very agreeable half hour; but, to describe it more fully I was treated as a brother ought to be.[10]

Edmund also sent Eliza a full account of his own religious beliefs, which were extremely tolerant even for the second half of the eighteenth century:

> We are neither bound in Nature nor in Reason to follow the code laid down to us by any particular church or any particular set of men. But as each of us must one day find sense enough to answer for ourselves, so it would appear unjust if we were not endued with powers sufficient to judge for ourselves. And this is my creed: that if anyone has used proper means to instruct themselves; or, to take it more largely, whatever anyone can firmly persuade themselves is to them apparently the true religion, to them it sufficeth and is to them the best.
>
> For if they act up to it, whether Jew, Grecian or Mahometan, it will certainly be found to them the first and most profitable religion.[11]

---

8   Edmund to Eliza, Letter 31, p. 196.

9   Edmund to Eliza, Letter 28, p. 185.

10   Edmund to Eliza, Letter 28, p. 185.

11   Edmund to Eliza, Letter 28, pp. 186-87.

Edmund's tolerance, however, did not extend towards blasphemy:

> Oh Eliza, and so you have learned to swear since you have been
> in Chester: a very pretty accomplishment indeed.[12] I can make no
> other excuse for you but that you have not yet been settled enough
> to go to church, and that you quite forgot the third commandment
> in Ireland. I should not have wondered much if you had acquired
> it there, but you really outdo Mr Corbet in your last letter.[13] And
> I must own I would rather have my head broken with a bottle or
> level than to hear 'Damn me'. My dear, what did you do that for? It's
> shocking in a man, it's disgusting in a woman to the highest degree.
> But you take the Lord's name in vain and, as I never knew you did
> it before, I thought it might be some new acquired talent of which,
> least it should increase, I thought proper to warn you – and to assure
> you then any aspersion you please to make to me will be full as
> strong, and as firmly believed, without an oath being added to it.[14]

There remained to be fixed the exact date of Edmund's arrival in Chester,
the proprieties of where he should stay and how they should travel back to
London. Edmund, on the grounds of not wanting to impose on the Eltofts,
proposed staying with his cousins in Liverpool. Eliza told him, however, on
the Eltofts' behalf, that he was being overscrupulous: 'Mr Eltoft bid me tell
you that when you are acquainted with him, but for one day, you will join
with him in laughing at your formality. That his house, not you, will receive
the obligation from your company'.[15]

Eliza's sisters, on the other hand, continued to worry about Eliza's
reputation, writing to her, and copying their letter to Edmund, to insist that
one of them should come to fetch her:

> they communicated the contents of their letter which I did not
> altogether approve, first in regard to the length of time they allow
> you to be in Chester and next that I am to be debarred of the pleasure

---

12   The swearing was in a letter which does not survive.

13   Swearing. The third commandment, 'Thou shalt not take the name of the Lord thy God in vain'.
Robert Corbet presumably swore frequently.

14   Edmund to Eliza, Letter 34, p. 201.

15   Eliza to Edmund, Letter 26, p. 180.

of escorting you here. These were proposals I could not agree to. And I will now make you mine: that, on condition you determine to leave Chester the second, or at longest the third, day of February, I will promise to be there on or about 31 January; and on no other conditions whatever.[16]

---

16   Edmund to Eliza, Letter 31, pp. 194-95.

Letter 25

Edmund Cobb Hurry to Eliza Liddell
London

Written January 1788; sent from London, January;
received in Chester, January

Happy was I, my dearest Eliza, to receive yours, which left Dublin on 31 December.[17] Still happier that I was able to read it, but happiest of all in that I can with sincerity assure of my being nearly recovered from as severe an indisposition as I have experienced for some time. Since I wrote my last to you I have not been out, and indeed been so weak and uncomfortable as not to be able to do anything.

On the first day of my keeping house, I wrote to your sister Barbara and enclosed it to Mr Barnes. A few minutes after, I received an invitation from Mr Barnes. This I replyed to as soon as I was able, requesting also that he would acquaint me with the abode of Mrs Collier. To these notes I have had no answer and am at a loss what to suppose is the cause. And now I have done myself the pleasure to rejoice so much at my own restoration, give me leave to congratulate you on the recovery of your spirits, or should rather have said your fortitude. Tho' your better spirits appear thro' the whole of your letter, yet nothing can be more conspicuous than your fortitude in the latter part of it. And I hope before this you will have found, once more, that those mighty waters are not so very dangerous as they are often represented.

I must now likewise tell you I find myself hurt, not at you. I can trace all those things to their true source in myself. But I must beg leave likewise to begin if possible to justify myself by telling you what reason I had, exclusive of the depravity of my own imagination, to suppose that you might think those not my friends who should oppose my inclination. It first arose from reading a letter of yours I received at Elsinore, in which you say a person turned of twenty-five certainly knows their own mind and may do as they please. What

---

17 Eliza to Edmund, Letter 23.

you meant to allude to I really cannot say, but at that time it in all probability struck me so as to cause the expression which hurt you so much. And I wonder not that it should, for the words placed by themselves appear the most absurd I possibly conceive, and I would be the first to alledge the contrary. And yet I think there are ways in which that sentence may be understood so as not to appear such a glaring absurdity.

'Inclinations', used as a word to express the desire of being united to a person in every respect worthy of me, and capable of making me happy: I say here he that would oppose my inclinations; nay, I'll go further, he that would not do all in his power to further such a union, may be my relation but can never be my friend. I do really understand you as you would wish in what you say with respect to money matters. And thinking as I do that it would hurt me to see you live differently from what you have been used to do: it might be the means of ruining us both together. For I am well persuaded we could not then be ruined singly.

I may say there lies my bane, but where the antidote is I have not yet been able to find. I mean it lies in that I have no fixed habitation, no comfortable dwelling. I have no place but my ship in which I can feel myself at home. Sometimes I pass the time with one, sometimes with another, but it is only passing it. For to enjoy some hours how often have I sacrificed to the goddess vice, and as often returned filled with apathy and discontent. I now live with a tender and affectionate sister, and yet I cannot feel myself at home.[18] Now I am well she has taken to her bed, but I hope in God she will soon be [restored].[19] Good health to all, for without it I wish not to live longer, and there are few I hope have taken such pains to destroy their own health as I have done.

You say you hope you shall see me in Chester. If I can crawl there you certainly shall,[20] but I fear I should feel myself under such obligations to Mr Eltoft as not to be able to make a long residence. A sense of obligation to others without any opportunity of returning them might make me detest him; nay, worse to me, make me fear

---

18   Mary Tolmé.

19   Word 'restored' supplied.

20   An offer which caused Eliza anxiety, Letter 27, p. 182.

him. Here comes a man I am in debt to, I cannot pay him, I must run off. But I shall go to my cousins at Liverpool and from thence visit you.[21]

However I am talking as tho' I had months to spare, when I must leave London 1 March and know not when I shall be able to get away from it towards you. For this sickness has set everything back. I have not even had industry enough to read a book, much less to write in one, and besides that I have now not less than forty correspondents. If you go on at this rate, I shall talk about burning letters. What must I do, who have written so many to hurt you? Therefore, on condition that you burn those of mine, I shall commit to the flames those you mention. I have written a parcel of the most unconnected stuff that ever any sheet of paper was in possession of it; and, but that I feared you should hear of my illness by other means, and that you would be disappointed at not having a letter in Chester, I would have deferred writing till tomorrow. Yours most affectionately, E.C. Hurry.

Cover, Miss Liddell, Mr Eltoft, Chester. Postmark, illegible.

---

21 Edmund Cobb Hurry's cousin, John Hurry (1747-1806) established a branch of the Hurrys in Liverpool. He married Alice Cross and had seven children. 'He was for many years one of the most prominent merchants and shipowners at Liverpool; and retired from business with an ample fortune some years before his death.'

Letter 26

Eliza Liddell to Edmund Cobb Hurry
Parkgate

Written 7-9 January 1788; sent from Chester, 9 January;
received in London, January

Parkgate, Monday

I took up my pen last night to write to you and Mrs Corbet; but, what with fatigue, bad pens and ink, I could not write intelligibly. We landed here at ten o'clock. Two tedious days were pent up in that delectable thing called a ship. Edmund, I am now in the same kingdom with you, thank God. Write to Mr Eltoft, Chester. Don't expect me to write more at present, but when I get to Chester. No, I will wait for you to write to me. Yours ever, E. Liddell.

Turn over.

Chester

I have received your letter. Send me word for God's sake. Are you better? Tell me when I shall see you. Perhaps I am foolish, but I don't like the style of your last letter, so low spirited. Oh tell me, are you worse than you chose I should think you are? Write I conjure you strictly.

Mr Eltoft bid me tell you that when you are acquainted with him, but for one day, you will join with him in laughing at your formality. That his house, not you, will receive the obligation from your company.

I wonder Barnes did not answer your letter. Barbara lives at Putney, Surrey. I am shocked to death about her and my other sister. Mrs Eltoft is afraid, so am I from the turn of their letters, that they have got connected with a set of Methodists and are fast imbibing their mistaken notions.[22]

---

22   Methodism was founded by John Wesley and at this time was still part of the Church of England. Its stress on personal belief and strong religious commitment were at odds with the Enlightenment values expressed by Edmund and accepted by Eliza.

I have not been in bed these three nights. My spirits are worn out. Good night.

Cover, Mr Edmund Cobb Hurry, Batson's Coffee House, London. Postmark, Chester.

Letter 27

Eliza Liddell to Edmund Cobb Hurry
Chester

Written 9 January 1788; sent from Chester, 9 January;
received in London, January

When I arrived here yesterday, your letter was put into my hands by Mr Eltoft, but I had scarcely read it when I found a necessity for putting it in my pocket, for they all surrounded me and were so happy at my arrival that, though I longed to get through your letter, I could not do it. Today I am ill. I feel my fatigue more sensibly than before I went to bed; and worse, I am wretched. You have I perceive (now that I have had leisure to again and again look over your letter) been ill, dreadfully ill. Great God! Are you yet so? Edmund, if you do not wish me to think I am totally indifferent to you, send for me to London. If this alarming disorder should continue, if anything should happen to you, if – oh God – what then would become of me? And if you do, may I then die. But why, why are you so low spirited? Alas, I too have rendered you uneasy. You are, though you deny it. You are hurt at what I said. I dwelt too much on that sentence in your letter and I am sufficiently punished for my taking it in the light I did. You say I write in better spirits than usual. Did I, could you see me now? Spirits I might now ask, what are they? If you can *crawl*, you will come to Chester.[23] Are you then so bad? Edmund, I am on the rack of anxiety. Oh, write tell me you are well.

You would hate Mr Eltoft – impossible. You would love him: plain, blunt, he says what he thinks, but he cannot offend, for his heart is excellent. He is partner to John Barnes, a wine merchant, and also he keeps a music and toy shop.[24] His wife is the best of women.

Cover, none. Postmark, none.

---

23   See Edmund to Eliza, Letter 25.

24   John Barnes and his wife lived in Crown Court, Westminster, near Covent Garden.

Letter 28

Edmund Cobb Hurry to Eliza Liddell
London

Written 8-9 January 1788; sent from London, 10 January;
received in Chester, January

Well I have sent you one off to Chester, but I have saved Mrs Corbet the trouble of sending you any from Ireland. And I hope for this reason, as well as many others, that Boreas will be so indulgent as to lend you his aid at the appointed time.[25] Besides I know, I cannot say by fatal experience, but I well know what it is to see every moment those whom we are every day expecting to be bereft of. And tho' it may not be an eternal separation between you and Mrs Corbet, yet it in all probability will be so. This adds greatly to the solemnity of parting, to part when every chance is against seeing each other on this side of the grave. To part with whom, with those whom time has endeared to us, nay perhaps made dearer to us than ourselves; as far as that is possible, there to part is misery to poor Mrs Corbet. And added to what you mention is enough to sink the most courageous mind in doubt, despair and gloom. I hope she has friends left to support her, and that your fortitude will not be too much shaken. May this find you safely seated besides Miss Eltoft relating the Wonders of the Stormy Deep.

When I received your letter last night I was not in a much better mood than Mr Turner.[26] I pity him poor fellow; he must have frightened you much, yet I think I should have affected you more. For I declare I do not think I should have spoken to you if you had been here. I would not to my sister. It was the effect of my disorder.[27] I again caught cold, but I thank God I am wonderfully well today. I cannot say that I have done more than exist ever since I came to

---

25   Boreas, the north wind. Dublin and Chester are on much the same latitude.

26   Turner's unnerving visit to Holles Street is described in Eliza to Edmund, Letter 16, p. 131; Letter 24, p. 167. See also, Appendix, A5, p. 289.

27   Melancholy was a fashionable and frequent complaint of lovers.

London; and, whenever I have been with my sisters and family, I have been as low and dejected, as sour and peevish as the greatest misanthrope that ever exists. I would not advise you ever to come to London again, at least whilst any of this part of the family are in it, for it's doubtfull with me what they might do with you. For they one and all declare you to be the sole cause: that my unhappiness is entirely on your account; and that I am so strangely altered of late that they know me not for the same person. But, as a lawyer makes up one part of the family, you may depend upon proceedings being legal and that no steps will be taken irregularly against you.

However, to prevent this piece of mischief, the best method I can think of will be first to recover my spirits with you at Chester, if that's possible. But I really do not know whether your company will not make me more gloomy than I am even now. It will make me reflect that we must part again; that I must again cross that multitudinous ocean, which indeed has no terror for me but its barring me the sight of you; and that perhaps for a long space of time.[28] I suppose if Mr Corbet remains in that situation I shall never hear from him. He never wrote me but one short letter since I left the Rosses and in that never once mentioned the account between us. I had every reason to distrust his honour and his honesty, as from appearances it seemed as tho' he would forget it.

Wednesday 9 January

I have this day been to pay the long intended visit to your Mary and your Barbara. And I shall freely tell you this, I apparently met with a more cordial reception from the former than the latter. But I must first go on so tediously as to relate to you every circumstance and then leave you to judge, but at the same time insist in your not mentioning it to them when you write. My first reference was to look in order to find a Putney stage, and by it the Bell Savage inn was the nearest;[29] but this I passed by without finding and luckily just met with one a going off from the Strand and one vacant seat in it.

---

28   Edmund was due to sail again to the Baltic in March.

29   The Bell Savage Inn was on the north side of Ludgate.

After being shut up near an hour with as disagreeable company as I ever wish to go with again, I at length arrived at the famous village of Putney; and fortunately the first house I entered was the one which contained Mrs Collier, to whom I immediately introduced myself. But from her I understood she was in London.[30]

Strange Mrs Collier should say she was in London, that's impossible. Well this must be Miss Collier. And then she talked of a sister, Mary, she had, who lived in the next village.[31] So I thought Eliza had three sisters: the one talking with me; one in the next village; and Mrs Collier in London. But afterwards, enquiring where I should find Mrs Collier, she informed me she was Mrs Collier and that her sister Mary was in London. This little mistake rather disconcerted me, and I think we rather passed two or three formal hours than friendly ones; but, be that as it may, it might be from the newness of our acquaintance rather than any other cause, and I am a strange person where I am not known. This is true more than in a literal sense.

At four I said I must go to London on account of the post, so off I tripped to Fulham, where the coach goes from. There I heard your sister Mary was returned and immediately sent to a friend's where she was engaged at tea; but I suppose they told her that a gentleman wanted her and not Edmund Hurry. However, she sent to beg I would come to her, with which I immediately complied. I was consequently ushered in; and, as I immediately knew her, I concluded she must know me by the message I had sent. However, we had talked together near five minutes before I perceived myself to be a stranger. Then, making myself known, I spent a very agreeable half hour; but, to describe it more fully I was treated as a brother ought to be.

The stage was ready; but, as they drove very slow, being rather overburthened, I lost the post, or I should this evening have sent off what I wrote two days ago.[32] And [it] was to have been a congratulatory letter on your arrival at Chester. But now I have really the pleasure of knowing you are safe there, and I condole with

30 Mrs Collier ran a successful millinery business with her friend Miss Wakeford.

31 Hammersmith.

32 See the earlier part of this letter.

you on your fatigue but congratulate you that you are once more safe amongst your friends in England. But pray, madam, supposing your sisters are turned Methodists, what right have you to be sorry for it? How do you know but that may be as ready a way of getting to heaven as the one you propose to yourself. Nay, if you are of the religion you profess, your opinions, I should rather have said your tenets, are nearly the same, but you are an hypocrite. Deny it if you can. Nay, I have positive proof of it. For you profess a religion whose tenets you do not believe. That is you give your consent to what you have told me you think unjust and horrid. I suppose you know what I allude to.[33] But I would have you consider, my dearest Eliza, that not only in the eyes of man but in the eyes of God, when we go constantly to church, it is taken for granted. Nay, we profess we firmly believe what is held in that church to be the true religion of the Gospel.

Therefore, if we do not believe it, we cannot deceive God; but we certainly are hypocrites to our fellow creatures. We are neither bound in Nature or in Reason to follow the code laid down to us by any particular church or any particular set of men. But as each of us must one day find sense enough to answer for ourselves, so it would appear unjust if we were not endued with powers sufficient to judge

Eastgate Street, Chester, 1791, by George Pickering

---

33 Possibly an Enlightenment dislike of damnation. See also, Edmund to Eliza, Letter 44.

for ourselves. And this is my creed: that if anyone has used proper means to instruct themselves; or, to take it more largely, whatever anyone can firmly persuade themselves is to them apparently the true religion, to them it sufficeth and is to them the best.[34]

For if they act up to it, whether Jew, Grecian or Mahometan, it will certainly be found to them the first and most profitable religion. Now this said Methodism, is it not a comfortable circumstance to feel oneself elected by God to Eternal Happiness, to be regenerated to a new life and not to have it in our power to sin? Is not this an admirable situation to enjoy on Earth? But there is one unfortunate affair (if your sisters should be in that way) which must damp every joy they can possibly feel here. I mean that of your being a reprobate: one who must be eternally damned for all your boasted goodness. They allow of none, but perhaps comfort themselves that God may of his infinite mercy take pity of you and bring you to a due sense of your own unworthiness.

I have written a great deal about religion, which I must own is mighty foolish, but your condemning your sisters for believing what they must think right was what led to it. I never bring it into discourse if I can possibly avoid it, for I do not think myself capable of defending my own opinions against your great logicians. And, as I believe what to me seems most consistent with the tenor of the sacred writings, I should be vexed anyone should by his advantage over me either in knowledge of those books or his superior capacity of reasoning make me acknowledge what on consideration I must deny.

I wish to obtain no proselyte to my way [of] thinking, but those who on a candid hearing of it prefer it to their own. I have filled my letter so much with this that I have scarce room to tell you I received this evening a letter from Mrs Corbet. She desires to have *The Shipwreck*, if I can get it.[35] Time enough tomorrow. I'll send it by the coach to you at Chester, as you will in all probability have an opportunity of sending it by one in whom you can trust. If not, keep it till I come and I will send it from Liverpool. If I could get away from hence by the 20th it would give me great satisfaction, but I have

---

34   Edmund Cobb Hurry's religion reflects the tolerant, Enlightenment side of Unitarianism.

35   *The Shipwreck* (1783). It is listed, new and neat at one shilling, in the Exeter catalogue for 1787.

met with some disappointments which may make it a rather later day. The earlier the more agreeable to yours most truly and most affectionately, E.C. Hurry.

I have not seen Mr Barnes yet; but, as am now got strong, I hope [I] shall tomorrow.

Cover, Miss Liddell, Mr Eltoft, Chester. Postmark 88.

Letter 29

Edmund Cobb Hurry to Eliza Liddell
London

Written 12 January 1788; sent from London, 12 January;
received in Chester, January

I am sorry indeed, my dearest Eliza, that your voyage should have had such a bad effect upon your health and spirits. I rejoiced to think that you had recovered them so far in Ireland, as you appeared to me from your late letters to have done, and I was in hopes you would never more have had cause but to rejoice. However, that is not likely to fall to the lot of any human creature; nor is it fit or necessary it should or it certainly would. That 'whatever is is right' has always been a favorite sentence of mine, but it will perhaps bear many different explanations from the light I take it in.[36] I have almost always hitherto enjoyed such a temper of mind as to be able in most cases quietly to acquiesce in every dispensation of an all-perfect being, tho' most likely precluded from the original formation of my disposition. But at present I find that temper has lately undergone a change greatly for the worse. I mean in regard to my own temporal peace; but whether it may not on some account be an alteration for the better time will discover. I am now exceedingly anxious for the future. When I say future, I speak only with regard to this life; and how short that future may be makes it almost madness to be anxious about it.

I sincerely congratulate you on having conquered the terrors of death, as you now talk unconcernedly about it. I suppose you will have no fear whatever when in a boat with me. As to myself, *God knows*, but I do not in the least apprehend that I am near my grave. Believe me, Eliza, grief killeth not so suddenly. It may be a gradual destroyer, but, except on very passionate people, I never heard of its causing immediate death. Now you have no passion, you say; you

---

36   Alexander Pope, *Essay on Man*, i, line 292, 'one truth is clear, "Whatever is is right"'.

have it not in the least degree.[37] In my present disorder, if any one will now allow me one, the effects of outward objects on the mind are the sole present causes of it.

I have sufficient reason to be sad, to be dejected. I could tell you such tales if I were with you as would require a more than common degree of credulity to believe. Our family, which was once the object of emulation and envy on account of the extraordinary harmony which existed between every one of the numerous branches of which it consisted, now bids fair to exhibit such a scene of discord as perhaps never was equalled.[38] This breach has been long gathering and has within these few years made several appearances in the most extended branches. It only affects me so far as it destroys the peace of those who are particularly dear to me. And, as I shall never forget the Fable of the Dying Fathers, I think it may and must be detrimental not only to theirs but even to my own temporal concerns.[39] While we stood connected as a body no small loss, nay a large one, could have little effect upon us; and if one rose we all rose together, which ought to be the greatest politick maxim of every family. Their interests ought to be so interwoven that one, if equally industrious and deserving, could not grow rich without the other; and consequently, when any misfortune happened, it ought to be equally borne. This was the case, but soon will be no more so. It was this caused them to stand firm amongst every shock and raised them to the wonder and the envy of every mean-spirited mind, who will now delight and exult at their disorder.

Yesterday I understood that Mr Barnes was seeking me on 'Change. Quite ashamed that he should give himself so much trouble to no purpose, I last night walked up to his house in Westminster,

---

37   Eliza's earliest letter, in which she made this claim, does not survive.

38   What this amounted to is unclear. There is no other sign of family disunity over business in the letters.

39   Aesop's *Fable of the Dying Father*: 'An old man on the point of death summoned his sons around him to give them some parting advice. He ordered his servants to bring in a faggot of sticks, and said to his eldest son, "Break it". The son strained and strained, but with all his efforts was unable to break the bundle. The other sons also tried, but none of them was successful. "Untie the faggots", said the father, "and each of you take a stick." When they had done so, he called out to them, "Now, break them", and each stick was easily broken'.

but had the misfortune not to find him at home.[40] So that it seems as tho' we are not to see one another. As to his not answering my note, Mrs Collier writing was quite sufficient. I expect she and your sister Mary will come and spend a day with my sister very soon, and then I'll see whether they are really Methodists by offering to attend them to the play. To that entertainment people of that persuasion never go. They may have imbibed stronger potations, and may write wonderful things, and yet may not be so bad as you expect. Pray be no longer under any dreadfull apprehension on my account. You have no reason, for there is more danger of my going mad than dying. My best respects to Mr and Mrs Eltoft and family, and believe that I sincerely subscribe myself affectionately yours, E.C. Hurry.

P.S. By directing to No. 28 Prescott Street, Goodmans Fields, I shall get your letter four hours sooner, as I never go to Batson's till three in the afternoon. I shall send *The Shipwreck* and one for you; also something to cover your black leather cap by the stage coach or mail.

Cover, Miss Liddell at Mr Eltoft, Chester. Postmark, 11 January 1788.

---

40 Spelt Wesminster in the original. 'Change was the Royal Exchange.

Letter 30

Edmund Cobb Hurry to Eliza Liddell
London

Written 13 January 1788; sent from London, 13 January;
received in Chester, January

London, 13 January 1788

Dear Eliza, I this day dined with your cousin Barnes, my sister being in the country and I quite alone. I thought I could not employ my evening better than by scribbling a few lines to you, and I was very sure I could not do anything more agreeable to myself except transporting myself into your company, but I fear that will be some time yet. They press me much to go down to Yarmouth; but I am certain I shall not before I visit Chester, unless any particular accident should happen, which God forbid.

I sent two *Shipwrecks* to my hatter yesterday, who is to press them up in a wooden box and to direct them by the Chester stage to you at Mr Eltoft's. It is also to contain something to cover that black cap which you had in Ireland and which may not appear so decent in Chester. He promised me he would fit your head exactly; and, if he does not, you have only to send it him back again.

A gentleman of my acquaintance, hearing I was alone, just called in to spend the evening with me, and so prevented me from proceeding any further. I could have dispensed with his company, as I should think myself happy in doing with all the inhabitants of this great place to be enabled to enjoy yours. But perhaps that's only because I know I cannot. For we are generally most desirous of possessing things beyond our reach, which we afterwards grow tired of and use as a child does its plaything. Now do not imagine that I should use you so, tho' you know I never pretend to answer for any action of mine. You have acted a very impolitick, nay a very imprudent part, in not listening to the attentions of that great gentleman in Dublin.[41] As to his having a wife was a mighty ridiculous reason: for I doubt not, if you had given him any encouragement, he would have found means to have been rid of her. And I am much mistaken if you would not have been greatly in favour with your Cousin Barnes, I mean Mrs Barnes.

I was very handsomely treated by them both and Mr Eltoft dined with us. I think their house very pleasantly situated indeed. As they are in the neighbourhood of such great folks, it's very excusable that Mrs Barnes should talk so much about them and appear to be so much acquainted with them. I think she is rather an agreeable woman in company, but if I am not mistaken she is not easily pacified when in a passion. Mum. You desired I would tell you truly what I thought of Mr Barnes. I have given you a long account of your she cousin; therefore say it's not so easy to give one's opinion of a man as of a woman, and at present I really cannot tell you what I think of him.

Your sisters are both very naughty girls, as they promised before this to write me when they would come and stay a day or two here, and I have not heard from them since I was there, tho' I wrote to inform them of your arrival the moment I got your letters. I shall perhaps write again to them today. Mary sent by me a very handsome hussif of her own making to my sister Tolmé.[42] I suppose I shall be favoured with a sight of your handwriting by this day's post. At least I shall expect it, as I have now written several since I heard from you. I shall be very angry if you be not wonderfully delighted with *The Shipwreck*. There are some very interesting and very moving parts in it to those that understand much less of the sea than you do. I do not expect to be able to leave London sooner than this day fortnight. May God bless you and preserve you in health and spirits is the sincere wish of him who is truly affectionately yours, Edmund Hurry.

Cover, Miss Liddell, Mrs Eltoft, Chester. Postmark, 17 January 1788.

---

41   For Sir Jerome Fitzpatrick, see Eliza to Edmund, Letter 23.

42   A hussif, or housewife, was a sewing kit. Mary Tolmé lived at 21 Great Prescott Street, Goodmans Fields, near Aldgate.

Letter 31

Edmund Cobb Hurry to Eliza Liddell
London

Written 25 January 1788; sent from London, 25 January;
received in Chester, January

London, 25 January 1788

My Dear Eliza, Why should you afflict yourself or be in the least uneasy when I informed you I should be satisfied you never meant to deceive me if your conscience acquitted you of any such intention?[43] For if we believe what we relate, tho' it is found afterwards to be quite untrue, yet is it no crime in us, but only a great foible. For in cases of this kind, we ought to say only what we are certain is true beyond a possibility of dispute. I believe I sent my last away in a very confused manner, and perhaps without a date, so I took care to date this before I began. I believe I informed you in my last that your sisters had written to me and that I was that day agoing to pay that visit, had I not been so unluckily prevented by my uncle, who came even before we had risen and staid that evening till 10 'clock.

The next day, which was yesterday, I had business in the afternoon and my sister Morgan was coming to town with her children, but I was determined on going.[44] Therefore [I] set off early in the morning on horseback and spent five hours very agreeably at Putney, where I also dined with your two sisters.[45] And they communicated the contents of their letter which I did not altogether approve, first in regard to the length of time they allow you to be in Chester and next that I am to be debarred of the pleasure of escorting you here. These were proposals I could not agree to. And I will now make you mine: that, on condition you determine to leave Chester the second, or at

---

43   Perhaps a reference to Eliza's admission of friendship but not love on Inishcoo. See Eliza to Edmund, Letter 1; and Edmund to Eliza, Letter 2.

44   The Morgans had two children, Sarah and George, at this time. They eventually had seven.

45   Mary Lawrence and Barbara Collier.

Eastgate Row, Chester, 1817, by George Pickering

longest the third, day of February, I will promise to be there on or about 31 January; and on no other conditions whatever.

At the same time, you are to promise not to be surprized or displeased at my spending ten days at Yarmouth. I must own it will appear a little particular to those who know not the cause that I should fetch you to London and then go and leave you. I must own it would be very pleasing to me if you could by any means make it advantageous to your sister Bab as well as yourself to join her in her business, as at present things appear darker to me than they have for some time. Murray has proved a rogue and I am afraid Corbet is not much better.[46] I have written them both two such letters that, if they have either shame or honour left (for honesty they certainly have none), they must do me justice.

I beg you not make so free as to show my letters to Miss Eltoft. They are not fit for the inspection of anyone not very deeply interested in them. They will give her no very favorable idea of me. For my own

---

46   Murray, unidentified.

father says in letters to my sister that Edmund's letters are not such as they used to be. 'I fear his intellects are a little disordered. I wish it was in [my] power to give him an independent fortune, as you think it the only thing could make him happy.' Little do they know from whence my uneasinesses proceed. It may be one source, but I have others which I have brought upon myself. And yet I cannot say I wish for an independent fortune. I only wish to be so settled as to be able by my own industry to earn a little more than I have occasion to spend. And now, according to their thoughts, you have been all along corresponding with a Bedlamite. Pray do your sisters think the same? In some respects I have acted very inconsistently towards them.

I have now recollected to beg you'll return my love to Miss Eltoft and tell her I am much obliged to her for the very great care she takes of you. But in regard to parting with you, I understand it will only be for a few weeks, as she is coming to London.

My best respects to Mr and Mrs Eltoft and believe me to remain sincerely and affectionately your E.C. Hurry.

Cover, Miss Liddell, Mr Eltoft, Chester. Postmark, January 1788.

Letter 32

Eliza Liddell to Edmund Cobb Hurry
Chester

Written 27 January; sent from Chester, 29 January;
received in London, January

Chester, Sunday evening, 27 January

Have you again seen my sisters? Have they informed you that I did not consent to their proposal? Let Barbara, if she has no other objection, shew you the letter I sent her. If she does, or tells you what I said, this will be unnecessary. You will find from that that I wished you to come here. I will return with you as soon as you please and should be unreasonable indeed, though I may wish it could be avoided, if I was to be dissatisfied at your going immediately to Yarmouth when real business takes you there.

I am sorry you have such a bad opinion of Corbet. I received a long letter from him yesterday in which he mentions having written both to you and your uncle, and I do hope in such a satisfactory manner as to oblige you to retract your opinion of him. His letter to me – but you shall see it; for I shall expect you, I think you say, the last day of this month.[47]

How could you be apprehensive I would shew your letters to Miss Eltoft, though I don't? But you deserve it for exposing mine to your relations. My sisters do not, I imagine, think your intellect in the least deranged, whatever other people may do; and I dare say like you so well as to be desirous to make a convert of you. But seriously do you find them far gone in their new doctrine? I hope not. I can scarcely see to write and the post office must receive this tonight or you will not get it before you leave London – that is if you come.

We have company to tea. I must attend. I have been twice round the walls and am somewhat fatigued. Pray have you ever been in

---

47   Edmund's uncle Samuel Hurry.

Chester? It is a strange built town, but the above-mentioned wall would, only too much crowded with company for me, be delightful.[48] There are some beautiful, romantic views from it.

This family request their best remembrance. Pray present mine to your sister, yours sincerely, Eliza Liddell.

'Thanks', you will say when you open this. For once she has not teased me with a long letter.

Cover, Mr Edmund Cobb Hurry, No. 21 Prescott Street, Goodmans Fields, London. Postmark, Chester, 29 January.

---

48   Chester's walls, measuring two miles and dating in outline from Roman times, were completed in stone in the twelfth century.

Letter 33

Edmund Cobb Hurry to Eliza Liddell
London

Written 23 January 1788; sent from London, 23 January;
received in Chester, January

Eliza, my dear Eliza, did I call you Belle, strange if I did, for I recollect not having done so since I was at sea.[49] However, I shall not do it for the future as you desire it not and have no title to the appellation. Your sisters are very eager for your coming to London. To say I were likewise so is needless, but not to Barnes's. That they cannot admit of, nor should I like you should either come there or to them without Barbara has so much employment as to be enabled to leave you no leisure, not as she expressed herself: if you were in the way she would set you to work. That I am persuaded neither you nor I should like.

I remember you mentioned in one of yours you expected to have been mistress of a considerable sum which you meant to have conveyed to your sister, but that you were disappointed of it.[50] Now surely you do not want any such sum or any other sum I have in my power. If you do, and I should by any means find it out, and you do not apply to me: remember, I write you no more. I think you need not scruple receiving anything from me, as I never wish anyone should know it but our two selves. On my part depend on it none shall; and, if you discover it, it's your fault. There is not a creature knows about the hat, for the maker knows me only by name, so you can do as you please with it.[51] It is I that run the hazard of being laught at and not you, for a cousin of mine is joked with to this hour on account of a lady giving him the fling after having received numbers of presents. You'll say what sort of a lady? A clergyman's daughter of this place. It's not much to her credit.

---

49   See Edmund to Eliza, Letter 5, p. 48.

50   The potential source of this money is unknown.

51   Eliza's rejection of the hat is in a letter which does not survive.

Your sisters will never go to a play again. Now I concluded this to proceed from Mrs Collier's present situation and pressed no farther, but at Barnes they again declared they had done with plays. I was dragged there last night, for I went much against my inclination merely to oblige my sister. We were to have seen Mrs Siddons in *Cordelia*.[52] This I should have had no great objection to; but, when we came, there no part of the house could be entered. So we hacked off for Covent Garden, where they were almost as full, and we came away by the time it was half done. I was much more entertained with my ride there and back again than with anything I met at the theatre.

I am going to visit your sisters and should have done so today but was prevented, for my uncle is come to sit with me so that I can hardly steal time to write this. He came and catched me in bed this morning and has been with me ever since. Beg to be suitably remembered to the familly you live with and believe me yours affectionately, E.C. Hurry.

Cover, Miss Liddell at Mr Eltoft, Chester. Postmark, 23 January 1788.

---

52   Probably with Mary Tolmé rather than Ann Morgan. Sarah Siddons (1755-1831) played Cordelia in *King Lear* opposite her brother, John Philip Kemble, as Lear, in 1788.

Letter 34

Edmund Cobb Hurry to Eliza Liddell
London

Written January 1788; sent from London, January;
received in Chester, January

Oh Eliza, and so you have learned to swear since you have been in Chester: a very pretty accomplishment indeed.[53] I can make no other excuse for you but that you have not yet been settled enough to go to church, and that you quite forgot the third commandment in Ireland. I should not have wondered much if you had acquired it there, but you really outdo Mr Corbet in your last letter.[54] And I must own I would rather have my head broken with a bottle or level than to hear 'Damn me'. My dear, what did you do that for? It's shocking in a man, it's disgusting in a woman to the highest degree. But you take the Lord's name in vain and, as I never knew you did it before, I thought it might be some new acquired talent of which, least it should increase, I thought proper to warn you – and to assure you then any aspersion you please to make to me will be full as strong, and as firmly believed, without an oath being added to it.

I should have sent this letter on Wednesday night, but your sisters have been here ever since. I could not well find an opportunity and I find by yours of yesterday it is of no consequence. For you do not intend to write me any more till I come to see you. And you do not care whether I come or not, but you wish me to go to Yarmouth and stay with my friends. For you think I make too great a favour of it. These are likewise I suppose some new actions you have picked up in Cheshire; but, if you really rather wish me to go home, it's out of my power now, for I have given my word to your sisters that I would visit Chester as soon as I could possibly leave this. Nay, I promised to take Mary with me; but, whether she goes or no, I am uncertain.

---

53   The swearing must be in a letter which does not survive, but see Eliza to Edmund, Letter 27, p. 182.

54   Swearing. The third commandment, 'Thou shalt not take the name of the Lord thy God in vain'. Robert Corbet presumably swore frequently. In general, swearing was considered an Irish talent or vice.

However, I should not wish to break my word and, for ought you know, I may have business there. Why not as well there as in Dublin?

The hat was improper for you. I am sorry for it, as my sole intention was that of sending you something usefull and showy. I declare I never saw it; and, if you think it too tawdry to wear, you may make a good use of it by giving it to some of your friends. Bab is determined to have you in London and that when I return from the north. Indeed, Mary's sole intention by coming was to fetch you up. I know not how she is situated, but I thought I understood you she had something settled on her. As to Bab, she says she has a very good business that is very profitable and no want of employ: that if you are in her way she shall set you to work.

I must beg you'll make no more secrets between us, nor ever pretend to sincerity where you are not in the strictest sense of the word so. Does your conscience never accuse you of having told me a falsehood when in Ireland?[55] And tho' I would hope you might not have known it at the time, yet as it must be discovered by those who may not think so partially as I do. It may cause them to suspect you very unjustly. Now if you cannot recollect the circumstance I allude to, perhaps you will never know it, for you then cannot have been conscious of uttering a falsehood if it does not immediately strike you. And if it does I am persuaded you will acknowledge it.

You have a monstrous good 'come off' at the end of your letter, and I think it will generally suit me to make use of it: i.e. to say I do not know what I have been writing. And then you know no part of the letter can possibly offend you. For in general you take things I write in so different a light from what I meant them that I often think I must make use of very improper words to convey my ideas. I assure you my sister and I were quite delighted with Bab and Mary, and I was very loth to part with them. But they could not make it convenient to stay longer, so we yesterday waited upon Miss Eltoft (I should rather have said Mrs Barnes), and staid two hours before they came home, they having been to see the Levee at St James. Being the Queen's birthday, they complained of being nearly lost in

---

55 Although the nature of this falsehood is unknown, Edmund may be referring to Eliza's denial that she loved him while they were together on Inishcoo.

the mob.[56] We then dined and drank tea there, and your sisters set off in the evening stage towards Putney.

Is there any thing else would be more usefull to you? If there is I should have a great pleasure in procuring it for you. Have you sent Mrs Corbet her book, or is it troublesome to you. If so, leave it till I come. Certainly he was not in your debt; if he was, and could not pay you, why should you keep it from me? Yours ever truly and affectionately, E.C. Hurry.

Cover, Miss Liddell, at Mr Eltoft, Chester. Postmark, January 1788.

---

56   Queen Charlotte (1744-1818), wife of George III. Oddly, her birthday was on 19 May.

London

we to were uninterruptedly to possess the enjoyment of
so much happiness as we did for a few days past
it would be so much above the scale of what we as
human beings might seem entitled to, as to render
us unfit to bear in a proper manner every calamity
which we might rationally suppose to be the attendant consequence of such a scene of felicity; but away with
distressing ideas my Eliza loves me, and I'll now
and by what means I arrived at my destined
Port in less than twenty four hours, as I had proposed
to spend this night with my aunt in Norwich
You will know I left the Bull Inn at 9 OClock, and had
only one Gent with me the whole way to Norwich, he
disturbed me at 10 OClock to take part of a Pigs foot
with him and as he was a very agreeable
man I joined him contrary to my usual custom
and ate a very hearty supper; but why should I
write abt such nonsense as eating and drinking
and tho I had determined to enter very minutely
into the merits of my Journey, I find it so
ridiculous that I can only tell you I got into Nor
it near half an hour before the Mail and
that means when it arrived was enabled to
come with it directly to Yarmouth. When I arri
d at four this afternoon

Edmund Cobb Hurry to Eliza Liddell, Letter 51 (below, p. 262), August 1788

5

London

After Eliza returned with Edmund to London in the first week of February, only two of her letters survive from 1788: one from February and one from August. In contrast, fourteen of Edmund's letters survive. Inevitably, the romance is now seen mainly through his eyes, as are the couple's plans for the future. He mentions the receipt of her letters to him, but the contents of her letters to him can only be inferred from his replies to them.

With Eliza living either with Edmund's sister, Mary, near Aldgate, or with her own sister Barbara in Putney, the couple saw each other frequently during February and March; but, on 26 March, Edmund sailed from Gravesend to the Baltic. There he spent the next four months, mainly at Derwinda and Libaw, returning to Great Yarmouth in early August. His letters express his grief at their not being together, but neither he nor Eliza was any longer in doubt about their mutual love. They looked forward in confidence to their future together.

Nevertheless, the departure of the *Fly* from Gravesend, on the Thames, was a great wrench to both of them, as Edmund wrote on the night before he sailed:

> if I am not writing to you, I am crying like a woman. I have been walking and crying this hour and, if you were here, it would be just as I told you. You would certainly go with me, for I could not part with you. I know you must feel as badly, if not worse, than myself; and I am sure I think no earthly thing shall ever part us again.[1]

---

1   Edmund Cobb Hurry to Eliza Liddell, Letter 37, p. 218.

At least he was only sailing to the Baltic, from which England could be reached within weeks; or even, with a favourable wind, within days. Edmund could therefore feel for a man bound for a far-distant land:

I have now joined company with an entire stranger to get a dish of tea with him, and I believe both he and I are now busily employed in the same manner. But he is parting for the Indies from whence he may not return for years, I only for a few months. If he feels as much as I do, how much more miserable is his situation than mine; and to suffer what I now endure I would not wish my greatest enemy to be tormented with. I am wretched and shall ever be so till I can again see my dearest girl; till I can see her to part no more till death.[2]

After working his way up the coast of East Anglia, before crossing the North Sea, Edmund was able to get on shore for a night at Great Yarmouth, where, as usual, he stayed at his grandparents' house:

The whole of yesterday and night were spent in Yarmouth. Chief of the evening was so employed in converse with my honoured grandparents on a theme most dear to me. You were the little heroine of my tale, and our future projects and prospects the chief subject: and whenever that happens it raises my spirits wonderfully, and I should never be tired were I not afraid of being tiresome to my hearers.[3]

Then, on 5 April, he was able to send a letter to Eliza from Elsinore, describing the 'mountains' of ice the ship had encountered when rounding the Skaw, the most northerly point of Denmark. In the Baltic the *Fly* also met ice, in the form of icebergs: 'we have again been retarded by large quantities of ice which has only now left the shores to seek its fortune on the waves, bad luck to it'. The *Fly* reached Libaw at 6 a.m. on 9 April.

Although Edmund's letters to Eliza from Courland are mostly about his feelings for her and his hopes for their joint future, they inevitably dwell on the problems of receiving and sending letters:

---

2   Edmund to Eliza, Letter 37, p. 219

3   Edmund to Eliza, Letter 38, p. 223.

And now I am only agoing to tell you that tomorrow morning I shall go with a very grave face to the postmaster and tell him that Eliza has sent me a long letter which must be in the Windaw bag. I shall therefore pray him to open it and, if he will not, I shall be fit to kill him.[4]

While 'to give you any account of the customs and manner of living of the people of this country, to one who is so great a lover of decency as yourself, must be disgusting indeed', the letters provide a few sidelights on Courland:

I was going on with some observations about creatures to whose society I was in the present confined, when I was called off by one of them leaping down who had some plank to dispose of. For in that respect they are quite sans ceremony, tho' in others they pay a most scrupulous attention to what we should look upon as the most childish trifles. For instance, to ask leave to mention any wearing apparel which is next to the skin. And numbers of such like ceremonies can in no wise be disposed with without being looked upon as a savage.[5]

Mostly, Edmund kept himself to himself, even in the house where he lodged at Windaw, which had its drawbacks:

For few will be either my occupations or amusements till they [Eliza's letters] arrive. For the present writing and reading are the only ones I can have recourse to, to pass the tedious hours and days, for I am full as much alone in this place as tho' I were shut up in a ship's cabin. To be sure I have only to go to the other end of the house and I may be amused by Mrs Blaesen's oratory. I believe no woman ever exceeded her and I am able to believe, with a certain Irishman, that her tongue is very glad when she is asleep. However, as she was brought up by a clergyman, she has read a great deal and is sometimes very entertaining. When she is otherwise I return to my books.[6]

---

4   Edmund to Eliza, Letter 40, p. 230.

5   Edmund to Eliza, Letter 40, p. 230.

6   Edmund to Eliza, Letter 42, pp. 244-45. Windaw, Windau or Derwinda in Latvia.

It is a pity that he did not send more of a description of his overland journey, accompanied by a Libaw merchant, Mr Hartwick, to Memel and Königsberg, aimed at making business contacts for the future. He clearly shared the common English suspicion of Prussian militarism when seeing troops exercising, but knew that this was of little interest to Eliza: 'I know you do not care a fig for the king of Prussia and so I will tell you no more about this demi-metropolis'.[7]

Their enforced separation did allow reflection on another subject of great interest to the men and women of the eighteenth century: religion. A christening in Windaw, which Edmund attended so as not to give social offence, brought out his disbelief in infant baptism, a strong indicator of his Unitarian views:

> Here I am called to attend at a christening. To refuse would be the greatest affront I could possibly be guilty of to the person who invites, and to go will be an affront to myself; but in matters of no convenience I will rather affront myself than other persons, tho' perhaps it may be the last time I shall ever see them. But were I such a railer as yourself I would say no, I cannot go; my religion will not allow me. And to give up one's religion rather than disoblige a person one cares not a fig for will seem to you the greatest wickedness as well as the greatest absurdity.
>
> Well I am now returned, and have *not* been renouncing the Devil and all his works, besides promising a great many more odd things for an infant of about five days old.[8] I cannot say but I pitied the poor thing to see it brought near half a mile into an old church, its limbs bound together like a bundle of tape, without power to move any joint or hardly any feature, and could not help looking upon it as next to a miracle if it should ever come to maturity ... to me the whole appears to be rather a mockery than what is really and spiritually meant by the office of baptism.[9]

---

7   Edmund to Eliza, Letter 42, p. 244.

8   The word 'not', expressing his disapproval, has been added above the line.

9   Edmund to Eliza, Letter 44, p. 251.

His attitude in general, however, was very much of the tolerance of the eighteenth century, inspired by the Enlightenment, rather than of the nineteenth, with its agonising over small theological points:

If they find it right, it would be foolish in me to tell them they are wrong. For if it is really so, i.e. that they think it from a full conviction, they are certainly right. And so I trust we shall all find that we have acted consistently, with what we from a mature consideration think and believe to be right, however differently each may think and act. The true Papists, Methodists, etc, etc, will all fare alike. For it cannot be necessary, nor is it possible: what idea must they have of their Creator who can think that one particular sect is more worthy or better entitled to eternal happiness than the millions who differ from them.[10]

Eliza shared his dislike of emotional religion, distrusting the enthusiasm shown by her sisters in their adherence to Methodism, though she was perhaps more formal than Edmund in her adherence to her religion.

At last, on 13 July, Edmund was able to leave Courland not in the *Fly* but in another of the Hurrys' ships, the *Elizabeth*, reflecting on his departure from somewhere where he had spent much of the previous five years:

It is a disagreeable situation to be in: to have to take leave of such a number of persons with whom I have lived so long, without even a prospect or chance of seeing them again. I might have added without a desire, for I flatter myself I never have been so guilty as to make them think I should part with any degree of regret. For tho' with you I should have been well satisfied to have spent that part of my life here in peace, in quiet, as we might have done, yet I would not spend another five years here, in the manner the last five have been spent, to gain thousands.[11]

After passing Elsinore on 23 July, Edmund landed at Great Yarmouth on 7 August and soon afterwards was in London, before returning to Yarmouth on the twelfth. The reunion with Eliza put an end to months of

---

10   Edmund to Eliza, Letter 44, p. 252.

11   Edmund to Eliza, Letter 44, p. 254.

separation and longing. As he wrote to her from Yarmouth on his return from London:

> I have often reflected that were we uninterruptedly to possess for a great length of time the enjoyment of so much happiness as we did for a few days past, it would be so much above the scale of which we as human beings might seem entitled to, as to render us unfit to bear in a proper manner any calamity which we might rationally suppose to be the attendant consequence of such a scene of felicity.[12]

All that remained to be finalised were their domestic arrangements, including their washing, and the exact date on which Edmund could return to London. This future included a decision to live at the house of Edmund's stepbrother, George Coldham, after their marriage, and the question of a servant.

A final delay inevitably made him impatient:

> That I am detained thus long here is to me most uncomfortable. I have not a moment's peace. I scarce ever know what I am doing, ever wishing to be with you, tho' conscious of the impropriety of it, till another ship is sent off to Windaw. Yet if possible on Monday or Tuesday you shall see me, and I think nothing shall prevent me.[13]

---

12   Edmund to Eliza, Letter 48, p. 262.

13   Edmund to Eliza, Letter 50, p. 269.

Letter 35

Edmund Cobb Hurry to Eliza Liddell
Great Yarmouth

*Written 15-16 February 1788; sent from Great Yarmouth, 16 February;
received in London, February*

Friday, 15 February 1788

My Dear Eliza, And so you thought I might be induced to show your secret, that you wrote such a fine postscript to it.[14] But pray, what right had you to think so? Did I ever show a letter of yours to anyone? No, never. That I once read a few passages to my grandparents is true. And ought I not to have done the same by this? Or at least I certainly must inform them all you say concerning my sister, for she has also friends in the world who would rejoice at her recovery or be more distressed at any ill accident that may befall her.[15] I too am amongst those who sincerely rejoice that she is better, and I hope, guided by your prudence and the authority of my uncle, she may be induced to remain so long within doors as to effect a perfect reinstatement of her health. If not, add the earnest desire and intreaty of a brother.

You too are ill, but, if it proceeds from those vile things which laid before the fire when I left you, I cannot much pity you.[16] But if it is from the irregular mode of life which I induced you to lead, I am extremely sorry for it. And for cure, know that on Sunday 19th I propose being with you to return to that same vicious course, which I believe we should continue in if left to ourselves, till we were no longer able to stir. But we must use resolution, and as it is so much easier to preach than to practise, suppose I go on for half hour on the subject, and then, the moment I am with you, act quite contrary to all I might have been writing.

---

14   Eliza's letter containing this postscript does not survive. About showing letters, see Eliza to Edmund, Letter 32, p. 197.

15   Mary Tolmé.

16   The nature of these vile things is uncertain.

I am sorry Mary cannot make London comfortable to herself. I am sure she is [of] an excellent disposition and must have a degree of charity scarce credible to talk as she did to me concerning Collier. I have a better opinion of the religion she professes than ever I had in my life, but I was always convinced that it is in general owing to the bad characters who pretend to profess any religion that makes us disgusted with any particular sect, and not from any material difference in their creeds on essentials. For where the heart is right it is of little consequence whether we are Jews, Pagans or Christians.

It gives me no little pleasure to hear my uncle finds himself so comfortable situated and, by the length of his absence from his son, I should think he was more than usually so. You will, I doubt not, contribute all in your power to further the continuance of his satisfaction, and I know my sister looks up to him as a second father, and I have every reason in the world to do the same. To tell you how earnestly I desire to see you again, or with what eagerness I look towards Monday as the day of leaving this, were out of my power.[17] And yet I must own to you there is a something which damps even the extreme pleasure I feel at this prospect, and that is the sorrow it gives some here to part with me, tho' they seem to join me in joys. When Eliza's in the case, all other things must give place.[18] And they ever shall do so, but when her way makes it necessary it should be otherwise.

Will you tell Mary her father dispatched a fine large cod by yesterday's coach. And indeed I hope when you receive this it will be nearby making its appearance; one also was sent Mrs Morgan. You will not be able to answer this as I should not get it; nor shall I be able to write again, as tomorrow we have no post.

Take care of yourself and my sister, and believe me sincerely and affectionately yours, Edmund Cobb Hurry.

Cover, Miss E. Liddell, at Mrs Tolmé, No. 21 Great Prescott Street, Goodmans Fields, London. Postmark, 16 February 1788.

---

17 Monday, 18 February 1788.

18 John Gay, *Fables* (1727), 45, 'For when a lady's in the case, you know all other things give place'.

Letter 36

Eliza Liddell to Edmund Cobb Hurry
London

Written 16 February 1788; sent from London, 16 February;
received in Great Yarmouth, February

Saturday, 16 February

You desire me to write again, but your sister says you are mistaken respecting the post and that you will certainly get this on Sunday evening.[19] So I cannot neglect my opportunity of telling you how rejoiced I am that you are soon to return. Selfish Eliza! For I find it impossible to lessen my impatience to see you by a consideration that your leaving Yarmouth is a source of regret to others.

Your uncle told us last night you were to return on Wednesday. Though I did not say anything, I was very much obliged to him for the news. He went out after tea to Mr Morgan's and I rallied to bed, for I was really very ill all day with a severe cold, but a comfortable potion of wine, whey and ten hours sleep has entirely banished it.[20] And I am today quite well.

Mr Hurry is very well. His son is better and, as to your sister, I think I may pronounce her perfectly recovered, so much so that she got up to breakfast this morning, which not a little pleased your uncle. Indeed her early rising was owing to a gentle lecture he gave her yesterday, and she was half afraid of disobliging him; so actually got up this morn, more than half asleep.

He seems quite pleased with his situation and I sincerely wish it was in my power to contribute to his satisfaction in any respect. For, besides the natural desire one must entertain to do everything to oblige and serve people advanced in years, he is your relation, and can I see a relation of yours without every inclination to administer

---

19   Evidence of the speed of the post between London and Great Yarmouth even on a Sunday.

20   Both Edmund and Eliza teased each other about the consumption of alcohol. See, for instance, Letter 48, p. 263.

to their happiness, though it may never be in my power to testify it to them [or] to you.

Your fish arrived safe last night; and Mrs Tolmé was doubtful till your letter came whether it was sent by you or your father.[21] So tomorrow she is to have Mr and Mrs Morgan to partake of it. And, as she is not to be quite alone, I wanted to go to Putney for the day, but am not permitted unless I will promise to return in the evening. That I cannot do, for I should be afraid to be parading the streets late by myself, though in a coach. Nor do I think I ought till my cold is quite well. I find my head affected by writing so shall conclude when I have told you my sisters are well and desire their best remembrances to you. Adieu till Tuesday.[22] May you arrive in health and safety to her who must ever remain yours most truly, Eliza Liddell.

Cover, Mr Edmund Cobb Hurry, Yarmouth, Norfolk. Postmark, unclear.

North-west view of the quay of Great Yarmouth, 1790, by James Butcher

---

21 Gifts of fish and game were often sent down by William Hurry from Great Yarmouth. A turbot was sent down by William Hurry's wife, Dorothy, to celebrate Edmund and Eliza's wedding on 20 August 1788.

22 Tuesday 19 February 1788.

Letter 37

Edmund Cobb Hurry to Eliza Liddell
Great Yarmouth

Written 24-27 March; sent from Great Yarmouth, 27 March;
received in London, March

Gravesend, 24 March at 2 o'clock afternoon

I hope, long ere this, my dearest Eliza has been refreshed by a few hours comfortable sleep by which she may be enabled the better to support her waking thoughts, which I know from sad experience are hard for her to bear.[23] I have used my utmost diligence to appear a little cheerful, thinking it a duty I owe my friends who so kindly accompanied me hither, but I might as well attempt to fly cross the seas. And I would not again suffer the pains of the past morning to gain thousands. Indeed I never knew what it was to part before and, except tears of joy, those I shed this morning are the first which have crossed my cheek these nine years past.

I have ever the disagreeable sensation of parting with any of my friends with whom I had lived a few weeks, but they were the feelings of the moment, or at most of a few days. But nothing can alleviate my present sorrow, for lost pleasure enjoyed in your company, but the delightful and near prospect of a speedy return, which I shall ever hope is not far distant.

We stayed till too late for the stage and, as Mr Cockle agreed to join the party, we took a post chaise and got down here by 10 o'clock, but were disappointed at not finding the ship here.[24] But I hope she will be down in a few hours, for rest to me is misery when absent from you. O, how gladly would I have had you with me, but the parting here would have been still more dreadfull! And I thought, if the ship was here, it would have been hurry and confusion.

You will have a great advantage over me in one respect, as you

---

23   The first letter after six weeks together.

24   Mr Cockle, unidentfied.

will be enabled to talk about me, which is one of the greatest reliefs that I know of in these cases, at least to me. I am sure it would be so, but what am I to employ my tongue about? I might as well have my mouth sewed up, for to speak of you is a theme I shall not once dare to touch on. To whom should I open my heart? There are none can sympathise with me. They feel it not. They would only stare, wonder what I meant and perhaps pity me as one beside himself; so I must smother my feelings, appear at least merry and sometimes laugh when it would be easier and more suitable to the temper of mind to lock myself up in a dark room and cry most terribly. I shall expect to hear from you at Windaw. It is the only thing can give me any hours of peace; and should Captain Ward of the *John and Mary* sail, in about ten days or a fortnight, for Riga, a letter by her may reach me some time before the post, should she have a speedy passage.[25]

I forgot to give 1s. 6d. to Mr Spurling's man for sharping my razors.[26] This you will either pay or desire my sister to do so. I have just been called off to line, and we have got to a place where we are as ill-treated as you and I used to be on the road from Chester. The man just now brought us a bottle of port with an epithet of its being 'the best wine in England', but it is mere hogwash.

I am raving, I am mad. They are gone to London and I would not send this away till the post went at night. From them you will hear that the ship is not yet down, and here am I left to my own thoughts. I never wished so much in my life to get rid of them and, if I am not writing to you, I am crying like a woman. I have been walking and crying this hour and, if you were here, it would be just as I told you. You would certainly go with me, for I could not part with you. I know you must feel as badly, if not worse, than myself; and I am sure I think no earthly thing shall ever part us again. This is the most incoherent stuff that ever was written; but, if I was not to write on, I fear I should lose my reason. I only wish my father could now see my feelings. If that were possible, it would [move] anyone to pity both you and me. I once thought I had a little courage, but I find I

---

25   The *John and Mary*, one of the ships belonging to W. & S. Hurry and Co.

26   Mr Spurling, unidentified.

am a coward indeed. I am truly miserable. Here not a soul that cares for me or my sorrows; not even a room to weep alone in.

I have now joined company with an entire stranger to get a dish of tea with him, and I believe both he and I are now busily employed in the same manner. But he is parting for the Indies from whence he may not return for years, I only for a few months. If he feels as much as I do, how much more miserable is his situation than mine; and to suffer what I now endure I would not wish my greatest enemy to be tormented with. I am wretched and shall ever be so till I can again see my dearest girl; till I can see her to part no more till death. Recommending you to the protection of the highest, I am sincerely and affectionately yours, E.C. Hurry.

Past 8 o'clock the *Fly* is now got down, but they will not clear us to night, so here we must lie off in the morning.[27] Had I known this, I might still have been with you. And it requires me to make use of the greatest quantity of resolution I ever yet wanted to prevent myself from coming back to you; but, if I was, I never could return without you. I hope to be a little more composed tomorrow, for to feel as I do now, if the wind was so that we could not sail tomorrow, I should certainly come up, however imprudent the step. Is it not very hard that I must write this to you and cannot get a line in return? I feel hardships I never felt before, but we must submit and suffer in silence. I hope it will prove finally advantageous to us. At least we shall be able to pity others who may be under like circumstances with ourselves.

Great Yarmouth shipping, 1790, by James Butcher

---

27   Clearing was the process of passing official checks before a ship could sail.

And now let me recommend you to the care of that Being who never errs, praying that he will strengthen us both to suffer and bear whatever his infinite mercy has found to be for the good of that chain of which we are links. Remember me to your sisters, busy yourself with writing what you promised me and writing to me. For by the *John and Mary* you may send what you please, i.e. as many letters in one packet as you can get ready. I shall now go on board and hope fatigue may make me sleep and forget the woes which waking torment me. Believe me ever your most affectionate E.C. Hurry.

A brig at Great Yarmouth, 1790,
by James Butcher

P.S. Just now sailed out.

At sea. 9 o'clock, Tuesday night, 25 March 1788

I could not go to bed without saying something to my Eliza, tho' it should be ever such nonsense. Yet without communicating my thoughts to you in the best manner that my situation will allow of (would to God I had a better one), I could not have slept a wink, but I have been endeavouring to walk away my thoughts all the day. And, if I may count by time, twenty miles is the least distance which I have perambulated on the *Fly*'s quarter deck.[28] Your dear image was ever present to me, and I was sometimes almost deluded by my imagination to suppose you present, but how bitter the disappointment, how hard to be borne. I find no ease but in flattering myself with prospects of future happiness to be enjoyed in your company. My views are more confined to this world than ever they were; and, tho' not afraid of death, when I contemplate the beauties which I have discovered in your mind, I see reason to be thankfull to my Creator for the preservation of my past life, and earnestly to beg for its continuance on your account as much as on my own. For I hope I shall have the means, and I am sure I shall not want the inclination, to make you as happy as it is possible for a finite being.

I shall endeavour to draw my wants into as small a compass as possible; and, when I am once more in the possession of your society, I am much deceived if I shall wish for any other. I have been writing thus far that, if I should meet a ship bound for England, I may not omit the only opportunity in my power of giving you pleasure, of making you happier; and in so doing I enjoy an inexpressible happiness myself. So that this proceeds from a very selfish motive. It is a happy circumstance for me that you are what you are; misery surest have attended me had you been otherwise. For to have fixed my affection in the manner that mine are on a person who could have misused my fondness, I am so weak that I should in all probability in a few years have made my final appearance on the great stage before Newgate.[29] You see what power I think you have over me. I charge you to use it as you have done hitherto and I shall be happy.

I shall now wish you a good night and, praying that you may have support under every trial and affliction, recommend you to the power who alone is able to defend and preserve us. May it be consistent with his dispensations that we speedily enjoy each other's presence is the sincere prayer of your E.C. Hurry.

We have just now past Orfordness and are got into the open sea.[30] Half past 10 'clock, Tuesday night.

How happy to think that I shall this morning be able to send you

---

28   The *Fly* was a ship of only thirty tons.

29   Public hangings had been moved from Tyburn to outside Newgate Prison in 1783.

30   Orford Ness, south of Aldeburgh in Suffolk.

this from Yarmouth, as we are now going into the Roads, but how patient a joy do I feel to what I should do were I sure to find my Eliza there. This is written at 6 o'clock Wednesday morning and I am not certain whether I shall get on shore myself or not. And, if I do, I may not have time to add anything more, but rest assured that I am and ever shall be yours most affectionately, E.C. Hurry.

I am got on shore at Yarmouth, but only for an hour or two as the wind is fair and I have no time to lose. For now, if it were possible, I wish to be conveyed to Libaw in an instant; or rather, if it were possible, not to go at all.[31] I even deluded myself for a moment in waking up here in supposing it so; but I know it is for both our interests that it should be so, how much we may suffer from it. But let us look forward to a few months, a time which, tho' now it appears so far distant, will when passed surprize us that we should think it so long. I could write to you for ever, nay it is what of all other things I should struggle the hardest for. For, next to being delivered of your company, to be debarred writing to you would be the most dreadfull to your sincerest friend, E.C. Hurry.

P.S. Tell Mary I would have written to her but I had this morning no expectation of seeing Yarmouth. I did not prepare a letter and by this she will learn I am well, that is I am in bodily health, but my mind is sick indeed. My best love to your sisters and to her. Farewell once more, farewell. Adieu.

Past 10 o'clock, Wednesday, 26 March 1788

Cover, Miss Eliza Liddell, at Mr Tolmé, Great Prescott Street, Goodmans Fields, London. Postmark, 27 March 1788.

---

31   Libaw or Libau in Courland, the modern Liepaja in Latvia.

Letter 38

Edmund Cobb Hurry to Eliza Liddell
Elsinore

Written 3-4 April 1788; sent from Elsinore, 5 April;
received in London, April

I yesterday sent you a sheet full from Yarmouth and here am again scribbling to my dearest Eliza. You will have reason to think me distracted, and indeed you must have kept some essential parts of me, for I cannot apply to any one thing whatever, so fully does your image occupy my mind. And as a convincing proof of it, I this day at dinner was so absent as to call the kitten by your name. The poor animal was purring and using all the little artifices in its power to attract my attention, which made me offer it a bit of meat. Finding it did not eat, I exclaimed, 'Here, Eliza, why take it'. Magill stared. Ives did not hear me and I recollected myself.[32] What pleasure would it have given me had Eliza been really present. She should have had the best morsel on my plate.

The whole of yesterday and night were spent in Yarmouth. Chief of the evening was so employed in converse with my honoured grandparents on a theme most dear to me. You were the little heroine of my tale, and our future projects and prospects the chief subject: and whenever that happens it raises my spirits wonderfully, and I should never be tired were I not afraid of being tiresome to my hearers. This and my being much fatigued prevented me from having had another sheet ready, and this morning at five I was obliged to decamp, and am now once more where nought but sea and sky can be seen. And pray where are you? Let me see, past two o'clock. You are sitting by the Putney fire side, and perhaps talking of me; but you are out for once, Miss Prophet, for I have not yet stirred from London.

I find myself a great deal eased by writing the above and I'll try if I cannot write something more necessary, but I find it almost as

---

32   Ralph Magill, a sea captain with a long association with the Hurry family. Ives Hurry was Edmund Cobb Hurry's youngest brother.

hard to leave off writing to you as to part with you. Good afternoon to you, pray take care you do not get a great cold. I have not been able to sit to write with any comfort since I penned the above and now is Tuesday 1 April, such strong gales and such high waves have we been continually entertained with. Add to that the cabin, one continued cloud of sulphurous smoke, and you may easily think that, as I value you so much, I am on your account happy you were not with me; tho', if I search my heart to the bottom, I know not whether I may not justly be compared to the fox, who cried some grapes because he could not get at them.[33] Be that as it may, you must certainly have been very uncomfortable; and, whatever gainer I might be in the case, yet to see you so at any time must be a source of the greatest uneasiness to me; and, notwithstanding all this, I am not sure whether I should not be unhappy if I thought you were quite as comfortable now as you would wish to be.

Whilst writing the above I was called to look at to me unexpected phenomena, the whole surface of the sea, as far as eye can reach, covered with ice. But I should first have told you where we were and have informed you that on Sunday morning we saw Norway. On that coast we were detained by a severe gale till yesterday evening, and this morning we past the Scaw, the north-eastern extremity of Jutland. And, at the distance of about ninety miles from Elsinore, were met by this vast body of ice, so that we have retreated under the Scaw, where we now have it quite calm, and have purchased seventeen large halibuts from the Danish fishermen for four English shillings, and two are to be boiled for supper.[34] I wish I could convey half of them to you; tho' should rather you would come to partake of the mess. For my own part, on any other terms, I would as soon eat dry bread. We are likely to have a calm night, but when [we] shall get to Elsinore I know not. Mountains must first be moved. I mean mountains of ice. I was fairly made an April Fool today, for I expected to have gathered up and dispatched this letter. However, I must leave off or I shall write my sheet full presently. So good night, Mrs Eliza, and mind and be a good girl, and God protect you and preserve you in health and grant us a speedy [reunion].

---

33   Aesop's fable about the fox and the grapes.

34   Skagen, Denmark's most northerly town, was known to English sailors as the Scaw.

Since April Fools' Day have we been cruising along the edges of the ice, and never durst attempt the passage till this day, 4 April, when we found that the mountains were overturned, but tho' much separated required a skillfull attendance to avoid destruction. Thank God we have this day saved the port at Elsinore. We were wafted up last night having escaped every danger, and I have now learnt that we have nothing further to fear with regard to ice, as the Baltic Sea has long been clear. I am happy to think that in ten days' time this will be handed to you, and in a little more than that time I shall be expecting to hear from you. I am sure it will not be your fault if I am disappointed, but must be owing to the eastern gale with which this month is so frequently attended.

I have a great deal more to say to you, but there is always so much gabbling, so much news to be heard, and so many praters, that upon my word it is impossible to write any thing connectedly. Therefore I can only tell you that I shall earnestly expect to hear from you: that you are well, that your sisters are so, and that every thing goes according to your wishes, amongst which I shall place my speedy presence in London, will ever be conducive to the happiness of him who hopes he may in the fullest sense of the word stile himself your sincerest and most affectionate friend, Edmund Cobb Hurry.

Elsinore, 5 April 1788. Wind fair for Libaw.

Cover, Miss Eliza Liddell, at Mr George Coldham, No. 11 Leman Street, Goodmans Fields, London. Postmark, 21 April 1788.

Letter 39

Edmund Cobb Hurry to Eliza Liddell
Libaw

Written 6-10 April 1788; sent from Libaw, 10 April;
received in London, 8 May

East Sea, Sunday, 6 April 1788

This is the fourteenth day since I enjoyed the society of my dearest Eliza. I shall never forget what a night we passed, and what a dismal day the next and each succeeding one has been to me; and may they still continue dismal and joyless till I again see and am seen by you. I yesterday sent you a sheet full from Elsinore, and I trust it is now travelling fast towards you.[35] Would to God I could arrive as soon, but that is impossible, so I must be satisfied with writing and writing on, and perhaps in two or at most three weeks' time I shall hear from you.

Let me see. I will give you till the 21st of this month and then I must have a letter. And I do not think I shall write again before that time after I send this (i.e. by post), as I shall limit both you and myself to one per fortnight, which I shall expect to receive regularly after I get your first. But when you have other opportunity by ships, you know how pleasing it would be to me to be continually hearing from you. Of this you may judge by yourself. And you may depend on it, I shall let no opportunity of the kind pass by without telling you what you must be already well acquainted with: I mean my sincere and unalterable affection for you.

We are now within 230 miles of Libaw; but we have again been retarded by large quantities of ice which has only now left the shores to seek its fortune on the waves, bad luck to it.[36] Two or three weeks ago one might have passed without seeing any. I long to hear where you are. I am tired of prophesying. I want also to know what you are doing. Have you been well employed today? I am tired of asking you

---

35   Edmund to Eliza, Letter 38, pp. 223-25.

36   Icebergs.

questions, for it must at least be six weeks before you can answer them. So, if I have a mind to know (no, not to know but to have an answer), I must make it myself. And I will venture to say you have been doing what you ought to do. And that you will ever use your utmost endeavour to do so.

I left off last night without wishing you a good night, but I trust it was not the worse on that account, and so now good morning to you. I think you would have enjoyed the sea had you been with me. Since I left Elsinore, it has been so smooth and so pleasant, not once rougher than the Thames.[37] Did I not go on deck and look around me, I might fancy I were on shore, so little motion can I perceive whilst in the cabin. Add to that the pleasantest sunshine that you can possibly conceive. To be sure we do feel a little cold, and it freezes pretty severely every night, but I never go abroad in the night, except by way of a walk after supper. How long will it be before I can again walk with you? I hope not very long and that I may be able to guess pretty nearly, when I write again, as I shall then be some judge how long my concerns here are likely to detain me.

By the above you might conceive I was got to Courland, not quite so fast but not far off neither. I will not tell you how far till I go to bed. Yes, we are, as near as I can guess, just a hundred miles, and if we have good luck may get there tomorrow; but, if we do not, I must be satisfied. There is one reason why I wish it much, because it's post day and I want to give you the earliest intelligence of my arrival that is possible, that you may be easy that I am once more on land, and, according to your ideas, somewhat safer; but in this on some accounts I differ from you.

Good night and do not forget to dream of me. I do every night of you, in short sleeping or waking you are scarce ever from my thoughts. And the thought of my being in yours gives me so much pleasure that, were I almost sure it was not so, I should glory in the deception, which is indeed the only pleasure that I can hope to enjoy until we meet again. Some find great pleasure in things which, when thro' the necessity of my situation I am obliged to join in, are quite irksome and disagreeable to me; and tho' by no means an unsociable

---

37 'Ruffer' in the original.

being, yet I long to be by myself again. Since I have left you I have had no company to tire me, for I cannot be said to have any society on board the ship. Indeed, except at meals, I do not know that I have exchanged one word that was not absolutely necessary. I write, read and think of you, and I do not know that I have found one hour hang heavy on my hands. Once more good night or I shall leave no room for tomorrow.

Tuesday, 8 April. This afternoon disappointed [of] getting in by only a few miles, it being dark; so obliged to keep off till morning.

Wednesday, 9 April. This morning before 6 o'clock got safe into Libaw after the pleasantest passage from Elsinore that ever I was making; but now I cannot send this away till Fryday, as here are only two post days in the week.

Fryday, 10 April. This day every thing was discharged from the ship. Have made a sad market of the fruit. I suppose Mr Brander and I shall lose £50 between us.[38] And in another article I have been cheated by those whom I thought would not have found their interest in it, nor can they (even here). It is almost the only thing one can trust in in these times, whether it is a person's interest to cheat or not. I mean worldly interest, for as to other interest they think not of. Dear Eliza, remember me to your sisters and believe me ever yours most affectionately, E.C. Hurry.

Cover, Miss Eliza Liddell, at Mr George Coldham, No. 11 Leman Street, Goodmans Fields, London.

---

38   Mr Brander unidentified.

Letter 40

Edmund Cobb Hurry to Eliza Liddell
Libaw

Written 16-23 April 1788; sent from Windaw, 23 April;
received in London, May

My dearest girl, this is 16 April and I am still in Libaw and likely to be so for some days to come. Last Fryday I sent you a sheet full and the latter part contained some lamentations, but God knows all things will ever cross and go contrary to our reasonable expectations.[39] Yet, whilst I am in possession of your heart, I will not repine. And let the outward appearance of things be ever so gloomy, yet will I not despair or indulge thoughts unreasonable, unjust complaints and murmurs ill with one who has so much of this world's goods in regard to what many others have who appear and I dare say are perfectly content. Contrary I am so or ever shall be whilst absent from you. Yet, as far as lies in my power, I will endeavour to be so and, by looking forward to that time which I trust is not far distant when we shall again meet, endeavour to console myself for what I suffer whilst absent from you.

I could always be writing to you and yet I have nothing to write about. For to tell you what passes here, and what disappointments and crosses I have met with and all in the way of business, cannot be pleasing either to you to hear or for me to relate. And to give you any account of the customs and manner of living of the people of this country, to one who is so great a lover of decency as yourself, must be disgusting indeed. There are no doubt a few amongst the numerous inhabitants of this country who are not only possessed of sensibility on that head but have hearts worthy of cultivating and friendship, but they are so few that it would be next to a miracle for a stranger to meet with them. Nor is it fit we should meet with those whose good qualities we must esteem and whose friendship we must loth to part with. It would make it as easy in every place as at home.

---

39 Edmund to Eliza, Letter 39.

I was going on with some observations about creatures to whose society I was in the present confined, when I was called off by one of them leaping down who had some plank to dispose of. For in that respect they are quite sans ceremony, tho' in others they pay a most scrupulous attention to what we should look upon as the most childish trifles. For instance, to ask leave to mention any wearing apparel which is next to the skin. And numbers of such like ceremonies can in no wise be disposed with without being looked upon as a savage. Whereas to us the most obscene discourse, and to fill the conversation with double entendres when in company with the ladies, is reckoned both polite and witty.

I have not written to you now of some days, having been in the country and this is 20 April. And now I am only agoing to tell you that tomorrow morning I shall go with a very grave face to the postmaster and tell him that Eliza has sent me a long letter which must be in the Windaw bag. I shall therefore pray him to open it; and, if he will not, I shall be fit to kill him. For I know there must be a letter from you, and directed to Windaw, for I think I did not tell you to write here, as I did not expect to stay half so long. O how I long to see the letter. I am so anxious to hear from you. If you sent it ten days after I sailed, I shall get it; and, if I do not, you shall hear of it tomorrow.

How chagrined, how disappointed no letter, and that thro' my own fault. Business prevented me from applying this morning. And, as I know the post had never been in till eight in the afternoon, I contented myself with going after dinner. But you can scarce conceive what I felt when I was told the Windaw post had come in, in the morning, and that the bag was already gone off. I asked the postmaster several times if he was sure it was come in, and I believe he thought me distracted. And so indeed I was for a short time, for I was almost sure I must have had a letter by that post.

We are now clear to leave Libaw and I hope tomorrow morning to make a still farther remove from you, so much do I endeavour to shun your company that I rejoice at the prospect of still increasing distance tomorrow; but because it is the only means by which I can reasonably hope soon to see you. So good night.

Wednesday, 23 April. Yesterday I left Libaw with the ship, as I expected, and this morning came in here, so you may easily guess at what a small distance these two ports are separated. Another bit of news. The post which came on Monday to Libaw comes today here, so the letters are much longer in travelling the distance than I have been, but I must make haste on shore, for I expect to get a letter, aye, a letter from Eliza. Why I would swim thro' the Windaw for it, cold as it is, and we have not done with ice here yet.

Well, I have got a letter, but not by this post. It has been laying here ever since Sunday, but it has put me into such a flurry I know not what to write or do. I have already read it three times over and done a hundred inconsistent things. Well may you say there were two hearts so dear to each other. I only wonder how it was possible to part. I am sure before ever I would suffer it again I would live on bread and water. But we have better prospects, Eliza, and more than I can tell you in this instant. I too will send you letters by the *Fly*, for as much time as I can possibly spare from business shall ever be as far devoted to you, my dearest girl, as lies in the power of him who is truly and sincerely your Edmund Cobb Hurry.

Cover, Miss Eliza Liddell, at Mr George Coldham, No. 12 Leman Street, Goodmans Fields, London. Postmark, unclear.

Letter 41

Edmund Cobb Hurry to Eliza Liddell
Windaw

Written 23 April to 7 May 1788; sent from Windaw, 7 May;
received in London, May

Wednesday, 23 April 1788

Tho' I have but this moment finished a long epistle of different date, yet I cannot sleep without telling my Eliza that I am now again got to my old lodgings at Mr Blaesen, and was he gave me your letter.[40] And I believe he might easily guess what sort of letter it was. It caused such extraordinary behaviour in me that I was several times asked what ailed me without their ever being able to get any answer from me. In short, some times I am about the room and others was quite with you. I thought I saw you sickening on your usual seat. I would have assisted you, but had I been there you would have wanted no assistance. I have an hundred times since I read your letter, nay hundreds of times before, wished we had resolved, in spite of the world and everything else, when last together, to have lived and died together. How often have I imagined to myself what pleasure could I enjoy were Eliza now with me. How many lonesome hours have I spent in the midst of large companies; how often laughed when my heart has been ready to burst.

Here have I again been telling you my feelings when, to follow your example, I ought to have endeavoured to hide them from you: but I cannot, Eliza, no I cannot, tho' I always reckoned myself an adept at hypocrisy. Here my art fails me. I know not why I should not be able to conceal them from you, for I am sure I would do anything to prevent you from a moment's uneasiness. O how often do I bless not only the first but second cause of my visiting the island in which you were immured.[41] How often do I flatter myself with

---

40   Mr Blaesen. Name difficult to read.

41   Edmund visited Inishcoo as a merchant but also found Eliza, and love, there.

being speedily blest again with your loved society. Nor business, nor pleasure, nor things earthly or divine, can cause my thought to wander I might almost say a moment from you. For whatever I do, whether eating or drinking, I continually have your image before me. And when I sleep I dream of you. The watchman informs me that it is after midnight, and yet I know not how to leave off writing or how to make my pen run fast enough, but I must say good night and may God grant you all you can enjoy here and hereafter. Adieu. I shall lay many a waking hour thinking of you this night, and I will think of my bark as you desire it, tho' thank God I do not want it, for I cannot say I have been so well this eight months.[42]

Good morrow, Eliza, good morrow. I have risen very early this morning and thus I have slept but little, yet I find myself more refreshed than tho' I had been a long time in bed. Thank God for it. It enables me again to read your letter again, to write to you, than which nothing can be so agreeable to me, except it were possible by any spell to convey you hither; and that would be delightfull indeed.

This day must the *Fly* be cleared and then she begins to load here and will in all probability be ready to bring you this letter in a few days, perhaps before you will get my last by post. This evening I cannot go to rest till I give you some account of my present plan, which God only knows whether I shall be able to put it into execution. First then, as soon as the *Fly* leaves this, and the roads are a little more passable, I intend to go to Libaw, Memel and Koningsberg, and there endeavour to form such connexions as may be of use to me when I return to London.[43] By the end of this journey, which may be in the beginning of June, I hope to find one or two ships ready to take the rest of the goods which I have here. And I shall immediately ship myself off in the last, so that I now was in the greatest hope to see you in the beginning of August at farthest. Is that not good news? Don't you rejoice at it? Yes, you do and so do I with all my heart. I look eminently forward to that time and shall think it very, very long in coming.

---

42   Medicinal bark was a common cure.

43   Memel, on the River Nieman, now Klaipeda in modern Lithuania; Koningsberg, Königsberg, now Kaliningrad.

Had my residing in this place been approved of by my father, I am sure we could have lived much better than we shall be able to do in London; but I doubt not, if please God to preserve my health, that I shall be able in a short time to have at least a very comfortable sufficiency, as the business which I shall enter into seems an increasing one, if I have but industry enough to look well after it. Now go to sleep and dream of what I have been telling you. And when you write to me, after you receive this, pray go and buy some fine paper, tho' it need not be so thin as this. Yet if it is not much thinner than the last I shall always meet with a great disappointment. That is I must pay for a double letter and only receive a single one. Nor was it really double you know. I should not value a guinea at more than a straw when put in comparison with a letter from you. But to pay for a disappointment is too much, if I must pay for it. Pray let me have double letters indeed.

Another post is come in but no letter from Eliza. Well, I have no right to expect one and yet I must say I did wish for one. For after I have received one letter, and read it, I immediately want another; so that were you to be continually writing yet would you never have power fully to satisfy me. But you must not think because I did not receive any of yours that I got no letter this post. Yes, I did, two: both of which will be some trouble to me to answer, and yet they cause no emotion whatever in me. For I can answer them immediately. But had I but one from you, I could neither answer them nor any thing else, so continually would my thoughts be lost in that pleasing dream of soon revisiting my native country. Not as before, coldly to meet those from whom I can part at any time I will not say without a sigh; and yet I may say so, if that parting is to be the cause of my meeting you.

Do you not, Eliza, does not your heart already anticipate the day on which I shall leave this country, or rather that day on which I shall again partake of your society, I trust never more to be deprived of it? Mine does. I have already imagined to myself a thousand pleasures, for you know I do not then suffer from looking forward to the dark side of my prospects. I have already in my own mind an hundred times left this and there met you in Putney. How long does it appear when we look forward to next August? And yet if we count the time, 'tis not such an age either: three or at most four months, which when past will seem as nothing. Yet now I cannot help facing years. Yesterday and the day before I could not command a single half hour to converse with my Eliza and this is Wednesday 30th, another post day, and I am now in the greatest expectation of hearing from you.

I know not how it is but I feel such an impatience to see your letter. So tho' it could not make me quite easy, true, it will tell me how you were about three weeks past. But how you are now? What are you now doing? That dreadfull uncertainty takes away considerably from the pleasure which would otherwise be great indeed. And yet I trust you are not only now, but that I shall find you when we meet, in good health; and, had you not too much feeling on that head for your own peace, might add in good spirits. That I shall find you so I doubt not. But that you are so now, tho' it might perhaps contribute to the preservation of your health, yet it would have this one disadvantage, that neither you or I should care how long it was before we we're again under the same roof. And if you could see me sometimes without your being visible to me (for if you were visible I should really be in wants of no one thing whatever), you would think that I was as easy and happy as could possibly be. But this is only when [I] am looking into futurity or not thinking at all. By looking towards future events I only mean when I am amusing myself with prospects of happiness to *be* enjoyed in your society.

I have got a letter from Eliza, yes I have, and I have read it already four times over.[44] And if I can but collect my thoughts a little I will endeavour to reply to it, for I expect the *Fly* will sail tomorrow. But it has put me in such a tremor again I hardly know what I do. And you were again at my sister's entirely by yourself, and you can't think of nothing but me. You may at least be sure that, tho' I cannot frequent places where you have been, yet are my thoughts so fully occupied about you as you could possibly wish them to be. And I do indeed agree with you, and I believe I have already mentioned it in this letter, that I will suffer any hardship rather than be again parted from one whom I may truly say I value full as much as myself; and

---

44   This letter does not survive.

to whom no sacrifice would be thought too dear. You did indeed conceal from me what you should feel at my being separated from you. But how strange that I should scarce have an idea of what I should suffer by it; for, if I had, it would have gone hard indeed with me. I should have wanted fortitude to have fulfilled my promise, had you discovered any unhappiness equal to what we now both are obliged to endure. I should at least have taken you with me.

I perceive by the tenor of your letter that my cousin Samuel Hurry is dead.[45] I wanted not this instance to convince me of the instability of mortality, nor to show me the vanity of riches, of the good things of this world. He certainly had as many as would make any reasonable man satisfied. And yet he never appeared to me either as a happy man, or one whose possessions could in any wise be envied, with a sufficiency to live handsomely upon. Without any relations who wanted his assistance, he appeared as busy and anxious as one who had to seek for not only his own daily bread but that of a large family also. Let his failings rest with him. He has undoubtedly done much good. Let us endeavour to do more.

I also observe that my father had expressed a wish that I should have the furniture. And yet it is astonishing to me that he, who supposed I was going to room myself by either taking lodgings or a very small house, which you know was my proposal, should ever think of my purchasing such furniture as there is in that house or such a quantity. For there is at least twice as much as I could possibly dispense with, without any good person would put me into the way of making £400 or £500 a year. And then I should by no means wish to set off at first at such a great rate. To be sure, if the necessary kitchen utensils and such like indispensable affairs are to be disposed of, it might save me some pounds to get them. But whether my cousin had lived or died the furniture was to be sold, it being too extravagant for him. How much more so for me. Besides, was it just such as I wanted, before I would ask for it I would make a shift with a house half furnished. It does not appear to me to be necessary that we should immediately purchase a large quantity of moveables, or even what some people may think necessary ones.

---

45 Samuel Hurry, Edmund Cobb Hurry's first cousin, who died in Clapham in 1788, was the son of Samuel Hurry (1727-1800). He was unmarried.

What are really so I doubt not but we shall always be able to procure, and I dare say your thoughts have been much the same on this head, tho' you say very little about it.

Yet it cannot but give both you and me pleasure to find that my father thinks about us. I know he was always a very kind parent to me and I dare say he would himself lay out the money for them. Yet it is what I do not desire. I have had already many advantages over my brothers and sisters by having had considerable sums lent me. And, tho' they have not turned out as might have been reasonably expected, yet I am not the less obliged to my father and uncle for them.

I know my grandmother would be particularly happy to have you with her, and on some accounts I must wish you had accepted the invitation. You will have no other opportunity of getting acquainted with them; for, when I once come to London, I shall most likely not have any time in which I can be absent from the capital, no not even a week. And if my sister Morgan go this summer, and any further proposals be made, you would not find it disagreeable to be two or three weeks there with her. However, I approve of your resolution to write a letter to my grandmother. And I am sure, if her eyes will permit, she will not omit corresponding with you.

If my aunt had been once acquainted with you, she would have made no difficulty of suffering Mary to be released; nor, as it was, could anyone have opposed it.[46] But for her to have done it would have been plainly saying, 'Aunt, I am heartily tired of being with you'. However, she must have been pleased with your attention.

In regard to your sister Bab, I rejoice with you and her that she has escaped I hope her worst dangers and her greatest difficulties; and that she has now the prospect of being at least tolerably happy and easy. But as to Mary being desirous of converting you is to me no wonder, for she certainly loves you. And do you suppose she could suffer any one she has the least regard for to run headlong to perdition? (For, if a true Methodist, she certainly thinks so of every one that differs from her.) Can you wonder then that she should use every means in her power to save you? I dare say, if she could, she would think it a meritorious act to confine you and Bab to bread and water, or even to

---

46 Aunt Ives, Edmund's grandmother's sister, and his sister, Mary Tolmé.

make you suffer almost any distress whatever. Nay, she must think it her duty to do so. And, if she thinks thus, you may act as you please but you cannot blame her. I long to have your letter by the *John and Mary*. I suppose you and Mr Terry had a most entertaining tête á tête and wish much to read your description of it.[47] However, I find your heart was hardened, and I suppose you were too dead in sin to feel the weight of his anathemas, if he used any.

This is Wednesday, 30 April, so that your letter has been only twenty-three days, did I say only, why it is almost an age. And those I shall get by Windaw will be still older, and I fear I shall not hear again before I set off for Koningsberg, which I propose to do next Monday se'ennight. It is now near twelve, so good night. Tomorrow I have all the ship's papers to prepare, and I must write to Mary, in whose letters I shall inclose this book. For when it goes above two sheets I shall call it a book. And do you know that this is page the tenth? God bless you.

The *Fly* did not sail as I expected yesterday and I shall now have an opportunity of filling another page. The wind remains quite contrary; but, as it has been in this quarter ever since I left London, it is not probable that it will continue much longer. I wish the ship could get away, as I am in hopes she will arrive sooner than the post. And the sooner she gets home, the earlier may I expect to be relieved, as they will, I suppose, immediately send out another ship or two, as I have been obliged to buy six hundred pieces of timber more in order to get some of those debts paid which were due to me in this place.[48] This will cause me very constant employment for some days to get them prepared for shipping.

I am now obliged to seal this, as I am informed there is a prospect of the ship getting to sea immediately. I shall write again before I set off for Koningsberg. And I am in hopes long before that to receive yours via the *John and Mary*, and one more I expect by post Sunday se'ennight. Remember me affectionately to your sisters and believe that I am truly your Edmund Cobb Hurry.

---

47   Garnet Terry, an engraver who adopted the biblical name of Onesimus, was a Methodist writer.

48   'They' refers to Edmund's father and uncle, William and Samuel Hurry.

Saturday morning, 3 May

I was agoing to close this packet when intelligence was brought me that the ship could not get out, so I was determined to keep it open, expecting this post to receive yours by Captain Ward; which I have just now done, and I cannot say they give me any satisfaction. On the contrary, they make me almost desperate. The thought of being obliged to pass so many weeks without your society makes me look upon it as a madness not to have taken you with me. In short, the more I reflect on it, the more plain my folly appears. What was I or you to have lost by it? I know what I should have gained by it. I should have escaped many, I may say very many, miserable hours. I could go on, but that am I tormenting you as well as myself by talking of the misery I ought to have avoided had I been wiser. I am afraid there are few that cannot with justice cast this reflection upon their own conduct at one or other period of their existence.

My letters must appear to you often very strange. They do so to me, but I am not myself, nor shall I ever know a moment's peace till I am with you again. There is nothing but the prospect of its speedily taking place, and the consideration that whatever I am here obliged to do is to hasten that period that could in anywise make my life supportable or make me fit to do anything. Whenever I get a letter from you it is like the opening of an old wound. My heart bleeds whilst I am reading it and I am mad that I cannot immediately go to you. Mad I should have been indeed if your last letter had not been preceded by that of 5 April,[49] for I should have fancied you in distress and out of my power to relieve you. That you are not so alleviates my distress and makes me thankfull to the Great Father of Mercies that, as it is out of my power personally to assist you, you also, thro' his goodness, are not in want of it. I too, like you, when I look around me, cannot but fancy I have no just cause of complaint.

Is not my lot in every respect to be preferred to thousands? But of myself alone do I complain. Is it not my own fault that I suffer what I do? Had I not the means in my power to have prevented it? Yes I had indeed, and it is that alone gives me uneasiness. Yet perhaps it ought not. It may be very advantageous to us both: 'tis absence alone can

---

49   Eliza's letter of 5 April is lost.

make us know the real value of each other's company; and my being assured that when we do meet we shall meet with all that mutual affection which each other can desire.

You seem to doubt. You seem to think it possible, I had almost said probable, that I should forget you. I scarce know what I say, and if you find anything you do not like you must suppose I did not mean it. For you may be assured I should be sorry to write anything that would give you uneasiness, and yet I write nothing else. How strange: unhappy to think of tormenting you and yet continually doing it. I wish I had a little more of my sister's temper: a momentary sensation and then it's over, how happy. No, no, no. I once thought my feelings were something in that way, and I was always very distrustfull of myself on that account, but I find to my cost that time in this instance only increases my sorrow.

If you do not see me in August you may depend upon it I shall go mad. I am half crazy already, as you may easily perceive by my writing, so I'll write no more at present but wish you a good night. And may the author of all good support us under every trial and supposed or real affliction is the sincere and fervent prayer of your E.C. Hurry.

Monday 5 May 1788, past 11 o'clock

Tuesday, 6 May

No fair wind for the ship. Hard at work all day getting the purchased timber out of the water. No Eliza in the evening to greet my return, so have been playing at cards, by way of drowning reflection, and I have lost my money. It is a happy circumstance I am not fond of liquor, or I now should be much tempted to use it and perhaps gain such a habit of it as would never be lost again. Of card playing I am not so fearfull, as I am sure I shall neither have opportunity or inclination in your presence to practise it. But as you know you are much given to drink yourself, I ought to be very carefull to set you an example. I suppose the dram bottle is the only relief you have at present, and cards, when business allows of it, mine. In your next tell me whether you prefer French or Ratafia that I may furnish you with a stock.[50] Joking apart, I have almost been wicked enough to wish that I could by any means stifle my sensations or in short remain in a torpid state till the fine weather comes. And I know no sun so genial as your presence. Good night again. I am happy to think I have one day less to suffer than I had last night.

Wednesday morning. I am now again called to seal up my packet. I must do it in good earnest, so God bless you. Adieu. I shall write again next post.

Watermark with crown and two lions in paper. Cover, none. Postmark, none. Sent via the Fly.

---

50   Ratafia is a fortified wine made of a mixture of brandy and the unfermented juice of the grape. Another joke about Eliza enjoying alcohol.

Letter 42

Edmund Cobb Hurry to Eliza Liddell
Libaw

Written 28 May to 2 June 1788; sent from Windaw, 2 June;
received in London, June

Libaw, 28 May 1788

I (as last night is come a postbag from Koningsberg and Memel) immediately enquired for letters, reasonably expecting to have heard from my father, but no letter of any kind was arrived. And was ruminating on the causes that might have prevented them, I was agreeably surprized by a person from Windaw bringing me a whole packet in which yours of the third instant was enclosed and consequently twice read before the others were even looked at. I found none from my father, which I own surprized me not a little, but if he had been indisposed you would certainly have mentioned it. So I shall rest satisfied and suppose that he thinks there is nothing of consequence to communicate, as long as he is with you.

I am glad you like my sister's company and that you have such an opportunity of getting acquainted with some whom I can really call my friends. I thought my uncle might have invited you to go to Yarmouth with him. Had this been the case, I should have been glad you had accepted of it. I am sure you would with great pleasure have staid at my grandfather's. Also you might have been as relaxed as you please. I am certain that, from what I know of you and my grandmother, that you would have been loth to part with each other's company, and next to my being there is no person so dear to me. It would give them both the greatest pleasure they could enjoy.

And so you like Mr Tolmé. I will not give you my opinion of him or any other person on paper, for you might be tempted to betray me, and tho' there are few persons to whose faces I would not declare my thoughts of them, yet it is not always necessary. You inform me of the arrival of the *Wycombe* and I hope your next will

bring me the good news of your having seen my brother William.[51]
I never looked on Mr Tolmé as a man of fashion, but only a great
stickler for decentness (and here it is, I fear, my brother is wanting),
and it is a kind of half virtue which can scarcely be carried to an
extreme. Finery I despise but the former I admire in every one, tho'
I cannot bring it so much into my own practise as I could wish.
And for you it is very improper, as we have a common saying that
there is nothing can poison a sailor but the cleanliness of his wife.
That profession I wish not to follow when you are mine. Indeed you
are so now in every respect but the form and it is the thought of
that inward security, that point to which all my thoughts continually
tend, that gives me the greatest ease and affords me the greatest
satisfaction in this separation from you. The single thought that
there were a possibility of a doubt could not but be attended with the
most painful distress. But, thank God, that is not the case, tho' you
threaten me with such a rival as long as he remains [*unclear word*]
at least.[52] I have no being to fear and you may employ all the doctors
in London. There are none can impart that faculty of speech to me.

I was prevented from finishing this letter [in] time enough for
yesterday's post, having had several of the greatest consequence
both to write and copy. So I shall take this to Windaw with me,
where I hope to be tomorrow. And tho' I cannot reasonably expect
a ship there already, yet I trust many days will not elapse before one
arrives. But whether I can with propriety come home in her, or must
wait for the *John and Mary*, is as yet a great uncertainty, tho' you may
be assured of that nothing that lies in my power shall be omitted till
I have again the pleasure of embracing my Eliza. Few moments can
I spend with any degree of satisfaction. As I am not indulged with
any kind of information respecting what has passed at home, I wish
you to be particular on that head as you can.

 I did expect to have been able to have written a great deal to
you on my journey; but, my friend Mr Hartwick of Libaw having

---

51   William Hurry junior, Edmund Cobb Hurry's younger brother, the second son of William Hurry
senior.

52   Unclear word.

joined us, I never had an hour I could call my own.[53] If on the whole it was as agreeable a journey as any could be, where you do not make one of the party, the shortness of our stay gave little opportunity of seeing any curiosities that may be in Koningsberg. And the place itself makes but a poor appearance for the capital of so large a province, and which might be called the capital of so large a kingdom as Prussia is at present. For altho' the court is removed to Berlin, yet the coronation of the king of Prussia must be held in this place;[54] tho' I should rather have said where a despotick prince governed has heretofore been held in this place. I know you do not care a fig for the king of Prussia and so I will tell you no more about this demi-metropolis.

Our time when not occupied by business was chiefly taken up by paying our respects to all my friend Hartwick's acquaintances. And tho' I would gladly have been excused accompanying them, yet rather than disoblige them I not only unwillingly made many formal [calls] but also [rose at] 5 in the morning to see the Prussian troops exercise. [According to my] fellow travellers this was a prodigy for more than eight regiments were yet arrived, for the number that they had ever seen did not exceed fifteen soldiers and a corporal. They certainly cut a great figure and their discipline is very strict, but it is a pity they are not more usefully occupied.[55]

Thank God I am got back again to Windaw, but I shall soon grow tired of it if the ships do not come. For few will be either my occupations or amusements till they arrive. For the present writing and reading are the only ones I can have recourse to, to pass the tedious hours and days, for I am full as much alone in this place as tho' I were shut up in a ship's cabin. To be sure I have only to go to the other end of the house and I may be amused by Mrs Blaesen's oratory. I believe no woman ever exceeded her and I am able to believe, with a certain

---

53   Hartwick, whose name appears at intervals in the letters, often as Herzwich, was a Libaw merchant. He visited London in 1792 and stayed with the Hurrys in Homerton.

54   Frederick III, elector of Brandenberg, had himself crowned king of Prussia in Königsberg in 1701. Königsberg, now Kaliningrad, was the capital of Prussia. He was able to do so because his duchy of Prussia, unlike Brandenberg itself, was outside the borders of the Holy Roman Empire.

55   Expressing a common English attitude towards the excess militarism of Prussia. Words in brackets supplied.

Irishman, that her tongue is very glad when she is asleep. However, as she was brought up by a clergyman, she has read a great deal and is sometimes very entertaining. When she is otherwise I return to my books.

How many times have I wished but in vain that you were here. How agreeably would we have passed the summer together in a strange land, but I flatter myself that the time is not far distant when our present suffering will give an additional pleasure to our future enjoyments. You say it's a mighty matter to write once a fortnight, but if that letter by its date did not accuse me, I should have pointed out to you that the distance between the dates of some of your letters will allow three weeks too long without any danger of being rushed.[56]

Remember me suitably to your sisters and do not forget to tell me you are quite well. And pray let me hear no more of those violent colds in the head; or, if you must have them, do not gad about from town to country to make them worse. I think my father will certainly be in London when Mr Tolmé arrives, and then you will have an opportunity of getting acquainted with him. Have you written to my grandmother? And, tell me, has she fixed the time of her coming to London? Perhaps it may be when I come home. I shall very likely land at Yarmouth. God bless you and believe your most kind Edmund Cobb Hurry.

Windaw, 2 June 1788

Cover, Miss Eliza Liddell, at Mr George Coldham, No. 12 Leman Street, Goodmans Fields, London. Postmark, unclear.

---

56   Two of Eliza's lost letters were dated 5 and 30 April.

Letter 43

Edmund Cobb Hurry to Eliza Liddell
Windaw

Written 22 June 1788; sent from, Windaw, 22 June, via the Fly;
received in Putney

Windaw, 22 June 1788

Another and another post but without any news from Eliza. The *Fly* has returned, and I was not a little angry with Ives that he did not write you that he was agoing to return hither. It was not your fault you did not send a letter by Ives, and this morning yours of 25 May came,[57] but in such company that I hardly know whether I was glad to receive it or not, and my mind is at present in such a state that I hardly now what I write.

The one I allude to was one from Atkinson of Hull, to whom I had written for a ship on certain conditions; which, if he had complied with, would have been the cause of my immediate release from this detested prison, for I can call it nothing else.[58] Instead of conforming to my orders, he has engaged a ship on very disadvantageous terms, as not only to cause a considerable loss but likewise to give me a deal of trouble and oblige me to wait the return of the *Fly*, by which ship you may expect me, should no unforeseen accident prevent. There is a possibility of its being by some earlier ship, but possibility is all I see at present, and I am sorry I should already have flattered you with too sanguine hopes of my earlier return. But you have been brought up in the school of disappointment, and early taught to bear the frown of fortune; and, tho' it is said that custom is next to nature, and that by it you may bear it the better, yet I am uneasy. As, tho' I know you will bear it with patience, yet I cannot suppose it will cause you no unhappiness or disquiet.

I would not have anyone know that I write you anything

---

57 Eliza's letter of 25 May is lost.

58 Probably Peter Atkinson.

that passes concerning business, altho' I know this caution to be unnecessary. Yet you have only to say I was disappointed. And now I have run on all this while with just what was uppermost, without once taking any notice or endeavouring to justify what I wrote you by last post; but this I must postpone till another opportunity, for my mind is full of bitterness and anger; and, till I have endeavoured to make Mr Atkinson feel the weight of my resentment, I cannot do anything. Well I have been giving it to him in the politest manner that the first impression his letter made on my mind would allow of.

And now I am going to tell you. I am very angry I wrote what I did to you last, as I am afraid it will make you unhappy, but at the same time it will show you I cannot bear anything like neglect.[59] I forgive you for not writing from the 5th to the 25th, and you must forgive me for writing so hastily, but what in the name of goodness could make you send your letter to Libaw? O, it was my Cousin Thomas's advice![60] Why, surely you must know better than he could whether I should be in Libaw or Windaw. And now I'll tell you a secret that you knew before, if you read the letters that I have sent you, and that when I am in Libaw, if I go to the postmaster, and speak very prettily to him, he will always open the Windaw packet for me. But if I am in Windaw, and the letters are directed to Libaw, then they must lay five days there before they can be forwarded; and this was the case with your last letter, for I received one from England per same post of 1 June, and the *Fly* sailed from England 1 June and came here in fifteen days. And this letter I shall send by her, and you will have an opportunity of sending me as many packets as you please, and you must have a great deal to communicate to me that must be very interesting, where as from hence the only thing that I can inform you of which is of the least importance to you is the force of my affection for you, if I may call it so; and which you will easily discover is in my last letter as in every preceding one so strong and immutable as is possible for a person possessed of so much indifference and so much insensibility.

You give me reason to expect I shall find you in Putney, and you

59 His complaint about not receiving letters, Edmund to Eliza, Letter 42, p. 245.

60 Edmund Cobb Hurry's first cousin Thomas Hurry (1749-1828), son of Thomas Hurry (1719-1801).

seem to like it better than either London or Clapton.[61] Indeed I am sure I should do so too, but we are often obliged not only to live where we do not like, but to do things so contrary to our inclinations that we must often wonder how we could possibly have forced ourselves to do them. It is what happens to me every day in this place. I suffer myself to be persuaded, either to ride, walk or visit, when the whole time I am fretting inwardly to think I have been so foolish. And indeed it is seldom that I am able so far to conceal my thoughts as but some of the company perceive that I am discontented and uneasy. I wish it would so far cure them as to dispense with my presence. In fourteen days the Baron and his whole family will be here. I dread it, for without I could plead [*tear*]. Thank God I cannot for I have not been so [*tear*] years. I do not expect to have one hour to [*tear*] when I am asleep. Would to God my mind was [*tear*] body. Your presence would cause it to be so, but when [*tear*] I try by way of remedy, if I can fix my thoughts for a moment [*tear*] that moment's ease, the next they are with you, [*tear*] as if one moment's satisfaction were too much to enjoy in your absence. It is indeed a mournfull and melancholy occupation to keep scribbling to you in this manner when I would give everything I owned to be with you. And the longer it is, I find it still worse and worse. When I think of the *Fly* going again without me I am half mad, but it must be so!

I have been exceedingly taken up with the *Fly*'s account, and the other ships arriving, that I have only just time to tell you I remain sincerely yours, E.C. Hurry.

Write when the *Fly* returns. I hope it will be but a few weeks, least they will appear years.

Cover, Miss Eliza Liddell, at Mrs Layton's, Putney. Postmark, Yarmouth. Sent via the Fly.

---

61   George and Mary Morgan lived in Clapton, near Hackney, in north-east London.

Letter 44

Edmund Cobb Hurry to Eliza Liddell
Windaw

Written 29 June to 5 July 1788; sent from Windaw, 5 July;
received in London, 2 August

I last night sent you a few lines per the *Fly* and was extremely chagrined that I was prevented from writing more, tho' it was much alleviated by her speedy dispatch for home, having every reason to hope that it may not be very long before she returns; and I am as fully determined, as changeable mortality will allow of, that nothing shall prevent my returning in her. This is Sunday 29 June and the wind is still favorable for her. It is vanity and vexation of spirit to wish to have been in her, for it could not be.

I have this moment received yours of the third instant, and I am surprized you never thought of sending your letter to George Coldham before, as I know he would always take care to forward them immediately.[62] You are still at Putney, and I would hope it will not be long before I shall also be there. You speak of the brightness of your prospects, and God knows I am well satisfied with mine, if I could but do as I like when I return to England. My friends seem to have many plans in agitation for me. I have but one, and were I but allowed to follow that one I doubt not but I should be as happy and content as any earthly being. I wish not for riches, nor do I even know whether I should be so happy if I had so much as to have no reason to toil for more. Yet I think I should, for I believe we are both fond of quiet and retirement; and I know for my own part I am as lazy as any lord need to be.

If you recollect, I just mentioned to you that I thought it would be both a frugal and desirable plan to live with George Coldham. He likewise was desirous of it, provided he had no prospect of changing his situation before my return. And as it was such a doubtfull matter

---

62   George Coldham, Edmund's stepbrother, the son of William Hurry's second wife, Dorothy. He lived at No. 12 Leman Street, Goodmans Fields, London.

I never spoke of it to anyone but he and you, tho' I believe my sister heard of it. And it is since come to my father's ears, with I doubt not a great many other tales of what I designed, perhaps never to do – but he seems to be displeased that I should keep everything, as he expresses it, a secret from him. Were it really so, I should certainly be wrong, for he always has been a most kind and most indulgent father to me, but I hope I convinced him that I had no design but implicitly to obey him as far as I ought.

But to return to the said plan, which I have often seriously thought of, and I find full as many reasons for not pursuing it as I can find advantageous in it. The first and greatest objection is we should never be alone. And I rather think the expense of his housekeeping cannot be less than £400 per annum. For the half of this sum, I think we might most certainly have a small house to ourselves. But as every plan or proposal of this and every other kind must so much depend upon future causes and circumstances, tho' it may be attended with some pleasure to think, to talk and to propose them, yet we may reasonably expect from the uncertainty of human events that they will in the end be very different from what we have examined. And I always flatter myself much better than the appearance gave me in reason to hope for. In short, tho' no one can raise higher palaces than myself, yet I am conscious that it is uncertain whether their durance would be the source of happiness or misfortune to me.[63]

You seem to wage continual war with Methodism. Are you infallible? If not, I think you may as well let everyone do as they like in those things. I am well satisfied that it's of little consequence, provided we use the best means in our power to get all the information we can, and to do our utmost to act up to what our reason tells us is right. What sect or profession we belong to, if our religion is not of the heart it must be vain. For to our fellow creatures we may always pretend to be what we please. I am one of the lukewarm Christians, which Mr Tolmé says is worse than an Infidel or Turk. I cannot help smiling at him. And if we smile at anyone, take it for granted we think ourselves at least for that moment wiser. I believe in general when we laugh at any person it must be from a comparison which we draw between that person and ourselves, and in which ourself

---

63   Uncertain word.

has flattered us at least we are superior. I suppose it is for some such a reason that you cannot bear being laughed at. But because those who laugh at us think themselves above or rather superior to us, it does not follow that they really are so. And really often proves the contrary.

Wednesday 3 July

I believe this is the first date I have put to this letter, and I am not certain whether my last had any date at all. I am now this morning going to oblige others at the expense of my own ease, as I am frequently obliged to do. Here I am called to attend at a christening. To refuse would be the greatest affront I could possibly be guilty of to the person who invites, and to go will be an affront to myself; but in matters of no convenience I will rather affront myself than other persons, tho' perhaps it may be the last time I shall ever see them. But were I such a railer as yourself I would say no, I cannot go; my religion will not allow me. And to give up one's religion rather than disoblige a person one cares not a fig for will seem to you the greatest wickedness as well as the greatest absurdity.[64]

Well I am now returned, and have (not) been renouncing the Devil and all his works, besides promising a great many more odd things for an infant of about five days old.[65] I cannot say but I pitied the poor thing to see it brought near half a mile into an old church, its limbs bound together like a bundle of tape, without power to move any joint or hardly any feature, and could not help looking upon it as next to a miracle if it should ever come to maturity. Can custom, foolish custom, make it necessary that every child should be thus treated, so contrary to reason and common sense? And can religion or the allwise Being demand that they should thus hazard the life of a tender infant to perform what any person who reflects must look upon as nothing more than a ceremony? But so long as they think they are doing right, they must be right. Tho' to me the whole appears to be rather a mockery than what is really and spiritually meant by the office of baptism.

---

64   Unitarians were strong believers in adult baptism.

65   The word 'not', expressing his disapproval, has been added above the line.

Your church demands, nay insists on, three sponsors for every child, and in short every minister is reprehensible if he should to perform the office without their being present.[66] And the father and mother, who are certainly the only persons that ever can fulfill that office, are expressly excluded. Here were not less than forty. All except myself solemnly promised that this child should renounce the Devil and all his works, should be brought up in the Christian faith, and lead a godly and pious life. At least one half of them will most likely never see the child again. How can what they have promised when seriously looked at be anything more or less than a mockery of essential ordination? If they find it right, it would be foolish in me to tell them they are wrong. For if it is really so, i.e. that they think it from a full conviction, they are certainly right. And so I trust we shall all find that we have acted consistently, with what we from a mature consideration think and believe to be right, however differently each may think and act. The true Papists, Methodists, etc, etc, will all fare alike. For it cannot be necessary, nor is it possible: what idea must they have of their Creator who can think that one particular sect is more worthy or better entitled to eternal happiness than the millions who differ from them.

I do not intend to send this till the *Elizabeth* (Captain Davison) is ready, which may be Saturday or Monday; and when you receive this I hope I shall be near coming away.[67] A thousand and a thousand times have I already ascended the staircase at Putney, but only in imagination. Would to God it was once realized. I am afraid the *Fly* has had a sad passage hitherto; for, tho' the height of summer, we have had nothing but heavy showers and that directly against them. I drove them away the moment they were load[ed] but I suppose they will not thank me for it.

And so you went to steal some of my books in Prescott Street.[68] Why do you not take them all home if you have room for them? Indeed there are not so many, and of those few worth having, but you must be certain that I should never wish them in anyone's possession but yours.

---

66   Church of England practice.

67   *Elizabeth*, another of the Hurry ships.

68   Eliza was living in Putney at this point.

Putney, 1799, by William Pickett

This is Saturday, 5 July, and it is now two days since I have written a line to you. I have been so employed in preparing to depart from hence in the *Elizabeth*, but I see so many obstacles yet remaining that I fear I shall not be able to overturn them all, and least not with propriety. And tho' to us four or five weeks may seem of such consequence, and indeed it really is so, when we consider the perhaps short duration of existence, yet there are few if any that would be indulgent enough to pardon any mistake which might happen by my not staying those few weeks.

Should it happen that I can get away, I shall send this by post, tho' I shall then most likely be with you before you receive this, without I should be detained in Yarmouth. And that you may be sure would not be long. I am half mad when I think of there being a possibility of my getting away now. I can think of nothing else. It will be a great disappointment to me if I do not.

I hope you will get the letter I sent by the *Fly* before you receive that by post, in which I could not help expressing my vexation at your long silence. For it was a month between the receipt of one letter and the other. And indeed you did not write for three weeks, so that you deserved partly what I said to you, tho' not all. But, tho' you are the aggressor, I shall be the greatest sufferer, and particularly if I should stay here another month. For I there desired you not to write me any more to Windaw; so that, should you comply with that desire, I may have the vexation of being so many weeks without hearing from you, and that merely by my own hastiness. For it were better for me that two or three of your letters should lie here than for me to be so long without.

This is another of the many Saturday nights; and I pray God it may be the last I may pass in this place. So good night and do not forget me. It is now Sunday night and I think I am pretty certain of getting away this week, but I have only time to tell you this, for I have now to write morning, noon and night as long as I can keep my eyes open. So good night to you, and I trust before you read this I shall be in Yarmouth.

The ship is laden and clear, part of my cloaths are on board, but the wind is not yet fair. This is Wednesday and I shall send this by tomorrow's post; but, if I am not too sanguine, you will have one from Yarmouth at least as soon, if not before, you receive this. I shall stay as short a time as Yarmouth as circumstances will admit of.

It is a disagreeable situation to be in: to have to take leave of such a number of persons with whom I have lived so long, without even a prospect or chance of seeing them again. I might have added without a desire, for I flatter myself I never have been so guilty as to make them think I should part with any degree of regret. For tho' with you I should have been well satisfied to have spent that part of my life here in peace, in quiet, as we might have done, yet I would not spend another five years here, in the manner the last five have been spent, to gain thousands.[69]

I only get time to write by starts, so that I suppose this letter will be a compleat piece of nonsense. I am continually called away before I have finished a sentence, and I am already got to Fryday morning and I must now close for the post. The wind is still vexatious, but it is a time of year in which I flatter myself it will not be of any long duration. Remember me suitably to your sisters and believe me to be most truly and affectionately, Edmund Cobb Hurry.

Cover, Miss Eliza Liddell, at Mr George Coldham, No. 12 Leman Street, Goodmans Fields, London. Postmark, 2 August.

69　This indicates that Edmund had spent the previous five years at Windaw or at least in the Baltic.

Letter 45

Edmund Cobb Hurry to Eliza Liddell
Elsinore

Written 23 July 1788; sent from Elsinore, 23 July;
received in London, August

My dear Liza, your Edmund is once more upon the bounded ocean, for it would be very improper to call it boundless, when its opposite shore is separated by only a few miles in comparison to the Atlantic or Southern Seas. Yet, small and limited as it is, I think every mile a degree, and every degree which still separates me from you appears a space unbounded, a distance which my eagerness to partake of that mutual joy which I trust my unexpected return will cause, is a distance immeasurable. Already have we left that wretched country fifty hours, and unimpeded by contrary blast we find ourselves advanced to the small distance of only seventy miles. So gently blows that eastern breeze that should waft me to you, to happiness. O may the duration of that happiness be as permanent and lasting as the distress caused by our separation was, and I believe would have been as long as might have continued. If ever I was impatient at sea it is now. My mind has no rest, ever anticipating our meeting. It leaves me no power to enjoy the present moment in the least degree, ever contemplating on our future prospects. Books appear as blank leaves and I have no enjoyment in them, or in anything around me. I have been reading your three last letters and, at the same time they convey a kind of consolation to my mind, they render me if possible still more impatient. Indeed to do what appears to me very right will be to go on reading away at the old rate, but I suffered so much at the thoughts of what uneasiness my last but one might cause you, that tho' you really should deserve it, as to all appearance you do, yet I will not reproach you any more. For tho' I have not heard from you for several post days, yet I have heard of you, heard of breaking your resolution of remaining quiet and retired in Putney, to encounter once more the noise and disturbance of half a dozen wild ones at least, besides the children in whom I suppose you find some assistance to pass away the hours very tolerably.

Surely you might have just made one scrawl in Mr Morgan's letter.[70] It was the most expeditious one I ever received, for tho' directed to Libaw it came to hand two days before it was written, for it was dated 15 July and I received it on the thirteenth, the day I sailed from Windaw. Note I have none from your ladyship since 3 June, and they have come this summer in nineteen days from London, but I have ordered all that may come after my departure to be sent in the *Fly* back to Yarmouth, when she returns again. Perhaps I may send you this from Elsinore to inform you how forward I am got in my return towards you, yet if I do I would hope that you will receive another from Yarmouth before you get this, as perhaps you may be there, for Mr Morgan seems to talk something like as tho' there was a proposal of that kind stirring, tho' he seems to have entirely declined making his intended visit; and, if he is got to his new house, perhaps I may have the pleasure of bringing my grandmother up with me. I think you wrote me she had partly promised to come, and I am much mistaken if my company will not be a very additional inducement.

The only objection will be that I shall not be able to get my grandfather from Yarmouth at that season of the year, on account of his fishing of which he is so doatingly fond. And distracted must be the mind of your Edmund when he cannot find at least a solitary satisfaction in writing to you, my dear Eliza. That he cannot must be plain from his having omitted it for so many days and during such a tedious passage, when the numbered hours of a long day in which he has no occupation have not been so employed. And yet there are few moments in each day in which his thoughts are not continually fixed on her, in which he is not suffering and I had almost said repining that he has it not in his power to command the winds and waves. Yes, my dearest Eliza, your Edmund sighs indeed, but he will not repine at what he cannot prevent.

This is already the tenth day since I left Windaw, and I have yet a considerable distance to make before I arrive at Elsinore. What

---

70   A letter from Edmund's brother-in-law George Morgan. Presumably it had been written, but misdated, on 15 June 1788.

distresses me considerably is this the thoughts of having left Windaw without previously [having] acquainted my uncle and father. Indeed I could not do it, for till within a few days I was undetermined whether I should be able to leave it or not. Now I am fearfull least they should send out another ship before the *Fly*, imagining that I am there such should be the case, I will be attended with considerable loss and could [*tear*] with their displeasure. I must leave a little room to fill up at the end, as I shall now most certainly send this off when I get there.

Wednesday, 23 July

This afternoon got down to Elsinore and hope now in a short time to have the unspeakable satisfaction of showing you with what sincerity I subscribe myself your Edmund Cobb Hurry.

Cover, Miss Eliza Liddell, at Mr George Coldham, No. 12 Leman Street, Goodmans Fields, London. Postmark. 5 August.

Letter 46

Edmund Cobb Hurry to Eliza Liddell
Great Yarmouth

Written 7-8 August 1788; sent from Great Yarmouth, 8 August;
received in Putney, August

Tuesday, 7 August

It is past eleven at night and I am now, thank God, safe up into my bedchamber and shall at length be able to write to you, my dearest Eliza. For which opportunity I have been earnestly wishing the whole day, as if you only look in your own breast you may judge what I feel, that I cannot immediately fly to you. Yet you must not expect that I shall be able to write anything coherent or connected; but, if it serves to show you the strength of my affection, it will answer the end which I propose to myself in writing.

And first I must tell you that I arrived safe this morning, just time enough to scrawl six lines and send by the post which, if you are in Putney, you must receive tomorrow.[71] But, as I am very dubious from yours of the 28th whether you may not be in Hampstead, I shall write Mr Coldham tomorrow and beg he will inform you of my arrival. If he can find out where you are at the same time, these will lay in Putney till you return, as you did not say for certain you were going to Hampstead.[72] And indeed I was so confused, and so vexed with myself when I read your letters, that I saw nothing about Hampstead or Clapton either.

For God's sake get rid of that slow fever immediately, and let the prospect of seeing me in a few days entirely cure you. Tho', with all your sufferings on that head, I scarce think you have suffered more than I have ever since I wrote it, and I am sorry to say that I find myself very easily offended. And, tho' I suffer so much myself by it, and am exceedingly displeased with myself, yet I know not how it is:

---

71   This note does not survive.

72   Eliza's reason for being in Hampstead is unclear.

if I meet with disappointments in the world it sours my temper, so that I could quarrel with my own self. But I am tired of the subject and I hope to be able in some measure by my future conduct to make you and myself amends for what we have both suffered on that head. So you see I will not allow you to be the greatest sufferer.

I suppose you will stay in Putney till I come up, which I am afraid will not be possible till the latter part next week. As if I get my accounts settled before, I can't refuse staying a day or two for Betsy, who I suppose you know is coming to be with her sister Morgan a month or two. And if you could but see what pleasure my being here gives my grandparents, you would think it very hard that we have it not in our power to live with them. I assure you I prefer their company, aged and infirm as they are, to any which I have in this place. And when I tell you that but for you I would never leave them whilst they live, you may certainly believe that I love you as well as I do myself. But how often do I ever vex myself with my own ill conduct. You must not wonder then if I sometimes give you uneasiness. Nay, I have before told you: you must expect it; and, if you are not prepared for, it you will often be disappointed.

We cannot avoid at least for a time living with George Coldham, for it is so firmly fixed. And my father is persuaded it is just the thing for us; that, tho' for many reasons I differ from him on that subject, yet we cannot now avoid it. For some reasons it is most convenient to me. First, we shall have no trouble in preparing anything for housekeeping; nor shall we want scarce any furniture. George Coldham's good temper will, I doubt not, make every thing easy. And tho' we may meet many things which may not be agreeable to us, yet I hope to see you happy; and then there will be nothing wanting to make me so.

I should have written very little to you on this subject did not Mrs Hurry press me to know your mind as speedily as may be with respect to a servant, who has lived I think five years at my father's, and is now agoing to leave it for no other reason than that she cannot agree with her fellow servants.[73] As you are a stranger in London, and perhaps not acquainted with any servants there sufficient to trust them, it might not be amiss to take her. She is a good cook, but I believe a very dirty one. However, that I think depends much on

---

73 Mrs Dorothy Hurry, the second wife of William Hurry. The servant in question was Ann Reece.

the mistress. Yet if you see any good reason for refusing her, or know of one you would like, let me know by return post, that she may look out for a place here. I am also desired to inform you that she understands washing well and can put a great deal of work of hand.

At the same time, I think George should be consulted. Mrs Hurry says neither he or I has anything to do with it. I do not wish to have any, I assure you, and so pray do not refer to me in this matter. And if you have no opportunity of communicating with George on the subject, and his mother answers for him, you must say yes or no. If no, you have only to say you know of one. Now pray do not forget to write about it in your first letter or I shall hear of nothing else all the time I am here.

I shall write George tomorrow. I believe I have already told you so. If he has time, I shall beg he will go over to Putney; and then you will have an opportunity of talking on that or any subject that may be necessary to him or you to know before I come up. Remember me to Bab and Mary, and believe me truly your Edmund Cobb Hurry.

P.S. I shall write again Sunday.

Cover, Miss Eliza Liddell, at Mrs Layton's, Putney. Postmark, none.

Letter 47

Edmund Cobb Hurry to George Coldham
Great Yarmouth

Written 7-8 August 1788; sent from Great Yarmouth, 8 August;
received in London, August

Yarmouth, 8 August 1788

Dear George, I was happy to learn from your mother that you approved of the plan I just hinted to you ere my departure from London. And I do assure you that nothing shall be omitted on my side to make it as agreeable to you as you could wish; and I have no doubt but Eliza will not be wanting as far as lies in her power to make your dwelling more comfortable than you can possibly be alone. If you know where she is, I have to beg you will acquaint her with my safe arrival in England, after a disagreeable passage of near a month. I long to be with you immediately, but that is not possible, as I have several little affairs which I wish to get settled. And I shall perhaps have to wait a day or two for Betsy, who is coming to stay with her sister Morgan.[74] I beg you will also acquaint her and Mrs Tolmé that I shall write to them very soon, but we have no post tomorrow.

Your mother wishes we should take Ann, who lives at my father's as a cook. I have written to Eliza about it and told her, if she had an opportunity, to speak with you about it. Perhaps you have no time to go over, if she is in Putney; and there would be no haste, did it not prevent Ann from applying to another place, as she wishes much to remain in the family and has been used to London.

You'll excuse this scrawl as I have not been bed since two yesterday morning and it is now two o'clock Fryday morning. Perhaps I may have an opportunity to scrawl some more in the morning – perhaps. Remember me to all enquiring friends and believe me yours sincerely, E.C. Hurry.

Cover, Mr George Coldham, No. 11 Leman Street, Goodmans Fields, London.
Postmark, Yarmouth, 9 August.

---

74 Edmund Cobb Hurry's sister Elizabeth, known as Betsy, was planning to visit their sister Ann Morgan.

Letter 48

Edmund Cobb Hurry to Eliza Liddell
Great Yarmouth

Written 11-12 August 1788; sent from Great Yarmouth, 12 August; received in London, August

Little more than four and twenty hours ago and I was enjoying the company of my dearest Eliza; and now I find myself transported into the company of my most honoured grandparents in a much shorter time than I could possibly have expected, and with much less fatigue than I ever remember to have travelled before. I wrapt myself in my boat-cloak. Even before the carriage had left the known streets of the great metropolis, the whole world was lost to your Edmund. And even Miss Eliza made no impression on my imagination, for you know I cannot be answerable for what passes in my sleep; but I may safely say to my waking thoughts your dear image was ever present, and I could sooner have gone to bed without adorating my Creator than have omitted the earliest opportunity of informing my Eliza what I know she most wished to be acquainted with: I arrived here safe and in good health; and that I do not care how soon I can congratulate you and myself on my safe return to London. And you may depend that nothing in my power shall be omitted to render my stay here as short as possible.

I have often reflected that were we uninterruptedly to possess for a great length of time the enjoyment of so much happiness as we did for a few days past, it would be so much above the scale of which we as human beings might seem entitled to, as to render us unfit to bear in a proper manner any calamity which we might rationally suppose to be the attendant consequence of such a scene of felicity. But away with distressing ideas. My Eliza loves me, and I'll now tell you how and by what means I arrived at my destined port in less than twenty-four hours; and I had proposed to spend the night with my aunt in Norwich.

You well know, I left the Bull Inn at 7 o'clock and had only one youth with me the whole way to Norwich.[75] He disturbed me at 10 o'clock to take part of a part of a pig's foot with him; and, as he was a very sociable, agreeable man, I joined him contrary to my usual custom and eat a very hearty supper. But why should I write about such nonsense as eating and drinking, and, tho' I had determined to enter very minutely into the merits of my journey, I find it so ridiculous that I can only tell you I got into Norwich near half an hour before the mail and by that means, when it arrived, was enabled to proceed with it directly to Yarmouth, where I arrived at four this afternoon.

Now mind and be a good girl and go to bed early, get up at 7, walk round the tenter ground,[76] get my uncle his breakfast, and of an evening, when you play whist, be carefull always to lead from your strongest suit. And if you have four trumps, lead one off boldly and be sure to follow your partner's lead when you can. Study this every morning after breakfast; read some book which you have not till dinner; and then drink plenty of wine or brandy to raise your spirits for the evening.[77] This with works, and now and then dropping me a few lines, may enable you to fill up your time as that you may not afterwards be [tear] to reflect that you have not done anything; for if you do all this you will do a great deal.

I am determined to go as little as possible into company here, and so my stay shall be short; so shall as much time as business will admit to be spent in the company of my grandparents and father. Mind and write me when you expect to see Bab; and I shall be very angry if you did not send Crozier at night again for your cloaths.[78] You have a right to make as free with my servants as I would do myself. I here give it you. I quite forgot, as I missed him in going to the stage, and it vexed me a great deal when I thought of it after. Give my love to Mary and Bab. To my sister I have written and enclose this. God bless you, believe me sincerely and affectionately, your Edmund Cobb Hurry.

---

75 The Bull and Gate, in Holborn, an ancient inn known as the starting point for coaches to Norwich.

76 Tenter grounds were used for stretching newly-woven cloth.

77 Another joke about alcohol.

78 Crozier (first name unknown) was a servant living in the house of George Coldham.

Mine, this cannot go till tomorrow noon, but I could not have existed if I had not written it tonight. 10 o'clock, Tuesday 12 August 1788.

You'll tell Barnes I am not in London, or he may think it strange if I do not call on them.

Cover, Eliza Liddell. Postmark, Stamp, illegible.

Letter 49

Edmund Cobb Hurry to Eliza Liddell
Great Yarmouth

Written 9-12 August 1788; sent from Great Yarmouth, 12 August;
received in London, August

My dear Eliza, how happy I was when I this evening rather unexpectedly received yours of the 8th instant. And how much that happiness was increased when you informed me you were well you will much easier conceive than I can describe. When I say unexpectedly, you must think from your last I was uncertain whether you were in Hampstead, Putney or perhaps even Clapton, to which I imagined the irregularity of the Putney post might prevent your getting my letter immediately. Yet was I willing to give it a chance of getting to you the soonest possible and it succeeded better than expected. However the next day, that you might be sure of getting a letter, I enclosed a sheet to you to Mr Coldham, which I doubt not but he would forward to you on.

There is one very disagreeable part of your letter where you inform me of the ill health of your sister.[79] I am truly concerned for her, and hope by your care that she may have her health restored, as she has sufficient afflictions to bear without that greatest of evils which the human race are subject to. I mean ill health.

You say you expect me Sunday or Monday. Is it not unreasonable Eliza, or rather what good would it do either you or me, if I were to come today or tomorrow and then have to return again for a week to Yarmouth? Not but I wish as much as you possibly can do to set off this very moment, nay the moment I arrived. For I find myself in the strangest state you can possibly conceive to be so near you and not to have it in my power to come immediately to you. But I think it best to settle such things as are absolutely necessary before I leave this; and, tho' I must leave many undone (for I shall not have patience to stay longer than the end of this week), yet I shall get the most important ones completed.

---

79   Barbara Collier.

Monday the 18th is the day we propose to set off.[80] For I told you in my last I waited a day or two for Betsy, who is to come with me; but I assure you it appears an age. And had I not pretty full employment, which will not allow of much time for reflection, I should be miserable. The nights are the only times I can manage to get my letters written, when the rest of the family are retired. I generally sit two or three hours at my writing desk,[81] and I assure you I rise very early notwithstanding, for 6 has been the latest hour, tho' I seldom get to bed before 2 o'clock – but I cannot lay awake.

I need not tell you what I think of and, tho' it gives me pleasure, yet it makes me uneasy and impatient. I am happy if I can write till I am quite sleepy and then as soon as I wake in the morning jump out of bed. You may keep writing me till Thursday. I would not have you write after that, as perhaps, tho' only perhaps, I may get away on Saturday; but I would not have you flatter yourself with seeing me before Tuesday. And if I can come sooner so much the better.

I have some reason to think, since I wrote you last, that, if you know of no servant you would like, the one I then mentioned would suit you very well; and tho' changing of servants must ever be very disagreeable, yet you know, if she does not, she need not be kept longer than a quarter. And now I am only afraid that you are going to be placed in a situation that will be very disagreeable to you. Yet I do not see how it can be avoided, as you will have the whole management of a considerable large family, for we shall be at least seven of us when alone.[82] You have, however, a right to expect that we shall use our utmost endeavour to make you happy. And I flatter myself very small mentions on my part will be necessary to that end. So, if I know myself, I could not suffer any greater torment than to see you wretched for a moment.

Give my sincerest love to Bab and Mary, the former I hope to find fully recovered from her indisposition when I get to Putney.

---

80   Edmund set off on Monday 18 August and arrived in London the following day. He and Eliza were married at St Mary's, Putney, on Wednesday 20 August.

81   'Set' in the original.

82   George Coldham, Edmund and Eliza Hurry, Mrs Briggs, Crozier, a boy, plus one.

That it may be very soon, I earnestly desire, and hope to find you in as good health and spirits as when you wrote your letter without the help of hartshorn.[83] God bless and preserve you to be the comforter of Edmund Cobb Hurry.

Sunday evening, 9 August. My grandmother is very poorly with her eyes. She desires her love to you.

Cover, Miss Eliza Hurry, Mrs Layton's, Putney, London. Postmark, Yarmouth, 12 August 1788.

---

83 Hartshorn, made from the antler of a male red deer, was used for a variety of medical treatments and as a smelling salt.

Letter 50

Edmund Cobb Hurry to Eliza Liddell
Great Yarmouth

Written 9-12 August 1788; sent from Great Yarmouth, 13 August; received in Putney, August

Yarmouth, 13 August 1788

My dearest Eliza, I received yours of yesterday this evening, and am sat down immediately to reply to it. I am sure if you think one servant sufficient I do; and particularly as there is a boy in the house. It therefore only depends on George to know whether he is satisfied therewith; and, if so, Mrs Briggs must certainly have the refusal.[84] But the best way will be to let it rest entirely till I have the pleasure of being with you; and indeed it cannot well be settled till we are all three together. As to what I said respecting a good cook, I only repeat Mrs Hurry's words; for I think you know I care not a farthing about either eating or drinking, or whether the meat is burned or raw. And the style of living in my father's house is just such a one, excepting company, as I should chuse to adopt. For I can assure you it is a very frugal one; and the expenses being divided will give us room to live better than we could otherwise have done. At the same time I assure you I am exceedingly unhappy to see that it will be disagreeable to you; but, situated as I am, I do not see how it can well be avoided. But this I promise you, if upon trial it should prove more disagreeable than I can possibly imagine, we can and will change.

You say I would live with my grandparents but for you. Yes, Eliza, I would; and you say what difference does it make. Believe me such a one: that with you I would not live in Yarmouth on any terms without I had an independent fortune. We should be both miserable, for I have no idea of its being possible for one to be so without the other. If you knew what I now felt from only a little discourse that has passed this

---

84   Mrs Briggs proved to be an undesirable servant, below, Letter 51, p. 275. Eliza's letter, to which this is a reply, is lost.

evening, and which I may possibly relate to you when I come, you would pity and condole with me. But were you here (I mean situated and bound to stay here), for to be sure if you were here this moment only for a time we should be as happy as the happiest of mortals, but if as I said before situated here, doubly miserable. In short, you can have no idea of what your situation would be, or of what mine ever will be, if condemned to stay long here at any time. For I cannot complain of a parent, and I cannot bear to see and suffer what I ever must here.

That I am detained thus long here is to me most uncomfortable. I have not a moment's peace. I scarce ever know what I am doing, ever wishing to be with you, tho' conscious of the impropriety of it, till another ship is sent off to Windaw. Yet if possible on Monday or Tuesday you shall see me, and I think nothing shall prevent me. I now scarce think Betsy will be suffered to come with me, which will be a great disappointment to her indeed. She has had an invitation from both her sisters, but my father I think this evening seemed to be determined she should not go.

I'm glad your sister is mending. I hope she will soon be perfectly restored. Give my best love to her and Mary, whom I suppose you have not seen lately by your not mentioning her. I do not intend to write again, but am in hopes that my presence will do as well.

In respect to the washing, I say nothing about it, as a thing I am quite ignorant of. Only if we had two servants, it would then I think be looked upon as very extravagant. The servant I wrote about is quite willing to undertake the whole, and I am informed very capable; but the present one must certainly be first spoken to about it. So let it rest. I dare say you will have an invitation to meet me in London, in which I would have you act as you please. Yet I think I had rather meet you where you are, and you may be certain I shall make no stay in London.[85]

All friends are well and desire to be particularly remembered to you. Believe me ever most sincerely and affectionately, your Edmund Cobb Hurry.

Cover, Miss Eliza Liddell, at Mr Layton's, Putney, near London. Postmark, August 1788.

---

85   Edmund left Great Yarmouth on Monday 18 August and reached London the following day.

Marriage

Eliza Hurry to Dorothy Hurry, Letter 51 (below, p. 275), August 1788

6

Marriage

On Wednesday 20 August, Edmund and Eliza were at last united at St Mary's, Putney, on the south bank of the Thames, near where Eliza's sister Barbara was living. Weddings, held in this case on a weekday, were often small-scale and private events at the time. Eliza's sister Barbara was her witness. The other official witness was the parish clerk.

> Edmund Cobb Hurry of the parish of the parish of St Mary Whitechapel in the county of Middlesex and Eliza Liddell of this parish of Putney, spinster, were married in this church by licence this twentieth day of August in the year one thousand seven hundred and eighty eight by me, Henry Whitfield DD, minister. This marriage was solemnised between us in the presence of Barbara Collier, Edmund Harpham clerk.[1]

It is likely, however, that others were also present, including Eliza's other sister, Mary Lawrence, with her husband, and Eliza's cousins, Mr and Mrs Barnes. On Edmund's side, his sister Mary Tolmé and his step-brother, George Coldham, with whom the young couple were going to live, may have been there, as may Edmund's father, William Hurry, his brother William

---

1   A copy of the marriage certificate was made for the couple's son-in-law, Alfred Hardcastle, in 1820. 'The above is a true copy from the register of Putney in the county of Surry taken this fourth day of May in the year one thousand eight hundred and twenty. By me R.J.B. Sandilands, minister.'

and his sisters Betsy and Ann, the latter perhaps with her husband George Morgan.

How and where the couple and the wedding guests ate and drank after the ceremony, and whether they had a short honeymoon, is unknown, though nine days later, when she wrote to Edmund's stepmother to thanking for her good wishes, Eliza mentions a turbot sent up from Great Yarmouth, presumably for the wedding feast.

St Mary's church, Putney, by J. Dillon, 1783

Letter 51

Eliza Hurry to Dorothy Hurry, London

Written 29 August 1788; sent from London, 29 August;
received in Great Yarmouth, August

Dear Madam, I received your kind favour on Wednesday and should have answered it immediately but that that Mr and Mrs Tolmé, Betsy and William dined with us, and I could not with any propriety leave them.[2] I am truly grateful for your letter, not only as a flattering mark of attention to myself, but because it expresses so many good wishes for the happiness of Edmund Hurry, who is indeed deserving of the most partial regard from his friends.

In uniting my destiny with his, I have given the highest possible testimony I could of an attachment that originated from a conviction of the excellence of his heart and character. Unused to make professions, I shall leave it to time to convince his friends how sincerely I mean to devote my life to promote, as far as depends on me, his peace and happiness. To his father and grandparents I beg my most dutiful respects.

Mr Coldham is too sincerely our friend not to ensure our most attentive indeavours to render his abode comfortable and pleasant to him, and from personal merit is too justly entitled to our esteem to need even a mother's recommendation.[3]

Mr Hurry has, I believe, already thanked you for the turbot, which came very safe. I hope Ann will be able to come up very soon, as we have only a woman by the week, Mrs Briggs being in the country – and, if here, both unable and apparently unwilling to do what is necessary. I am, madam, your friend and humble servant, Eliza Hurry.

Cover, Mrs Hurry at Mr William Hurry's, Yarmouth, Norfolk. Postmark, 29 August 1788.

---

2   William, Edmund's brother.

3   Dorothy Hurry, the second wife of Edmund Cobb Hurry's father, William Hurry, was the mother of George Coldham. Ann Reece was a servant.

Following their wedding, Edmund and Eliza lived first with George Coldham, in Leman Street, Goodmans Fields, near Aldgate. They subsequently moved to a house in Cambridge Heath and then to one in Homerton. Their first two children, Anne and William, were born in London in 1789 and 1791 respectively.[4]

The couple were apart in 1792 while Edmund sought to set up his own business in France, at Le Havre, where Eliza and the children joined him towards the end of the year. Many in England welcomed the early stages of the French Revolution, bringing about the end of autocracy in France. Edmund clearly saw what was happening there as a major commercial opportunity. The deterioration of the political situation in France, however, which led to the execution of Louis XVI in January 1793, and to war between Britain and France the following month, forced them to return to England. There was a much longer separation in 1793, when a desperate business problem to do with the cargo of the *Bernstoff* threatened Edmund with ruin, forcing him to go to Copenhagen, and then St Petersburg, between June and December that year.

When they were apart, the couple continued to write to each other. Just under 250 of their letters survive between 1789 and 1796, amounting to nearly 150,000 words. Much of the correspondence is domestic in content, with a great deal about the activities and health of their two elder children, Anne and William. Many other subjects, however, are touched on, including business and travel, other family members, friends, house hunting, servants, shopping, books, religion and health.

Correspondence from other family members also survives. This includes letters from Edmund's father, William Hurry, his grandparents, Edmund and Anne Cobb, and his sister Priscilla. There are also a few letters from Eliza's sister Barbara Collier, who was often ill and died in 1795. In her will of 6 January that year, she left: 'What furniture I received from Mr Hurry to be left at his disposal. My watch I leave to Ann Hurry, to Mrs Lawrence my long shawl and white gown and everything else belonging to me Mrs Wakeford as a very poor recompense for all her trouble'.[5]

No letters survive between Edmund and Eliza after 1796. Eliza, whose constitution seems never to have been strong, suffered increasingly from

---

4   Their youngest child, Edmund, was born in Great Yarmouth in 1796.

5   Mrs or Miss Wakeford was Barbara Collier's business partner.

bad health. While there is no proof of the exact nature of her illness, it is possible that she contracted tuberculosis.

A late glimpse of Eliza is provided by the poet Robert Southey, who, on a visit to Great Yarmouth in May 1798 reported to his wife that:

> Mrs Edmund Hurry is a very interesting woman – an excellent mother, with a highly cultivated mind and manners. She is the only female there whose good opinion is worth having or from whose society I could derive pleasure. I could have wished to have seen more of her; she confines herself chiefly to her own family; the society at Yarmouth is not such as suits her; like the east winds of the coast it is too rude for her. She endures much ill health, and this with the kind of people among whom it is her lot to dwell has induced that kind of misanthropy which exists only in the better class of minds ...[6]

Eliza died on 29 January 1799, her last hours being movingly described by her husband:

> 29 January 1799, about half past 3 o'clock

> This morning my dearly beloved wife left this vale of tears, as a weary traveller retires to rest. At 10 o'clock the evening before I had been sitting by her side, talking of most of our absent friends, with as much cheerfulness as ever she did in her life, and altho' I had many days before dreaded her dissolution, yet I no more expected it that night than I did my own. I kissed her at parting, expecting from appearances she would have a good night.

> It seems from the report of the nurse, she sat up at 3 o'clock in bed, had a fit of coughing, took a little tea, then asked for her watch, which she talked about a great deal to Mrs Crisp, told her the man had repaired it very badly for she could not make it strike. After talking for half an hour, she said she should not want anything more and desired Mrs Crisp to come and lay down by her, which she did, supposing her to be asleep and she observed to the servant how

6   Robert Southey to Edith Southey, 29 May 1798, *The Collected Letters of Robert Southey*, ii, *1798-1803*, no. 320 (Romantic Circles, website).

easy Mrs Hurry breathes now. It was her mistake. She breathes no more. Oh! How happy to die so, without a pang and without even a regret, for she was so worn down by weakness that she hardly had any desire for life, at least she expressed none for many days before.

Thus ended to her family a most valuable life, one who never suffered any of the pleasures or vanities of the world to draw her one moment from her duties. If anything she carried her attentions and anxieties for me and her children to too great an extent, as I must fear they contributed to shorten her life, and they certainly robbed her of much comfort in this life. That her spirit is now in a state of happiness I cannot have the smallest doubt, but how and where we are not permitted to know.

Sunday, 3 February.

This day the mortal part of my Eliza was put in the vault under Mr Hill's meeting in Old Gravel Lane, where my grandfather and cousin Samuel [are] laid.[7] Ives, Ann and Mr Alderson saw this last sad office performed. As I was obliged to remain at Homerton as well on account of my own illness …[8]

* * *

After Eliza's death, Edmund continued his career as a merchant, travelling frequently between London and Great Yarmouth, and often further afield. His children lived mainly with his family, first in Yarmouth and then in Lowestoft, with his sister Priscilla, who was married to a Unitarian minister, Michael Maurice. Maurice set up an academy for Dissenting families, at Normanstone, near Lowestoft, on a small estate bought for him by Edmund.

---

7   Old Gravel Lane Independent Chapel, about 30 by 60 feet in area, with a small burial ground, was at the corner of Old Gravel Lane and Love Lane in Wapping. These streets have been renamed Wapping Lane and Watts Street, while the chapel has disappeared and the land on which it was situated has become part of Wapping Green. Noah Hill was the minister of the Old Gravel Lane Chapel from 1772 to 1810. According to the *Encyclopedia Londiniensis: or Universal Dictionary of Arts* (1815), p. 521, Hill possessed 'a strong reasoning mind. He readily seizes the prominent bearings of his subjects, fixes them in the clearest point of view, and is easily apprehended by his auditory'.

8   Note by Edmund Cobb Hurry, Templehouse Archive, M3.

Edmund subsequently established himself at Gosport, a major supply base for the British Navy during the Revolutionary wars with France, and purchased an estate, Holly Hill, near Fareham, where he was often visited by his children. On 7 June 1804, he married Jane Chambers, who had previously been his children's nurse. The many letters which survive between him and his daughter Anne record his poor health. It is likely that he too suffered from tuberculosis. He died on 26 August 1808 at the Hot Wells in Bristol, where he had gone in the hope of recovery, and is buried in the churchyard of the Unitarian chapel at Frenchay, just north of Bristol.

Of Edmund and Eliza's children, their elder son, William Cobb Hurry, described as 'a man of extraordinary talent', went out to India and established himself as a merchant at Calcutta, where he became editor of a leading Indian newspaper, the *Englishman*. Returning to England, he lived at Cook's Folly, near Clifton, where he died unmarried in 1862, aged seventy-two.

Their second son, Edmund Cobb Hurry junior, died of tuberculosis in 1814, aged eighteen. He is buried near his father at Frenchay. His life, character and final illness are described at length in surviving letters between him and his sister, Anne.

Anne Cobb Hurry was a highly intelligent and attractive girl, very well read and also musical. At Michael Maurice's at Normanstone, one of the pupils was Alfred Hardcastle, the son of a leading Evangelical merchant, Joseph Hardcastle, the founder of the London Missionary Society. Alfred fell in love with Anne and proposed, but the marriage was forbidden by Joseph Hardcastle on the grounds of her rejection, as a Unitarian, of the Trinity.

Several years later, hearing accidentally one day that Anne had become an orthodox Christian, Alfred drove posthaste to Frenchay, renewed his offer of marriage and was accepted. The couple were married on 2 January 1815, but Anne died tragically in September of the same year after giving birth to her only child, and Edmund and Eliza's only grandchild, Joseph Alfred Hardcastle (1815-1899), by whom their letters descended through the Hardcastle family to the Templehouse Archive.[9]

---

9   For Edmund and Eliza's correspondence after their marriage, see Templehouse Papers, N15-19, N22-25. See also N20 (Priscilla Hurry) and N21 (William Hurry). For Anne Cobb Hurry, see N26-32, N34, N36-39. For Edmund Cobb Hurry junior, see N30-31.

Appendix

A1

Thomas Mathews to William Burton Conyngham
Rutland in the Rosses, 16 June 1786

Rosses, 16 June 1786

Sir, Tuesday's post I had the honour to write to you directed to Dublin.[1] The arrival this day of Mr Gerredot must be of singular service to this country. When his colony arrives it will make my saltworks flourish. In my last I troubled you with an account of my proceeding on Edderness and requested a credit on Dublin, and my intention of erecting a brewery on Rutland. Yesterday I viewed the lake. There is a small island on it that will answer compleatly with a few acres of meadow, as a horse must be kept for a malt mill. If this meets your approbation, I make no doubt of sending you such ale to Slane as will be a credit to the Rosses. I am a judge of malting, having malted in Drogheda these twelve years past. I request your answer when you can spare time, as I only wait for it.

My business calls on me to go to Glasgow, Liverpool and Bristol, the moment I return to Drogheda. I plainly see now a good deal of business with care can be done here. I shall pursue it. The brigg with timber etc from Avendal returns here on my account loaded with iron, deal, bars and gunpowder. This sortable cargo must answer

---

1   National Archives of Ireland, Cliffe-Vigors Papers, 1096, section 9.

here and be of service to the country. I have the honour to be with great respect your much obliged and very humble servant Thomas Mathews.

Cover, The Right Hon. William Cunningham, Killibeggs, Postmark. Killibeggs.

A2

Thomas Mathews to William Conyngham
Rutland in the Rosses, 29 June 1786

Rosses, 29 June 1786

Sir, A state of uncertainty must be distressing to a person in a strange country.[2] It is unhappily for me at present my case. I beg leave to refer you to my letter from Drogheda wherein I proposed taking from you £2000 at 5 per cent with an expectation of an encouragement when my works were completed. I expected it out of the publick fund as a new letter. From Mr Forster's letter that you had agreed to my proposal, I accepted of it and of course I could not form to myself any other opinion, only to account to you for the yearly interest of £2000. On the word of an honest man, this is what occured to me.

My expenditure is far more than the £600 you gave me. I have few vouchers, as I did not expect to be called on for them. You made me a most generous proposal of money to erect a red herring house. I declined it, as I intended to consult my friends Messrs Mason and Bourn of Liverpool and lay their opinion before you. They are greatly in that line.

As a misunderstanding has taken place, you and only you I hope will settle it. I pay Mr Forster and Mr Fortescue near £600 a year. They are pleased at my dealings and I flatter myself a little time will I hope merit your approbation.

I am one of the first letters here and I claim your protection, and I am to pay you more than any man in the Rosses. A brewery will help your tenant to pay more cleverly your rent. I hope you have turned this plan in your mind. I remit 100 guineas to Connaught for sheep and I want seventy or eighty heyfers for Croi. I will thank you for a bill on Croi account and one for the saltworks.

I have the honour to be, Sir, your much obliged and very humble servant Thomas Mathews.

---

2   National Archives of Ireland, Cliffe-Vigors Papers, 1096, section 9.

A copy of an entry made at home in my pocket book which will show Mr Conyngham my intention as to the agreement with him:

> Tuesday 20 March 1786 agreed with the Right Hon. William Conyngham to build saltworks at the Rosses. He gives me £2000 at 5 per cent for ever and a lease for ever of the ground.

Mr Mathew's whole wish and desire was and is to please Mr Conyngham and ashure him any emolument he may make at the Rosses would be nothing to him without his friendship. In Drogheda he flatters himself he was deemed a man of his word. The Rosses shall never make him forget it.

In ten days I expect a letter from my friends Messrs N. and D. Abelaven of Amsterdam, with their sentiments on codd and herrings. If pleasing, will send them a cargoe.

I never suffered so much as I have done since I came to the Rosses. My men turned out twice, obliged to humer them and very distressing to account them. Up at work every morning at six; often I don't taste a morsel until six in the evening. What I take in hand I will finish. No price fixed on the bullocks or horses at Croi.

Wrote several letters to the Right Hon. William Conyngham and received no answer. Mr Conyngham must see my situation and put matters in some satisfactory form to setle his humble servant Thomas Mathews.

Cover, Right Hon. William Conyngham, Enniskilling. Postmark, Killybegs.

A3

Ann Cobb to Edmund Cobb Hurry
Great Yarmouth, 18 January 1788

I thank you, my dear Edmund, for your care to Thomas Crombie, but if I had known it would have occasioned you so much trouble would not have desired you to go after it.[3] We are quite sorry to find your spirits so low as to imagine any of your best friends should have any suspicion of your integrity in representing what passes in your affairs at London. So far from that, we have the highest opinion of your conduct, prudence and sincerity, and should rejoice to know you were in a situation that would make your life pleasing and comfortably to you.

But I hope you will always remember this is a state of probation. We must expect tryals. If we bear them as we ought, they will certainly increase our true happiness. We did hope for the pleasure of your company here with your sister Tolmé, but suppose from your father's letter you are going another way. I wish this intended journey may be a means to promote your health and give you an easy mind. Give our love to Mrs Tolmé and tell her we have received a box for her Aunt Ives which shall be conveyed to her the first opportunity, but she wants to know who she is to pay the money Mrs Tolmé has disbursed for her. Our most tender love and good wishes attend you, Mr Morgan, both your sisters, Ives and the dear children.[4]

I am, dear Edmund, with sincere prayers for your happiness, your affectionate grandmother, Ann Cobb.

Mr Cobb hopes you'll excuse his not writing to you. The badness of his eyes making it so painful to him.

Cover, Mr E.C. Hurry, Mrs Tolmé's, no. 21 Prescott Street, Goodmans Fields, London. Postmark, Yarmouth, 19 January 1788.

---

3 Templehouse Papers, Ballymote, County Sligo, Ireland, N13. Thomas Crombie had had a stroke.

4 Ann Cobb sends her best wishes to Edmund's sisters Mary Tolmé and Ann Morgan, and their children, as well as to the latter's husband, George Morgan, and to their brother Ives. Aunt Ives was Ann Cobb's sister.

A4

Ann Cobb to Eliza Liddell
Great Yarmouth, 14 April 1788

Yarmouth, 14 April 1788

I thank you, my dear Miss Liddell, for your pleasing and obliging letter, and tho' we are not personally known to each other, yet I entertain such an opinion of Edmund Cobb Hurry's *choice* that I doubt not but he will have an agreeable friend and partner in domestic life, whenever you are united in the most pleasing ties of matrimonial friendship.[5] And tho' you may suppose me partial to one I have loved tenderly from his infancy, from his former behaviour in every relation of life I think he will endeavour to make every one happy with whom he is connected. There is nothing in this world would give me greater pleasure as to see all my dear grandchildren happy and united in love to each other. Mr Cobb and Mr Hurry join with me in due respects to you and your sisters. I am your sincere friend, Ann Cobb.

Cover, Miss Liddell, at Mrs Tolmé's, No. 21 Prescott Street, Goodmans Fields, London. Postmark, Yarmouth, 15 April 1788.

---

5   Templehouse Papers, Ballymote, County Sligo, Ireland, N14. Thomas Crombie had had a stroke.

A5

Robert Symes to Robert Corbet,
Rutland in the Rosses, 2 June 1789

Rutland, 2 June 1789

Dear Sir, I received yours of 21 and 23 May, which brought me the first account of the *Fox* since she left.[6] She had as usual a tedious time of it. You will be the best judge what needs to be done with her, as there is nothing I know of that would answer, unless Kilkenny coal to Sligo or Ballyshannon. Hope you have by this got all your things, as I took very particular care in packing them.

The papers you wrote for Mackesy sent on Sunday as you directed. We were both glad to hear the few errors found were in your favour. I wish much the examining was over and the stores here given up, as there is a daily waste of the oatmeal running to [mites].

I dare not think of leaving this till the people are paid off, many of whom are grown very troublesome. I suppose they never will be paid. I got but six guineas from Mr Olphert when last there, but said if he could collect again [at] the fair at Dungloe (which was on Saturday) he would send it. I have not since heard of him. There is £71 due on the returns (not a penny coming to the store), besides Magowan and Hughes, since you left this. Mr Clarke is very uneasy at not hearing from you, as his year is now out, and is continually teasing for money.

The grass is beginning to look very well about Munmore, but the garden [is] in no great order and the walks very wet and very soft. Cummins still continues his family there and keeps a cow and makes use of the turf, as also Mary Clooney's husband. They both work at Lackebegg, where there are great improvements going on in gardens and lawns. Mr Cole went on Sunday to Ballybofey to the races and cockfights. He had 100 guineas on the main. He had a letter from Mr Conyngham the other day mentioning his intention of going to England immediately and bringing a party here the latter

---

6   National Archives of Ireland, Cliffe-Vigors Papers, 1096, section 9.

end of the summer. Mackesy and his family have been living at Burtonport these three weeks but are coming back again this day. I hear the two families did not agree well together. Coyle's family here still but talking of going every day. He had his horse in Edernishfree till Sunday. He said it was by your directions; however, he could not be kept in the fair part and I had him put off the island. There will be fine grass there this summer. I shall direct this to Ross, as you mentioned your going there as soon as you heard of the f[ire]. The light house is to go on [immediately]. All well here. Sandham desires to be remembered to you. With compliments to Mrs Corbet and family. I remain, dear sir, yours very sincerely, Robert Symes.

Cover, Robert Corbet Esq.

A6

Robert Symes to Robert Corbet,
Ballycasnell, date unknown

My dear Corbet, The severity of the weather has detained Richard some days longer than intended.[7] It looks well, however, this morning and promises to answer for his long passage to the eastward. I am thankfull to you for having spared him so long, as without his assistance I would have found it difficult to set out my clough this year.[8] If Turner has any iron proper for such work, I should be glad that he would [send] another ten hundredweight for me. One of the cloughs in Rosses may be fitted with it and that may bring it nearly to answer for the one I have here; at least a small alteration of a smith here may make it work.

I have yet heard not any thing of the office of sheriff, so remain still in doubt and expectation. Tomorrow we go for some days to [*unclear name*], but next balls are not yet determined upon, but when they are I shall be at leisure and know that he may come better shod that he did to the last.

All here desire to be remembered to you. I am, dear Corbet, your ever sincerely etc, Robert Symes.

Ballycasnell, Sunday morning

Should you be satisfied to leave the sopha bed of your drawing room in Inniscoo behind you, Mrs B. would be glad to purchase it, for whatever it may have cost you.[9] She means the bed only, without the curtains, as she remembers that they were to match other furniture of yours at Corbet Hill and would not suit any of hers here.

I have spoken to Dobson, our borough constable, about your bullocks. He may possibly go in a day or two to Rosses to see them.

---

7   National Archives of Ireland, Cliffe-Vigors Papers, 1096, section 9.

8   A clough is a narrow valley.

9   Mrs B. unidentified.

Beef is from a guinea to 25 shillings per head I find in the next market. Mr Rayner the butcher from Letterkenny should go to your deal only for ready money. He is a decent fellow but not in the same good circumstances as he was some years ago. Verbum sapienti.

Cover, Robert Corbet Esq., Rutland.

Index